Oxford Shakespeare Topics

Shakespeare and the Arts of Language

OXFORD SHAKESPEARE TOPICS

Published and Forthcoming Titles Include:

Lawrence Danson, *Shakespeare's Dramatic Genres*
Andrew Gurr and Mariko Ichikawa, *Staging in Shakespeare's Theatres*
Peter Holland, *Shakespeare and Film*
Jill L. Levenson, *Shakespeare and Twentieth-Century Drama*
Ania Loomba, *Shakespeare and Race*
Russ McDonald, *Shakespeare and the Arts of Language*
Steven Marx, *Shakespeare and the Bible*
Robert S. Miola, *Shakespeare's Reading*
Phyllis Rackin, *Shakespeare and Women*
Bruce R. Smith, *Shakespeare and Masculinity*
Zdeněk Stříbrný, *Shakespeare and Eastern Europe*
Michael Taylor, *Shakespeare Criticism in the Twentieth Century*
Stanley Wells, ed., *Shakespeare in the Theatre: An Anthology of Criticism*
Martin Wiggins, *Shakespeare and the Drama of his Time*

Oxford Shakespeare Topics

GENERAL EDITORS: PETER HOLLAND AND STANLEY WELLS

Shakespeare and the Arts of Language

RUSS MCDONALD

OXFORD
UNIVERSITY PRESS

Great Clarendon Street, Oxford OX2 6DP

Oxford University Press is a department of the University of Oxford.
It furthers the University's objective of excellence in research, scholarship,
and education by publishing worldwide in

Oxford New York

Athens Auckland Bangkok Bogotá Buenos Aires Calcutta
Cape Town Chennai Dar es Salaam Delhi Florence Hong Kong Istanbul
Karachi Kuala Lumpur Madrid Melbourne Mexico City Mumbai
Nairobi Paris São Paulo Shanghai Singapore Taipei Tokyo Toronto Warsaw

and associated companies in Berlin Ibadan

Oxford is a registered trade mark of Oxford University Press
in the UK and certain other countries

Published in the United States
by Oxford University Press Inc., New York

British Library Cataloguing in Publication Data

Data available

Library of Congress Cataloging in Publication Data

McDonald, Russ, 1949-
   Shakespeare and the arts of language / Russ McDonald.
      p. cm.— (Oxford Shakespeare topics)
Includes bibliographical references and index.
   1. Shakespeare, William, 1564–1616—Language. 2. Shakespeare, William,
1564–1616—Technique. 3. Shakespeare, William, 1564–1616—Literary style.
4. English language—Early modern, 1500–1700—Style. 5. English language–Early
modern, 1500–1700—Rhetoric. I. Title. II. Series.

PR3069.L3 M38 2001   822.3'3—dc21   00-062406

ISBN 0–19–871170–0
ISBN 0–19–871171–9 (pbk.)

1 3 5 7 9 10 8 6 4 2

Typeset by Kolam Information Services Pvt. Ltd, Pondicherry, India
Printed in Great Britain
on acid-free paper by Biddles Ltd, Guildford and Kings Lynn

Acknowledgements

Many people have assisted in the preparation of this book, but two have been especially generous. Stanley Wells and Peter Holland, although they must be as busy as anyone in the Anglo-American academy, have never been too busy to read drafts of chapters (and to read them rigorously and sympathetically), to answer queries about historical or bibliographical puzzles, to suggest additional (and usually superior) examples, to offer advice about organization and pitch, to rescue an author from embarrassing errors – and they have performed all these labours promptly and cheerfully. As general editors of the Oxford Shakespeare Topics series, they have been exemplary in making their supervisory presence both inspiring and reassuring.

For answers to questions, general advice, critical inspiration, and good-humored support, thanks to Denise Baker, Thomas Berger, A. R. Braunmuller, Christopher Hodgkins, James Longenbach, Catherine Loomis, and George Walton Williams. Stephen Booth and George T. Wright have not only written brilliantly on the topic of Shakespeare's language but have also been magnanimous to me in ways that frustrate attempts at acknowledgement. I am grateful to Hugh Parker for help with the Latin. Maggie DiVito did an expert job of helping me proofread; the errors that remain are my fault. Frances Whistler at Oxford University Press is such a scrupulous editor that she will probably object to my expression of gratitude: she has been unfailingly attentive, encouraging, and accommodating.

Many chapters have been improved by the responses of various audiences and readers. At meetings of the Shakespeare Association of America, members of Maurice Hunt's seminar (1998) and Ann Baynes Coiro's seminar (2000) offered useful advice, as did readers in John Drakakis's seminar at the International Shakespeare Conference in Stratford-upon-Avon (August 2000). I thank Janet Field-Pickering, Margaret Maurer, and Robert Watson for allowing me to present some of this material to students and colleagues at the Folger Shakespeare Library's Teaching Shakespeare Institute; Kate Levin at the Brooklyn Academy of Music and the City University of New York; Fran Teague at the University of Georgia; Russell Peck and Mervyn Willis at the University of Rochester. Staff members at several libraries have been helpful: the British Library; the Folger Shakespeare Library, especially Betsy Walsh; the Jackson Library at the University of North Carolina at Greensboro, especially Nancy Fogarty and Mark Schumacher; and the Perkins Library at Duke University.

I wish to thank my wife and son for their patience and good will: as usual, Gail McDonald has put aside her own work to read, discuss, and improve mine. Although this book comes with no formal dedication, I wish to express my gratitude to my mother, who purchased a copy of *Reading with Phonics* in 1954 and with it taught me to take pleasure in words.

Contents

List of Illustrations

A Note on Texts

All quotations from Shakespeare are taken from the *Complete Works of William Shakespeare*, ed. Stanley Wells and Gary Taylor (Oxford: Oxford University Press, 1986), except in a very few cases noted in the text. Most of the passages from other sixteenth- and seventeenth-century texts have been modernized for the convenience of the reader.

Introduction

Language can . . . be compared with a sheet of paper: thought is
the front and sound the back; one cannot cut the front without
cutting the back at the same time.

(Ferdinand de Saussure, *Course in General Linguistics*, 1916)

This book is designed as an overview of the 'arts' of Shakespeare's
language, an introduction to his unparalleled command of his verbal
medium. The chapters that follow examine his talent for stimulating,
through the conscious or unconscious manipulation of that medium,
certain responses in the bodies, minds, and hearts of the audience. As a
basis for exploring his artistic control of words, the study begins with a
brief treatment of the state of the English language when Shakespeare
took it up professionally. This historical discussion of early modern
English divides into two parts: in the first chapter, vocabulary, syntax,
grammar, and the cultural centrality of rhetoric, and, in the second,
Shakespeare's adoption of these basic rhetorical instruments. That
groundwork prepares for the subsequent examination of figurative
language in his works, first imagery and then its metaphoric or symbolic functions; of blank verse, particularly rhythmic permutations; of
the varieties and uses of prose; and of the immense importance of
wordplay. The last chapter treats Shakespeare's changing views of his
verbal medium over two decades of professional activity. Now, by way
of prelude, I want to articulate several common themes that recur in
these chapters, declare some of the assumptions that underlie them,
and attempt to situate this study in its critical context at the beginning
of the twenty-first century.

My conviction that the study of language is central to the understanding and appreciation of Shakespeare's work informs every page of
this book. That belief derives from the even more basic tenet that his
control of language—more than plot, characterization, theme—gives
his work its distinctive qualities and underwrites his demonstrated
theatrical sovereignty. To make such a claim is not to denigrate other
dramatic elements: for example, the stories he tells are irresistible.

Consider, for example, the numerous adaptations and versions that *Romeo and Juliet* has inspired: Gounod's nineteenth-century French opera, Prokofiev's twentieth-century ballet, Leonard Bernstein's *West Side Story*, Peter Ustinov's *Romanoff and Juliet*, down to the 1997 porno-slasher film called *Tromeo and Juliet*. But Shakespeare's 'original' is itself an English adaptation, created in the 1590s, of a story introduced into English in 1562 as a narrative poem by Arthur Brooke. Although Brooke had translated it from the Italian of Matteo Bandello, some form of the tale had been circulating in the European narrative tradition for centuries. Shakespeare appropriated it and gave it its most enduring form, thereby establishing the model that would come to be emulated over the next four centuries. The enduring appeal of his play is to be found in the extraordinary poetic embodiment that Shakespeare has given to the ancient story.

Style, then, that profound and enigmatic combination of sound, image, denotation, connotation, pattern, and a multitude of other properties, is a primary determinant of Shakespeare's theatrical success. Granted, many of his adaptors and admirers have come to the plays through the mediated form of translation rather than a direct confrontation with Shakespeare's English, but often those translations have been the work of artists such as Pasternak who capture in the translation the poetic power of the original. As with narrative, so with character: both make the effect they do thanks to the verbal medium. The eighteenth and nineteenth centuries tended to isolate and revere figures such as Rosalind and Falstaff and Hamlet, submitting them as evidence of Shakespeare's unparalleled insight into 'human nature', and if our own culture has been a little less susceptible to such idolatry, many people continue to admire what are now described as Shakespeare's psychological insights. We may thus need to be reminded that the character we call Falstaff, when reduced to his essential elements, is merely a collection of verbal signs and that Shakespeare's brilliant portraiture represents a talent for arranging words into meaningful patterns. Analysis of those patterns and how they create the responses and effects they do is a first step in satisfying our normal curiosity about what makes Shakespeare Shakespeare.

Drama depends upon a verbal medium whose individual units convey meaning in a way that other media—musical tones, oil paint— do not. In the study of music, no one disputes that notes and their arrangement should be the main object of scrutiny. The musicologist who analyses a Chopin nocturne or a rock-and-roll song, for example, cannot escape the dominance of melody, rhythm, harmony, and other such formal features, even though the biographical or cultural influences on the work may be compelling and useful. But words, or what we have come to call signifiers, deliver meaning on their own, before they are employed by the poet and placed in productive conjunction with other words. A solitary G-sharp or a C-natural does not automatically convey meaning; the noun 'flower' or the verb 'stab' obviously does. Musical meaning begins to emerge as notes are assigned to instruments and placed in relation to one another. Language, however, necessarily and immediately directs our attention away from itself to an idea or image, the 'signified' that the signifier represents. Paradoxically, then, words distance the perceiver from the text, discounting their own physical or material being and recommending contents or ideas or contexts. Recent criticism has accepted those recommendations with alacrity, devoting itself especially to social or cultural meaning and thus endorsing what has been described as 'our all too ready flight from [words] to the things they point to'.[1] That phrase was written in the 1960s, and since then the velocity of the flight has greatly accelerated, so much so that the materiality of the medium is often neglected entirely.

My treatment of Shakespeare's language thus proposes to reassert the physical contribution of the signifier. That aim is part of a larger desire to reaffirm the importance of pleasure in the study of early modern theatre generally. This book assumes the power of words to beguile by means of their sounds; of their weight, both semantic and aural; their connotative colours and nuances; the effects of sounds and colours when combined with others like them, or different from them; the pleasures and the affective possibilities of patterned language; the effect of sound when it 'seem[s] an echo to the sense' (Alexander Pope), and also when it does not; the music of ideas, harmonious or dissonant, that derives from arresting semantic combinations. My commitment to the non-referential qualities of the signifier implies that aural and other rhetorical pleasures have been slighted in recent years, and there is no denying that the current interest in historical conditions, political influences, gender conflicts, and other such contextual phenomena, renewing and constructive though it is, has necessarily diverted attention from the formal and material attributes of words. Inevitably, certain objects will be invisible to the gaze that remains fixed beyond the signifier. But devotion to context does not preclude attention to the verbal and discursive attributes of early modern drama: several recent critics have demonstrated that 'discourse in Shakespeare ... is inseparable from the social and political'[2] and have sensitively explored the cultural implications of Shakespeare's dramatic speech. But it is also vital to remember that those implications depend upon a corporeal medium. Thus I have tried to heed Patricia Parker's call—she is here endorsing the view of Catherine Belsey—for 'a more historically grounded study of language and culture, one that takes seriously the "matter" of language as part of the "material Shakespeare"'.[3]

Reference to recent critical debate introduces an important critical development of the late twentieth century, one with significant implications for questions of style: the revised conception of authorship. Although this phenomenon has sometimes been trumpeted as 'the death of the author', a more judicious way of describing it is as a recognition of the collaborative nature of literary agency. A corollary of this dispersal of authorial responsibility has been an expanded sense of what is considered a 'text'. Called 'cultural poetics' by Stephen Greenblatt, this broadened approach to writing and history is part of a normal cyclical reaction to the later (and narrow) phases of New Criticism, the practice that dominated the academy in the middle of the twentieth century. But literary study has hardly dispensed with William Shakespeare, dramatist and poet. Rather, the figure of the author has been elasticized somewhat so as to take into account the theatrical and social influences that helped to shape the theatrical artefact. The refashioned author is, as Greenblatt puts it, an agent for 'the collective production of literary pleasure and interest'.[4]

For students of theatre, the augmented or complicated author may be less perplexing than for others, since drama has always been acknowledged as a collaborative art. This redefinition of artistic 'authority' or agency properly rebuts the fiction of imaginative autonomy, assigning greater responsibility for artistic choices to theatrical and literary convention, shared cultural assumptions, and other contemporary ideas, discourses, and social practices. It need not, however, challenge the existence or value of verbal or theatrical effects. Rather, it seeks to relocate the origin of the stylistic choice, removing it from the solitary artistic imagination and resituating it in the interaction between that imagination and the various contemporary pressures to which it is subjected. Revision of authorial responsibility provides more abundant and varied opportunities for identifying the sources of auditory and semantic pleasure.

A related critical development is the renewed emphasis on the instability of the Shakespearian texts we possess, for consciousness of such textual uncertainty may seem to undermine critical claims made for subtle poetic effects. This is a justifiable concern, and it may very well be that in some cases what we take for a brilliant poetic stroke is attributable to textual corruption, not to genius. But problems of textual transmission pose no real threat to the analysis of a dramatist's *œuvre*. The number of poetic tropes and their indisputable contribution to the meaning and pleasure of Shakespeare's works make it obvious that for every illusory effect there are hundreds that arise from an unparalleled poetic imagination working in a receptive theatrical culture.

The semantic property of words affords rewarding work for those attentive to language. Because many words, their usage, and the cultural phenomena to which they direct the listener's intelligence have changed so drastically since the sixteenth and seventeenth centuries, the twenty-first-century reader may require assistance. It can be difficult to grasp even the literal meaning of a term or phrase, much less comprehend its contemporary nuances and its embeddedness in one or more significant cultural discourses. This book, then, is to some extent an exercise in historical philology, an effort to 'place' Shakespeare's words in relation to the development of the English language and to the flourishing of English poetic drama at the turn of the seventeenth century. Awareness of the historical ramifications of words and poetic practices is vital to a proper understanding of the Shakespearian text. To extend the parallel with music, we might say that the recontextualization of early modern diction approximates the reversion to original instruments in keyboard and chamber performances over the past two or three decades. The keyboard sonatas of Beethoven sound different when played on a modern Steinway grand from the way they do when performed on the kind of pianoforte for which he composed them. Many words that we think we know meant different things to Shakespeare's original audience. When Iago says to himself 'Cassio's a *proper* man', one's understanding is altered considerably by the discovery that in the early seventeenth century a primary meaning of the adjective was 'handsome'.

Shakespeare's language functions as a symbolic register, an instrument for recording, transmitting, and magnifying the conditions of the fictional world that the play represents—the conflicts, affinities, and changes occurring among the persons who inhabit it. In fact, dramatic speech or poetic language conforms admirably to the figure that critics call a symbol because it both represents or symbolizes something else, and yet commands attention as an entity itself. To borrow another formulation from Sigurd Burckhardt, poetic properties such as metaphors and puns are especially valuable to the artist for their power to 'corporealize language, because any device which interposes itself between words and their supposedly simple meanings calls attention to the words as things'.[5] The payment of such attention, the identification of similarities and differences on the surfaces of the text, creates moments of sensuous and mental gratification—there are thousands of such moments in every play—that add depth and texture to the inseparable semantic or referential response. Shakespeare's distinctive union of the referential and the material creates the ultimately indefinable attraction of the plays, the force that fills theatres, sells books, and sustains his role as cultural icon.

The nature of that attraction is dependent on both the formal demands and the formal comforts of verbal representation. The ordering of experience that the playwright has arranged in a play like *A Midsummer Night's Dream* provides, largely by means of its patterned language, a formal substitute for the clarity and assurance we seek in the more chaotic realm of daily life. To perceive these linguistic turns or patterns and to sense the security of an artistic structure is to achieve a small intellectual victory over the disorder of normal existence. We come to know such comfort, for example, when we connect the sounds of 'wake', 'take', and 'sake' in the charm Oberon speaks over the sleeping Titania; when we feel the incantatory repetition of Titania's 'And for her sake do I rear up her boy, | And for her sake I will not part with him'; perceive the intensity created by the alliteration in Demetrius' 'And I in fury hither followed them, | Fair Helena in fancy following me'; register the garbled allusion to St Paul in Bottom's

'The eye of man hath not heard'; absorb the rhythmic propulsion of Hermia's 'How low am I, thou painted maypole? Speak!'; relish the sensual luxury of Lysander's reference to the moon goddess's 'Decking with liquid pearl the bladed grass'. Such music permits us to inhabit, if only for an afternoon, an imaginary realm more meaningful and agreeable than our own. The same is true of larger patterns: the symmetrical relationships of the four young lovers, the contrasts and likenesses between Theseus and Oberon, Hippolyta and Titania, the antithesis of Athens and the wood, the reflective delights of the mechanicals' theatrical effort, the play within the play. Recognition of such parallels and contrasts exercises the intellect, attention to sounds and pictures fills the mind with images, and thus the theatrical experience both gratifies the senses and enlarges the imagination.

At the same time, however, the words gesture beyond themselves, offering guides and shaping responses to actions and persons represented on stage. Frequently these pointers function subliminally. During a performance of *King Lear*, for example, although the audience may not be consciously aware of it, the King's style of speech shifts radically from the grand imperatives heard at his first entrance to the more vulnerable interrogative mood he assumes on the heath. The visible change in fortunes and power is not merely reflected in the words but is communicated to the audience at least in part through the formal modulation of Lear's speech. And by the final scene that style has undergone still other mutations. Characterization is perhaps the most obvious contribution of verbal signs, but these sounds and pictures convey a good deal more than personality. The rhythms of a play, the regularity of the iambic beat and the departures from that regularity, give aural embodiment to the problems of government that pervade the histories and tragedies. The same may be said for the music of certain prose passages. Language serves as an auditory emblem of the conflicts and harmonies emerging from the action.

Language also manages to consolidate, to unify the audience, to stimulate community. The regular alternation of stressed and unstressed syllables in the pentameter line constitutes a model of social engagement, reciprocal relationship, and cooperative movement or progress. One iamb supplants another in orderly succession, with sufficient variation in the repeated pattern to prevent tedium. As the critic George T. Wright puts it, the verse is animated by a constant tension between the regularity of the beat and the syntactical or semantic pressures of the sentence, although the sentence ultimately yields to the line and restores the balance between order and liberty. Owing to this energetic but disciplined pattern of sounds,

[a]n aesthetic and an ethic of mutual dependence and obligation are deeply inscribed in Shakespeare's drama. More intently than in most nondramatic verse, we hear the elements of Shakespeare's language exercising a force on each other, one element compelling another to respond. Actor and audience, text and reader, require each other. Syllable, foot, phrase, line, speech, scene, even play invites or challenges its companion, its cohort, its rival, its reader to supply its needed complement.[6]

Wright demonstrates that the rhythms of the verse physically embody the theme of mutuality and moderation to which Shakespeare seems unfailingly committed, and his connection of medium and message typifies the method that I try to employ throughout this book. Recent criticism has sometimes bridled at the impulse to dwell on words, to 'fetishize' or 'reify' dramatic language: pleasing sounds are suspected of being palliatives that interfere with the social efficacy of meaningful language. But Shakespeare's witty exploitation of the sound and weight of words suggests that, at least in the theatre, the reification of language is a virtue, that stressing the materiality of the word is one of his principal goals, and that consciousness of its sensory properties unites the audience in common experience. It is not too much to say that Shakespeare's style performs a kind of social labour, not only in its power to delight listeners but also in its ability to create a community of thought and feeling.

But sounds alone are empty. Or as George Gascoigne put it, writing in 1575 about the task of the poet, 'it is not enough to roll in pleasant words'.[7] The skill at encoding information—and encoding so much information—in the mesmerizing verbal medium is one of the gifts that make Shakespeare a greater dramatist than any of his contemporaries, even the most talented and accomplished of them. To take one contrary instance, John Fletcher, the junior playwright of the King's Men and Shakespeare's collaborator at the end of his career, seems to have appropriated many of his mentor's formal structures and rhetorical flourishes without being able to infuse them with comparable significance. The listener apprehends the pattern but misses the wealth of implication. In Shakespeare's case, the language calls attention to itself and also gestures beyond itself. We have recently tended to concentrate on what the style points to, worrying obsessively about the message while doing our best to ignore the messenger. This book is meant as a modest challenge to that impulse. To reflect on the arts of language is to recall and learn to relish again the pleasures that attracted us to the theatre in the first place.

The Language Shakespeare Learned

Those who speak reverentially of English as 'the language of Shake-speare' might be surprised to find that, as a child, little Will learned to speak what many of his educated countrymen considered a crude and ignoble tongue. Not until the close of the sixteenth century did English attain something like the dignity and authority it now boasts, and it did so chiefly because Shakespeare himself, along with fellow poets—Marlowe, Sidney, Spenser, Donne, and Jonson—took it up as an artistic medium, exploiting and augmenting its possibilities and conferring upon it something like the prestige of the classical lan-guages. The beginning of Shakespeare's literary career coincides with the emergence of his native language as a significant expressive tool, for only recently had English replaced Latin as the primary medium for poetry. Early modern English, just having emerged from Middle English, was relatively undeveloped as a literary instrument, encum-bered with fewer regulations and conventions than the venerable ancient tongues. Thus, its plasticity afforded Shakespeare and his contemporaries rare freedom in shaping vocabulary, grammar, and other features of style. Moreover, these poets and playwrights ben-efited from an extraordinary cultural self-consciousness about their artistic medium, a widespread interest in words that resulted from decades of debate about the native language, the vernacular. This preparatory chapter will examine the state of the English language when Shakespeare took it up professionally around 1590: its new-found respectability and prominence, its dynamic instability, and its potential for eloquence. Such a groundwork will permit us then to place Shakespeare in relation to the language of his time. Without discounting his imaginative and poetic gifts, we can say that the emerging state of the English language at the end of the sixteenth century contributed much to making his plays what they are.

The Rise of the Vernacular

A convenient way of summarizing the linguistic revolution in the sixteenth century is to say that the English language became respectable. Throughout the Middle Ages the vernacular had served mainly for informal oral discourse, not as a vehicle for serious and permanent forms of communication. Those who wrote history or philosophy or theology usually wrote in Latin, and in scholarly efforts students followed the lead of their masters. Legal proceedings as well as many matters of state were conducted in French. Chaucer had written his great poems in Middle English, of course, a good deal of English and Scots poetry was written in the fifteenth century, and the popular drama, e.g. the mystery cycles, was written and performed in English, but until the middle of the sixteenth century a poet or fiction writer did not automatically compose in the native tongue: Thomas More, for example, wrote *Utopia* (1516) in Latin. From later in the reign of Henry VIII, however, the Tudor monarchs presided over a linguistic transformation. By the death of Elizabeth I in 1603, the vernacular had mostly supplanted Latin as the primary medium for written discourse, and the literary muse dictated in English.

A hundred years earlier, however, the English language stood in very low repute, with many social, historical, and political factors contributing to its second-class status. Its orality was perhaps its greatest liability: the learned disdained it because the untutored spoke it. Such considerations of class obtained throughout the Middle Ages and back to the time of William the Conqueror. When the Normans conquered Britain in the eleventh century, French became the proper tongue, and even 300 years later, at the courts of Edward III and Richard II (*c.*1350–1400), English was the linguistic stepchild. A survey of sixteenth-century views of education and writing indicates that English was often dismissed as crude and therefore unsuitable for literary or scholastic uses. In the culture of Tudor England labels such as 'barbarous', 'rude', 'vile', and 'base' would have had a more potent social charge than they do today, and the attacks on the vernacular, particularly compared to Latin and Greek, were frequently articulated in terms of class, high and low. The native tongue, it was argued, did not permit the writer to scale the peaks of eloquence available to the Latinist. English vocabulary was allegedly too limited for sophisticated argument, its structures too simple for graceful statement.

Hostility to the native tongue is expressed even by those who were masters of it. In 1563 Alexander Neville prefaces his translation of Seneca's *Oedipus* with an apology for having wrenched the high-sounding Roman playwright out of his proper language:

For I to no other ende removed hym from his naturall and loftye Style to our own corrupt and base, or as al men affyrme it, most barbarous Language, but onely to satisfye the instant requestes of a few my familiar frendes.[1]

Neville and other translators often deprecate English as part of the conventional declaration of modesty, suggesting that their shortcomings as translators are bound up with the crudeness of their verbal medium. But those who compose original works in their native tongue also betray mixed feelings about their endeavour, wanting to reach as wide an audience as possible but regretting the inadequacies of the medium to which they are reduced. Sir Thomas Elyot and Sir Roger Ascham, for example, authors of some of the most influential and respected educational treatises of the period, freely confess their distaste for the common language they feel compelled to employ. Ascham laments 'the rudenes of common and mother tongues': after Greek and Latin, all modern languages will be found wanting; the classical languages afford the writer an expressive range and polish impossible to achieve in English. In addition to metaphors of high and low, the comparison that appears repeatedly in such discussions of speech is sartorial: Latin is figured as the splendid and colourful coat in which a writer's ideas may be sumptuously clothed; English, on the contrary, is a threadbare and homespun garment. The vernacular may be useful for reaching the multitudes and can deliver an intelligible version of necessary information, but it cannot pretend to elegance. To quote Neville once again: 'In fine I beseech all together (if so it might be) to bear with my rudeness, and consider the grossness of our own country['s] language, which can by no means aspire to the high lofty Latinists' style.'[2]

That so many sixteenth-century writers spent so much time maligning their language and expounding its weaknesses attests, of course, to its growing strength as a cultural force. As more and more people learned to read, writers began to recognize that English, not Latin, was the most practical means of reaching the public. Although Latin was still the focus of a young man's education in the grammar schools, many thousands of people were taught to read English in dame schools or petty schools. Having learned as much as they needed to keep accounts or to read the Bible, widely available in English translations from the mid-sixteenth century, they made no pretence to scholarship and left the classroom to go to work. The increasing significance of English in the sixteenth century is chiefly attributable to the rise of literacy, but the phenomenon also owes much to three other related factors.

First was the influence of the printing press. Although sporadic private printing apparently took place earlier, William Caxton's publication of *Recuyell* [Anthology, or Gathering Up] *of the Historyes of Troye* in 1476 marked the birth of the publishing industry in Britain, less than a hundred years before Shakespeare started school. Until the end of the fifteenth century, the vast majority of oral communication was conducted in English, while the vast majority of writing was done in Latin. The production and widespread distribution of printed books began to tip the balance in favour of the vernacular. Writers sought readers, and printers, customers; thus, while many works were still published in Latin, English books became the principal product of the printers and the booksellers. The majority of English books published between 1500 and 1600 were concerned with matters of religion, and the most important book in the Renaissance was, of course, the Bible.

The vernacular also profited from the zeal of the religious reformers. In the early decades of the sixteenth century, tradition was so powerful and English considered so unworthy that Protestant converts such as William Tyndale and Miles Coverdale met with angry resistance in their efforts to translate the Scriptures from Latin. Indeed, most of the early Tudor English translations were printed on the Continent and smuggled into England. Opponents of an English Bible deplored the lack of eloquence available in the vernacular, but ultimately the Reformation succeeded in turning that very characteristic to its ideological purposes. Thomas Becon, for example, ironically defended the simplicity of the English Bible, compared to the Latin, on the grounds that 'The baser [it] seemeth, the higher doth it excel the other, not with windiness and vayne bablying, but with solidite and graue doctrine.'[3] Native simplicity was to be preferred to the painted rhetoric of Rome.

The third factor was a spirit of nationalism. The ascendancy of England as a force in European politics, a process that began with Henry VIII and came to fruition under Elizabeth I, conferred a new and unimpeachable authority on the native language. Educators and writers began explicitly to associate the English tongue with English values and national pride. The Elizabethan educator Richard Mulcaster put the matter succinctly in the 'Peroration' to his great pedagogical work, *The First Part of the Elementarie* (1582): 'I love Rome, but London better, I favour Italy, but England more, I honour the Latin, but I worship the English.'[4] These biases represent more than simple jingoism, however. Earlier in the same passage Mulcaster makes the use of English a sign of national maturity, of independence from Europe and its past, of freedom and a profitable future.

For is it not indeed a marvellous bondage, to become servants to one tongue for learning sake the most of our time, with loss of most time, whereas we may have the very same treasure in our own tongue, with the gain of most time? our own bearing the joyful title of our liberty and freedom, the Latin tongue remembering us of our thraldom & bondage?[5]

Repeatedly in *The Elementarie* Mulcaster defends the historical process by which nations and their languages naturally displace their predecessors, and his book is an eloquent witness that, at the end of the sixteenth century, English had finally bested its classical antecedents in the contest for sovereignty.

The Look of the Language

A playwright coming of age in the last quarter of the century inherited a dynamic language: English was relatively young as a literary medium, unfixed in structure and vocabulary compared to Greek and Latin, and subject to variation and shaping according to the needs of the artist. This plasticity was especially obvious because Latin and

Greek were (relatively speaking) fixed linguistic systems, with settled vocabularies and unalterable grammatical forms. English, on the contrary, was in a constant state of flux, owing especially to its hybrid origins. Its derivation from both Germanic and Roman roots was a source of passionate controversy. Enemies of the vernacular regularly seized upon and ridiculed this mixed parentage. The Anglo-Saxon foundations of the English language had been altered and supplemented by the linguistic equivalent of the Norman invasion, with hundreds of words appropriated from French—and thus, ultimately, from Latin—over the span of 500 years. By the age of Elizabeth, as English became more esteemed and more widely used, and as disciplines such as philosophy and theology and the physical sciences began to expand, many writers found themselves faced with a vocabulary insufficient to their needs. Even the most fervent promoters of the vernacular had to acknowledge its impoverished diction. Thus, in order to express a new idea or make a fine distinction, writers found it necessary to invent or borrow or adapt a word or phrase from another language, a process known as neologizing. Two contrary approaches to neologizing emerged, and the differences between them generated some of the most heated linguistic disputes of the day.

Some champions of English objected to the practice of borrowing from other languages, sometimes from patriotic motives. George Gascoigne, the mid-century poet and translator, endorses plain English words as a sign of national pride: 'the most ancient English words are of one syllable, so that the more monosyllables that you use the truer Englishman you shall seem, and the less you shall smell of the inkhorn.'⁶ (The advice is worth remembering given Shakespeare's obvious delight in the properly placed English monosyllable.) Usually, however, foreign tongues were dismissed on the grounds that readers unfamiliar with Latin or French or Italian would be unable to comprehend coinages from those tongues. As an alternative, advocates of the vernacular proposed to fill gaps of meaning by creating fitting and self-explanatory terms, particularly compounds, from native materials only. This prejudice generated some very ingenious fabrications. For example, in preparing his textbook *The Arte of Reason, rightly termed, Witcraft*, the logician Ralph Lever sought to protect his discourse from foreign contamination, refusing to import even with modifications the Latin terms appropriate to the discipline. He thus devised native substitutes, such as *witcraft* for 'logic', *endsay* for 'conclusio', *ifsay* for 'propositio conditionalis', and, perhaps best of all, *saywhat* for 'definitio'.[7] Such absolutism was hard to sustain, of course, and in time the opponents of verbal borrowing lost the battle, as the disappearance of all Lever's inventions implies.

The ultimate winners in this controversy, also enthusiasts for the vernacular, took a more pragmatic view of foreign influence. Reversing the argument about linguistic bastardy, they asserted that the mixed parentage of English was really a strength, that its disparate origins made it open to expansion and supplement as occasion or subject demanded. From the nouns, verbs, and modifiers available in the well-stocked stores of Latin, Greek, and (to a lesser extent) the modern Romance languages, they crafted new and necessary terms. Scholars have concluded that almost 30,000 words were added to English, mostly from Latin, between 1500 and 1659.[8] In defending this practice, the neologizers, here represented by Thomas Digges, appealed to classical precedent:

for as the Romanes and other Latin writers, notwithstandinge the copiouse and abundant eloquence of their tongue, haue not shamed to borrow of the Grecians these and many other terms of arte: so surely do I thinke it no reproche, either to the English tongue, or any English writer, where fit words faile to borrow of them both.[9]

Others echo Digges's historical justification and assert that English is made both more functional and more graceful by the judicious adaptation of other languages.

The line between necessity and affectation was often blurred, however, and the liberal neologizers were divided over how far to go in forging a new vocabulary. In *The Art of Rhetoric* (1560), Thomas Wilson cautions his readers about the dangers of loan words by introducing a brilliant negative example, an application from a job-seeker to a gentleman at court. The letter has become a famous instance of what Wilson and other critics of pretension called 'inkhorn terms', fancy words and phrases that seemed uncomfortably new (just come from the inkstand, or 'inkhorn'). One notorious sentence suffices to convey Wilson's point: 'I obtestate your clemency, to invigilate thus much for me, according to my confidence, and as you know my condign merits, for such a compendious living.'[10] In other words,

'I beg your kindness to watch out for me in this way, as I know you will, and as you know my appropriate talents for such a lucrative job.' Except for pronouns and auxiliaries, virtually every word in the letter is Latinate, and far from achieving the desired eloquence, the writer makes himself ridiculous.

These controversies and the examples that illustrate them call attention to the most notable feature of the English language in the last half of the sixteenth century—its lack of standardization. Dispute over the introduction of new words is an especially revealing instance of such instability, and one source of disagreement on such matters is that until the seventeenth century, English people had no dictionary of their own language. Latin–English and other bilingual dictionaries and similar instructional aids did exist, but nothing like the complete listing of English words and their spellings which we take for granted. The book usually considered the first English dictionary, Robert Cawdrey's *A Table Alphabetical* (1604), was not meant to be comprehensive but rather a helpful collection of new and unusual words. Moreover, the publisher assumed that learned men would not need such a guide: according to the title page, the contents are 'gathered for the benefit and help of ladies, gentlewomen and any other unskilful persons' (see Fig. 1(*a*) and (*b*)). Since Elizabethan readers had no authoritative source to consult for the definition of an unfamiliar word or phrase, they had to rely on context, on a synonym provided by a considerate writer, or on etymological clues supplied by their familiarity with Latin.

For similar reasons, spelling was utterly irregular. Perhaps the most famous case of orthographic confusion is that, according to the authenticated signatures, Shakespeare seems to have spelled his own name in at least two different ways: Shakspeare and Shakspere. Spelling was governed by such various determinants as sound, etymology, whim, and the physical requirements of the printing house. Manuscripts, for example, disclose that a single writer or scribe often spelled the same word in different ways for no apparent reason. In the only surviving manuscript believed by some to be in Shakespeare's hand, the fragment from *The Book of Sir Thomas More*, the writer spells the word 'sheriff' five different ways in three lines. If a printer setting type found his line running into the margin, he might omit an *e* or another dispensable letter; if he were running short on type he might

A

Table Alphabeticall, con-
teyning and teaching the true
vvriting, and vnderſtanding of hard
vſuall Engliſh wordes, borrowed from
the Hebrew, Greeke, Latine,
or French. &c.

With the interpretation thereof by
plaine Engliſh words, gathered for the benefit &
helpe of Ladies, Gentlewomen, or any other
vnskilfull perſons.

Whereby they may the more eaſilie
and better vnderſtand many hard Engliſh
wordes, vvhich they ſhall heare or read in
Scriptures, Sermons, or elſwhere, and alſo
be made able to vſe the ſame aptly
themſelues.

Legere, et non intelligere , neglegere eſt.
As good not read, as not to vnderſtand.

AT   LONDON,
Printed by I. R. for Edmund Wea-
uer, & are to be ſold at his ſhop at the great
North doore of Paules Church.
1 6 04.

1 (*a*). The title page of Robert Cawdrey's *A Table Alphabetical*, the book considered
to be the first English dictionary. Its principal function was to help with unusual or
unfamiliar terms.

A Table Alphabeticall,

contayning and teaching the true
writing, and vnderſtanding of hard
vſuall Engliſh words. &c.

$(\because)$

(k) ſtandeth for a kind of.
(g. or gr.) ſtandeth for Greeke.
The French words haue this (§) before them.

A

§ **A** Bandon, caſt away, oʒ yǽlde vp, to
leaue, oʒ foʒſake.

Abaſh, bluſh.

abba, father.

§ abbeſſe, abbateſſe, Miſtris of a Nunne-
rie, comfoʒters of others.

§ abbettors, counſelloʒs.

aberration, a going a ſtray, oʒ wandering.

abbreuiat, ⎫ to ſhoʒten, oʒ make
§ abbridge. ⎭ ſhoʒt.

§ abbut, to lie vnto, oʒ boʒder vpon, as one
lands end méets with another.

abecédarie, the oʒder of the Letters, oʒ hee
that vſeth them.

aberration, a going aſtray, oʒ wandering.

§ abet, to maintaine.

B.   § abdi-

make a similar alteration. Sometimes, to improve the look of a passage or for some other reason, he might fill out a line with a letter or two. Other features of grammar and sentence structure were undergoing change as well. Although many conventions of Middle English were still observed, especially verb endings (taken up below), numerous modifications and simplifications that we regard as 'modern' were beginning to be adopted. The language was in transition, retaining many of its ancient traditions but edging towards modernity.

In almost any sixteenth-century text, the grammar serves as a register of this unstable condition. Writers and speakers often had a choice of grammatical forms: a telling instance of this mixed state involves verbs and their endings, particularly the third person singular.[11] The inflected endings characteristic of Middle English (*go, goest, goeth*) were gradually being replaced with their simpler modern equivalents (*go, go, goes*). These distinctions were also regionally based, in that around 1500 *-eth* was the form favoured in London and the southern counties, while *-es* was a northern convention that migrated south over the next hundred years. Both forms were available around 1590, and Shakespeare avails himself of both. His choice was sometimes dictated by the demands of rhyme, and often by rhythmic patterns: *-eth* furnished an extra syllable, whereas *-es* was normally silent, elided with the previous syllable. Also, the two forms carried distinct tonal associations: *-eth* seems to have been the more formal choice, used as it was in sermons or other kinds of ceremonious discourse, while *-es* shows up more regularly in private and popular kinds of writing, such as letters and pamphlets.

By the time Shakespeare began to compose for the theatre, the earlier endings were being used much less frequently, especially in speech, and thus *-est* and *-eth* had come to sound outmoded or to connote unusual solemnity. In general the public playwrights of the time, Shakespeare included, favoured the simpler, less formal *-es* and observed the tonal distinctions described here. It is significant, for example, that speakers in scenes of low comedy rarely employ the older endings. In the case of a few simple verbs, however, Shakespeare conspicuously favours the older form, as in his use of 'hath' and 'doth'. 'Doth' is spoken almost three times as often as 'does', for example, with no obvious explanation or criterion for the choice. What is important about the two endings is that the late Elizabethan writer had options, and that such flexibility enriches the speech of Shakespeare's characters.

Similar choice was available with pronouns, particularly *thee, thou, thy,* and *thine.* The familiar (i.e. informal) forms of the second person, these pronouns have today been completely supplanted by *you* and *your,* a process of replacement well under way in the sixteenth century. But Shakespeare and his contemporaries still had access to both forms, and their audiences would have unconsciously registered the nuances of each, particularly the social implications. The difference between 'thou' and 'you' corresponds to the difference, still observed in modern Romance languages, between the informal and formal styles, i.e. *tu* and *vous* in French. At the risk of oversimplifying the complexities of early modern pronoun usage, we can summarize the most important distinctions as follows.

'You' was the more formal and respectful choice: servants addressed their masters this way, and common folk always used 'you' when speaking to the king or to a member of the aristocracy. The nominative 'thou' (as well as the accusative or objective 'thee') was more familiar, spoken in personal conversation and in friendly encounters between equals; lovers and family members used it; it was the customary form for speaking to servants and children. It also quickly conveyed distinctions of rank, in that high-born or respected people regularly used 'thou' to address their social inferiors. The prevalence of this convention also meant that 'thou' and 'thee' could be used to try to *establish* social superiority: a person wishing to insult another could shift from 'you' to 'thou' as a way of demeaning the adversary. Despite these clear distinctions of class, worshippers addressed God—or heavenly powers generally—as 'Thou'. Other sorts of pronominal difference obtained, such as that between the nominative 'ye' and the accusative 'you', but such subtleties are beyond the scope of this chapter. What matters is that the audience knew the connotations of each form, and Shakespeare carefully modulates his usage for a variety of dramatic purposes. He regularly clarifies social relationships among characters by his careful assignment of pronouns. His wooers shift from the more formal 'you' to the more personal 'thou' to indicate growing intimacy: in *Twelfth Night,* the Countess Olivia finds herself increasingly attracted to the young messenger Cesario (actually Viola in male disguise) but maintains the formal 'you' throughout their first interview; as soon as she is alone, however, Olivia confesses her passion to the audience in soliloquy, shifting immediately to the more personal 'thou' and 'thy'. The availability of the more and less formal styles allows the playwright to move abruptly or stealthily from one register to another to denote a change in relationship.

Other cases of linguistic instability might be catalogued, but there is space only to mention some of the most vital. Syntax, the placement of words in sentences, was flexible enough to provide a writer with a good deal of choice. Unlike Latin, in which the order of parts of speech was mostly fixed, or present-day English, in which the vast majority of sentences begin with the subject followed by the verb and then the object, early modern English afforded a number of structural alternatives. Writers could vary the position of key words and thereby achieve a particular effect without sounding stilted or confusing. Donne's famous injunction 'Send not to know for whom the bell tolls', based as it is on the inverted alternative to 'Do not send', efficiently conveys the power of the inversion. Lady Macbeth, likewise, breaks up the disastrous banquet with 'Stand not upon the order of your going, | But go at once' (3.4.118–19). In this case, as in others like it, the iambic rhythms support the syntactical reversal: 'not' occupies the stressed position. Variable pronunciation also created a range of effects. The language was undergoing the process known to linguists as 'The Great Vowel Shift', in which pronunciation of English was moving from its Middle English habits to something approaching its modern forms. When Shakespeare counted he probably pronounced the number 'one' as something like 'own' or the first syllable in 'only'. He probably rhymed the noun 'sea' not with 'bee' but with 'lay'. And he regularly rhymed the noun 'wind' (as in 'weather') with the long-vowelled 'kind'. None of these forms was exclusive, however: Shakespeare's rhymes indicate that certain words could legitimately be pronounced in more than one way. Moreover, there were regional variations, of which only traces remain today: Londoners spoke differently from their relatives in Yorkshire, and those differences involved considerably more than accent.

Many of these variations fall under the category of 'poetic licence', a phrase that had a much more technical meaning to the sixteenth-century writer and reader than it does today. George Gascoigne in 1575 offers the following description: 'This poetical licence is a shrewd fellow, and covereth many faults in a verse; it maketh words longer, shorter, of more syllables, of fewer, newer, older, truer, falser; and, to conclude, it turkeneth [twists] all things at pleasure, for example, *ydone* for *done*, *adown* for *down*, *orecome* for *overcome*, *tane* for *taken*, *power* for *powre*, *heaven* for *heavn* . . . and a number of others."[12] Shakespeare often takes advantage of such poetic licence, his shifting of accent being one of the clearest examples. In the first scene of *The Comedy of Errors*, for example, the word *confiscate* is pronounced with the accent on the second syllable (con-fís-ket), while in the second scene (five minutes later) it is spoken in the modern way (cón-fis-cáte). The linguistic transition that made these different forms available was a happy historical accident for the Renaissance dramatist. By the end of the seventeenth century the process of standardization was nearly complete, and the range of expressive possibility had narrowed considerably.

Artifice in Abundance

The decades of linguistic debate just described bespeak a culture that was extremely self-conscious about its language. A proper understanding of Shakespeare's artistic achievement requires that we recognize the nature and extent of this verbal self-consciousness, specifically that we comprehend the linguistic assumptions of the playwright's intended audience. Chief among such predispositions is the centrality of rhetoric. Perhaps more than any other single factor, this devotion to artfully arranged words separates early modern thinking from our own. Anglo-American culture at the beginning of the twenty-first century, shaped by the ideas of modernism, pragmatism, and other such intellectual and artistic movements of the past hundred years, tends to be wary of any kind of stylistic flourish. Expressive training nowadays emphasizes the virtues of economy, utility, and transparency. Despite the contrarian efforts of some post-modernist artists and thinkers, our attitudes about written expression are consistent with our views of spatial form and of decoration generally, ideas captured in the famous phrase of the modernist architect Mies van der Rohe, 'Less is more.'

Our Elizabethan predecessors would not have accepted such a proposition. The theory of composition in which they were trained held that ideas, in order to be transmitted effectively, had to be expressed eloquently. The verbal sign and its presentation mattered as much as the idea it signified. As Richard Lanham puts it, the age believed that words must be 'looked at before they can be looked through'.[13] And if words were to be relished as well as apprehended, then the writer was obliged to consider such principles as amplitude, patterning, and ornamentation. It would be misleading to imply that sixteenth-century literary education was monolithic, or that all teachers of writing agreed about every question of style. Writers were capable of understatement, to be sure, and as the sixteenth century advanced an explicitly anti-rhetorical strain developed, particularly among thinkers with Puritan leanings. Taken up by Francis Bacon and others, such scepticism became increasingly prominent in English thought in the seventeenth century, reflecting attitudes that would, after a series of turns and reversals, culminate in the austerities of modernism. Nevertheless, most Elizabethan writers, readers, artists, and playgoers were committed to the intrinsic value of the literary sign, especially to its physical satisfactions.

Artifice was considered an instrument for the transmission of thought, not an obstacle to it. Elizabethan critical theorists describe the poet as a 'maker', one who arranges verbal materials into delightful and instructive patterns. Another way of putting this point is to say that the age valued the performative quality of all writing, and in the work of an artist creating dialogue for the stage that consciousness of the performative takes on special significance. Readers and playgoers were expected to notice and to admire the skill with which artistic materials were arranged and presented. George Puttenham, in the analytical defence of the poet's work that concludes his *Art of English Poesy* (1589), addresses himself directly to the problem of artificiality. His last chapter in Book III (entitled 'Of Ornament') is headed '*That the good Poet or maker ought to dissemble his art, and in what cases the artificial is more commended than the natural, and contrariwise.*' Presupposing that the poet's task is the imitation of nature, Puttenham insists that in some cases artistic effort should be concealed, that the greatest art lies in disguising the artistry. In other instances, however, the artistry should show: physicians and gardeners, for example, are among those who must frankly manipulate and rearrange natural materials. Whatever the circumstances, the underlying assumption

throughout his discussion is the intrinsic artificiality of poetic discourse.[14] And it is worth noting that his remarks are addressed directly
to Queen Elizabeth, who knew something about artifice.

In the sixteenth century 'artificial' was not a term of opprobrium, as
it usually is today, but a term of praise. And having inherited their taste
for artifice from Greek and Roman literature, the Tudor pedagogues
set about to appropriate classical techniques for the arrangement of
verbal materials. Gabriel Harvey, friend of Edmund Spenser and the
Elizabethan version of a public intellectual, urged his countrymen 'to
imitate the excellentest artificiality of the most renowned work-
masters that antiquity affordeth'.[15] Those who wished to follow Harvey's advice had access to a number of instructional aids. For decades
English schoolmen, in an effort to dignify their newly respectable
language, had been converting to their own use the vast rhetorical
system of tropes, figures, and schemes set forth in the Latin writings of
Cicero, Quintilian, and the pseudo-Ciceronian *Rhetorica ad Herre-
nium*. Devised as guides for orators in a pre-print culture, these
classical treatises codify, describe, and illustrate formulae for achieving
distinct emotional and argumentative effects, and so the European
literary theorists applied their methods to the composition of poetry.
Puttenham's *Arte of English Poesy* is the most comprehensive of
the English guides. Others include Richard Sherry's *A Treatise of
Schemes and Tropes* (1550), Thomas Wilson's *The Art of Rhetoric*
(1553), Richard Rainolde's *A Book Called the Foundation of Rhetoric*
(1563), and Henry Peacham's *The Garden of Eloquence* (1577) (see Fig.
2). The immense popularity and influence of these guidebooks can be
indicated by the fact that Wilson's *Art of Rhetoric* was reprinted seven
times before the end of the century. And the aim of each author is
summarized in Wilson's stated intention 'to set forth precepts of
eloquence'.[16]

The pursuit of eloquence is perhaps the most distinctive characteristic of the Renaissance humanists. Although the early Tudor commentators had lamented the expressive inadequacies of the vernacular,
by the end of the century prevailing opinion had begun to change, and
the richness and variety of the language were regularly praised, promoted, analysed, and illustrated with excerpts from recent English
writing. Samuel Daniel, in the peroration that ends his poem *Muso-
philus* (1599), identifies and praises the ideal:

ℭ, THE GARDEN OF
Eloquence.

¶ The names of Figures.

Figures of the Grecians, are called Tropes and Schemates, and of the Latines, Figures Exornations, Lightes, Colours, and Ornaments of speeche. Cicero who supposed them to be named of the Grecians Schemates, as a iesture and countenaunce of speech, called them Concinnitie, that is propernesse, aptnesse, featnesse, also confoumations, foumes, and fashions, comprising all ornamentes of speech vnder one name.

¶ *A Figure what it is.*

A Figure is a fashion of woords, Oration, or sentence, made new by Arte, tourning from the common manner and custome of wryting or speaking.

¶ *A Figure how it is deuided.*

<pre>
                        ⎧ of wordes. 9.
              ⎧ Tropes ⎨ of sentences. 10.
              ⎪   ⎩
              ⎪   ⎧ Orthographical. 14.
A figure is ⎨ &c   ⎧ Grāmatical. ⎨ Syntačtical. 42.
deuided into ⎪   ⎪   ⎩
              ⎪   ⎪
              ⎩ Schemates ⎬ &
                       ⎪   ⎧ Of wordes. 24.
                       ⎪   ⎪
                       ⎩ Rhetorical ⎨ Of sentences. 25.
                                     ⎪
                                     ⎩ Of Amplificatiō. 60.
</pre>

B.j.   ¶ A

2. A page from Henry Peacham's *Garden of Eloquence* (1577) where he translates for English readers the Latin system of rhetoric borrowed from Johannes Susenbrotus' *Epitome troporum ac schematum et grammaticorum et rhetoricum* of 1540.

Pow'r above pow'rs, O heavenly *Eloquence*,
That with the strong rein of commanding words,
Dost manage, guide, and master th'eminence
Of men's affections more than all their swords:
Shall we not offer to thy excellence
The richest treasure that our wit affords?
Thou that canst do much more with one poor pen
Than all the pow'rs of princes can effect:
And draw, divert, dispose, and fashion men
Better than force or rigour can direct:
Should we this ornament of glory then
As th'unmaterial fruits of shades, neglect?[17]

From the Latin *ēloqui*, 'to speak out', the English word 'eloquence' in the critical writing of the period appears to be synonymous with both 'style' and 'rhetoric', and it further implies several related meanings, from smooth and polished writing to persuasiveness to copiousness of statement. This last quality, taken over from Latin *copia*, suggests that good writing depends upon the multiplicity and abundance of the words employed. It is the most frequently recommended means of achieving eloquence.

The noun 'copia' was interchangeable with 'eloquence' because fullness or variety of statement was considered a virtue in and of itself. As Thomas Wilson says of 'amplification', 'Among all the figures of rhetoric, there is no one that so much helpeth forward an oration and beautifieth the same with such delightful ornament as doth amplification.'[18] Revelling in the new possibilities of their language, writers (and readers) took pleasure in repetition, variation, exemplification, synonymy, and a host of other specific forms of verbal multiplication. Many technical names were assigned to these strategies: *epexegesis* (adding words and phrases to amplify an idea); *systrophe* (heaping up descriptions in place of a definition); *anacephalaeosis* (a recapitulation); *epizeuxis*, also known as *geminatio* (repetition of a word with no other word in between).[19] The various names suggest the popularity and utility of these tactics. Such formulae helped to reveal the 'bravery' or splendour of the English language and thus invited favourable comparison between the vernacular and Latin.

More than a decorative strategy, however, augmentation or ornamentation was understood to be essential to the process of defining and exploring the complexity of the topic at hand. Early in his treatise *De Copia* (1514), Erasmus asserts the value of 'turn[ing] the same thought into many forms, as the famous Proteus is said to have changed his form'. Variety stimulates the intellect and thus serves to engage the reader or listener: 'Nature herself especially rejoices in variety; in such a great throng of things she has left nothing anywhere not painted with some wonderful artifice of variety. And just as the eye is held more by a varying scene, in the same way the mind always eagerly examines whatever it sees as new.'[20] Embellishment, in other words, contributes not only to the articulation or analysis of the subject but also to the production of knowledge. According to Richard Sherry, in his *Treatise of the Figures of Grammar and Rhetoric*, certain figures are known as 'ornaments of matter, because by them, not only the oration and words, but the body of the matter groweth and is increased'.[21] This view of verbal material effectively captures the humanist belief in the *materiality* of words themselves, their intimate connection to the subject *matter* they represent. Thus, the wish to arrange words into patterns, the impulse that gave rise to the domestication of classical rhetoric, represents something more than an attempt to glamorize one's ideas or an effort to delight with ornament. The substantiality of words is such that to shape and form the language is to do nothing less than to begin to remake the world. Speech thus becomes a potent form of social agency. And yet the capacity of patterned speech to please the senses is not to be underestimated. 'At the heart of rhetorical reality lies pleasure.'[22]

Humanism and the Power of Language

The language Shakespeare learned—to conclude with a glance back at the original topic of this chapter—was the language of Renaissance humanism. His artistic achievement was, in other words, the product of a century of self-conscious debate about the power of the word in general and specifically about the potentialities of English for promoting the humanist ideals of eloquence and persuasion. He profited both from the dynamic growth of the vernacular and from the system of rules designed to control such unruliness. A helpful way of situating Shakespeare historically is to say that he was the ideal pupil of the Tudor schoolmasters, the student who absorbed the precepts of his teachers and transcended their comparatively limited systems by putting their recommendations to artistic use.

To the Renaissance commentators, language was God's great gift, the capacity for eloquent speech the property that made men and women, of all creatures, the most nearly divine. All their debates were essentially variations on the problem of power, discussions of how the possibilities of the word might most effectively be harnessed. Wayne A. Rebhorn reminds us that when the Elizabethan

rhetoricians define the nature and function of the art in their treatises and handbooks, they stress its power above all else, specifically the power it puts in the hands of the orator to control the will and desire of the audience. They conceive rhetoric as a political instrument, to be sure, but not one whose main purpose is to enable free political debate and discussion. Rather, they celebrate rhetoric for giving its possessor the ability to subjugate others, to place the world beneath his feet.... At its core, then, Renaissance rhetoric is animated by a fantasy of power in which the orator, wielding words more deadly than swords, takes on the world and emerges victorious in every encounter.[23]

When we consider that at no point in history have Shakespeare's plays been more popular and more frequently performed than they are now, at the beginning of the twenty-first century, we may recognize that this passage offers an apt summary of what he managed to do with the language he learned. The next chapter will be devoted to a demonstration, albeit a limited one, of some of those poetic victories.

Shaping the Language

Words, Patterns, and the Traditions of Rhetoric

It is necessary to state the obvious, although it is difficult to know how best to say it: that Shakespeare was a verbal prodigy? possessed of an extraordinary gift for language? amazingly sensitive to words? endowed with unparalleled poetic talent? a genius? Stephen Booth suggests the dimensions of the problem when he says that 'We generally acknowledge Shakespeare's poetic superiority to other candidates for greatest poet in English, but doing that is comparable to saying that King Kong is bigger than other monkeys.'[1] Having admitted the impossibility of the task, we must nevertheless persist in an attempt to define the nature of Shakespeare's particular gift for language. This chapter, then, will consider Shakespeare's relation to the language of his time. It begins with his manifest interest in contemporary debates about linguistic fashion, most of them controversies about vocabulary and syntax and style. It also takes up his contribution to the language *per se*, specifically his remarkable role in expanding the English vocabulary. The bulk of the chapter is given over to Shakespeare's treatment of rhetoric, particularly his changing attitude towards the vast system of schemes and tropes that the Tudor schoolmasters adapted from the Romans. In short, this chapter examines what Shakespeare did with the language he learned.

The topic of Shakespeare's verbal achievement must be prefaced, however, with a word about the problem of artistic agency. The literary text is now seen less as the creation of an individual artistic intelligence than the product of cultural forces articulated through the writer. The analysis of poetry, however, is not incompatible with this recent enthusiasm for discursive context. Indeed, it ought to be the beneficiary of such interest. Students of poetry should heed the motto of cultural materialism: 'Always historicize.' It is vital that we examine the origins and relations of Shakespeare's words just as rigorously as we do the physical spaces in which he worked and the political structures in which his plays were imbricated. Only by doing so can we identify and assess his distinctive gift for language. The plays and poems are shaped by linguistic pressures that belong specifically to the historical moment and the verbal culture in which the playwright worked, his characters speak as they do because their creator conceived them at a particular point in the history of his verbal medium, and the semantic and poetic rewards of a Shakespeare play owe much to the growth and vigour and instability of the English language around 1600.

Shakespeare was born at the right time. In a fortunate intersection of individual talent and cultural context, his unmatched sensitivity to words combines with the range and plasticity of the English language at this moment in its development. The Elizabethan self-consciousness about language described in Chapter 1 apparently acted as a powerful stimulus: first, to his recognizing and using the resources of the English language; and second, to his reflections about language as an artistic and humanistic medium—its value, its possibilities, its uses, its limits. Because language, specifically the potentialities of the expanding vernacular, was a central topic in the metropolitan milieu that he entered in the late 1580s, Shakespeare found a receptive and encouraging audience for the development of his own exceptional poetic abilities. The disputes over the vernacular that had occupied the intelligentsia for much of the sixteenth century had at last produced a mood of optimism about the artistic possibilities of the native tongue. That confidence was reinforced by national pride at the victory over the Spanish Armada in 1588, and this mix of patriotism and literary enthusiasm is partly responsible for our neglect of some of the depressing social and economic facts about the 1590s. But from a poetic standpoint, the age was golden.

The last quarter of the sixteenth century saw an outburst of literary creativity unsurpassed in any equivalent period. A brief account of works published or circulated would include Edmund Spenser's *Faerie Queene*; the sonnet sequences of Spenser, Sir Philip Sidney, Phineas Fletcher, Samuel Daniel, and others; Sidney's great prose romance *The Countess of Pembroke's Arcadia*; the court comedies and prose works of John Lyly; miscellaneous poems (short and long) by Sir Walter Ralegh, Isabella Whitney, Spenser, Robert Greene, Thomas Lodge, Michael Drayton, Sir John Davies, Mary Sidney Herbert, Donne, and Queen Elizabeth; Raphael Holinshed's *Chronicles of England, Scotland and Ireland*; the audacious plays and erotic poems of Christopher Marlowe; George Puttenham's *Art of English Poesy*; Byrd's and Dowland's books of songs and airs; Richard Hooker's *Laws of Ecclesiastical Polity*; Thomas Nashe's satiric prose fiction *The Unfortunate Traveller*; the initial instalment of George Chapman's translation of *The Iliad*; a number of other translations by Elizabethan women; some of Francis Bacon's early essays; and this is not to mention the multiple new editions of works popular in earlier decades, such as the collection of biographies known as *The Mirror for Magistrates*. Finding a common denominator among such disparate works is exceedingly difficult, but if there is one shared feature it is an implicit, and sometimes explicit, faith in the possibilities of the English language. Expression is one of the principal subjects, and the effect of their words is never far from the writers' consciousness, as one example will illustrate. Christopher Marlowe, addressing the audience in the prologue to his first theatrical success, advertises his poetic flair:

> We'll lead you to the stately tent of War,
> Where you shall hear the Scythian *Tamburlaine*,
> Threat'ning the world with high astounding terms...
> 　　　　　(*Tamburlaine, Part 1*, Prologue, ll. 3–5)[2]

Words could 'astound'; English had acquired the power to charm. In 1623 Ben Jonson looked back to the late Elizabethan theatrical culture from which Shakespeare emerged, referring specifically to Marlowe's 'mighty line'. The sound of Marlovian verse apparently had a palpable effect on listeners at the Rose Theatre in the late 1580s, and the poet's pride in his gift for exploiting the vernacular is not only a Marlovian but an Elizabethan trait.

Fashions and Controversies

Shakespeare almost certainly heard these 'terms'; we know that he read widely in contemporary literature; and he found his own artistic leanings and gifts consonant with the taste of the times. Although his fascination with the uses and abuses of language shapes a number of episodes in his early works—Petruccio's witty skirmishes with Katherine in *The Taming of the Shrew*, for example—one of the early comedies seems concerned with almost nothing else: *Love's Labour's Lost*. Shakespeare devotes virtually every scene of this play to an exploration, much of it conducted ironically, of the problem of appropriate expression. The central characters, most obviously Biron, struggle with the proper way to speak the language of love, and the wooing plot resolves itself in Biron's apology for the derived and overdone language of his courting.

> BIRON Taffeta phrases, silken terms precise,
> 　　Three-piled hyperboles, spruce affectation,
> Figures pedantical—these summer flies
> 　　Have blown me full of maggot ostentation.
> I do forswear them, and I here protest,
> 　　By this white glove—how white the hand, God knows!—
> Henceforth my wooing mind shall be expressed
> 　　In russet yeas, and honest kersey noes.
> And to begin, wench, so God help me, law!
> My love to thee is sound, sans crack or flaw.
> ROSALINE Sans 'sans', I pray you.
> BIRON　　　　　　　　　　　Yet I have a trick
> Of the old rage. Bear with me, I am sick.
>
> 　　　　　　　　　　　　　(5.2.406–17)

The ironies of this confession are typical: characters talk at length about the proper uses of words, their style contradicting the substance of their arguments. Biron regrets the use of 'figures pedantical' while summoning a figure ('these summer flies') to denounce their ill effect; as Rosaline notes, he relies on an affected term (the French *sans*) in his disavowal of affectation; and the entire apology, a critique of the way that self-regarding poetic forms can misrepresent genuine feeling, is delivered in rhyme. The historical ramifications of this play are profound because it foregrounds the linguistic controversies that had divided English pedagogical theory for nearly a century, questions of vocabulary, foreign terms, highly patterned speeches, appropriate syntax, and rhetorical flourishes. Shakespeare's personal view of these matters is difficult to ascertain, of course, chiefly because *Love's Labour's Lost* is a theatrical entertainment, not a tract. As Inga-Stina Ewbank aptly puts it about his practice in general: 'in the end Shakespeare was neither a rhetorician nor a philosopher of language but a practising dramatist. The problem of the relationship between language and truth is one that he *uses*, rather than solves.'[3] He seems in this play to have entertained many conflicting thoughts about proper discourse, and such complementary thinking about language (as well as about almost everything else) continued until his retirement.

Shakespeare had an ear for argumentative extremes, and in *Love's Labour's Lost* he assigns the most eccentric verbal follies to the cadre of minor figures who animate the margins of Navarre's court. Holofernes, the pedantic and self-satisfied schoolmaster, emerges as one of the most colourful speakers, as indicated by his entrance speech about the royal hunt:

The deer was, as you know—*sanguis*—in blood, ripe as the pomewater [apple] who now hangeth like a jewel in the ear of *caelo*, the sky, the welkin, the heaven, and anon falleth like a crab on the face of *terra*, the soil, the land, the earth. (4.2.3–7)

This is *amplificatio* gone wild, a parody of *copia* according to Thomas Wilson and an exaggerated version of one side in the pedagogical debate over English vocabulary. Holofernes' speech is peppered with Latin phrases, multiple synonyms, pretentious nouns and verbs, and ostentatious rhetorical patterns. And yet he considers himself a sensitive critic of others' language, as when he reproaches Armado because 'he draweth out the thread of his verbosity finer than the staple of his argument. I abhor such fanatical phantasims' (5.1.16–18). This assessment, like Biron's speech on affectation, and like the play as a whole, delights in the very foolishness it mocks. The playwright asks us to recognize a fundamental paradox: for all the excesses and follies into which language can lead us, its faults are closely related to its attractions.

In a historical version of that theatrical paradox, Shakespeare himself was engaged in the coining of English words even as he was mocking his characters for doing so. The target of his ridicule on this point is the hilariously affected Armado, 'a man of fire-new words' (1.1.178). At the same time, Shakespeare's own contribution to the expansion of the language was noticed in print as early as 1598, when the commentator Francis Meres, applauding the increasing status of English literature in relation to the classics, places him among those writers who have recently dignified their language. Meres praises Shakespeare, along with Spenser, Sidney, Marlowe, and a few others, for creating works by which the 'English tongue is mightily enriched, and gorgeously invested in rare ornaments and resplendent habiliments'.[4] Here we recognize the sartorial imagery and connotations of 'bravery' familiar from the Tudor theorists. But later, in the eighteenth and nineteenth centuries, critics and scholars began—inaccurately— to doubt that Shakespeare could have helped significantly with the expansion of English vocabulary. Some of these sceptics were committed to the neoclassical image of Shakespeare as a poor Latinist, while others, particularly some Victorians, seemed eager to deprecate his classical learning and thereby to preserve him as a Saxonist. This critical prejudice, predictably, fostered an overreaction, so that one early twentieth-century writer, using (it must be said) a faulty method of calculation, credited Shakespeare with having coined nearly 10,000 words![5]

Recent scholarship has proposed a more judicious estimate of Shakespeare's neologisms. Calculating the number of new words he invented is a very complex and technical business because what you find depends on what you count. For example, the results depend on the definition of a coinage: should variations of existing words be included? or should two forms of a given word be registered separately? what about an existing word to which Shakespeare has given a new meaning? do compound words count? To complicate matters further, our access to evidence about the extent of English vocabulary in the sixteenth century is limited. The *Oxford English Dictionary*, which lists the first printed appearance in English of a given word, is not an infallible resource. Words are more likely to be considered Shakespearian inventions simply because his works have been more thoroughly scrutinized than other early modern texts. Since the first publication of the *OED*, many new words previously ascribed to Shakespeare have been 'antedated', or located in the earlier writings of his contemporaries. And yet the identification of an earlier usage does not preclude the possibility of a Shakespearian coinage: especially in the absence of dictionaries, Shakespeare and another writer may have devised the word independently of each other.

The difficulty of arriving at precise figures notwithstanding, Meres was right. Shakespeare significantly enriched the English language with coinages, many from Latin, some from French, some from native roots. Estimating very conservatively—that is, disallowing such questionable forms as compounds or participial expansions of existing words—the most recent expert finds that Shakespeare used Latin to invent some 600 words over the course of his writing career.[6] A high percentage of these, perhaps as many as one-third, have not survived, for a variety of reasons. Several were what are called 'nonce-words', terms created to answer a momentary poetic or theatrical need: for example, 'unprovokes' in the Porter's scene in *Macbeth* was apparently coined to make a comic match with 'provokes' in the previous line. And many words simply did not catch on, such as 'convive' meaning 'to feast' (*Troilus*, 4.5.272); 'crimeless' meaning 'innocent' (*2 Henry VI*, 2.5.64); 'facinorous' meaning 'extremely wicked' (*All's Well*, 2.3.30); and 'unseminared' meaning 'castrated', literally 'deprived of seed' (*Antony and Cleopatra*, 2.5.11). On the other hand, some words that we use every day appear to be Shakespearian coinages: 'countless' (*Titus*, 5.3.159), 'assassination' (*Macbeth*, 1.7.2), 'unreal' (*Macbeth*, 3.4.106), 'frugal' (*Much Ado*, 4.1.128).

The topic of Shakespeare's vocabulary has warranted so much space because it is fundamental to an understanding both of his cultural debts and of his originality. Words were the principal issue in the early modern debates over language and its functions: as a recent scholar has explained, sixteenth-century educators and commentators thought and wrote much more extensively about words than about grammar and syntax; not until the seventeenth century did those structural topics begin to take precedence.[7] Thus, Shakespeare was very much of his time in his enlargement of the language. And yet he was exceptional too. Difficult though it is to be sure about numbers, it appears that of the neologisms added to English between 1590 and 1612, Shakespeare contributed a substantial percentage. That he had such liberty to invent words permitted him to colour his plays in a manner that would have been much more difficult either 100 years before or 100 years later. Clearly, he took advantage of the plasticity, the unruliness of the English language.

For all the vigour and instability of the vernacular, however, it was not without structural rules. The English language was being shaped into forms by the great Tudor rhetoricians, and Shakespeare's relation to contemporary systems of rhetoric is an immense topic. Although experts disagree on whether he knew this or that rhetorical handbook, all admit his absorption in and fascination with the discipline. If, as some have urged, the young Shakespeare spent some time as a private schoolmaster, perhaps in Lancashire, then his familiarity with Cicero and Quintilian and their English followers would have been total. And even if he never taught, it is obvious that his own teachers and his habits of reading had inculcated in him the principles and particulars of Elizabethan rhetorical theory. As Brian Vickers points out, 'every person who had a grammar-school education in Europe between Ovid and Pope knew by heart, familiarly, up to a hundred figures, by their right names'.[8] If this is true of most educated Englishmen, then a dramatic poet, someone with a professional interest in language, must have been even more adept at the art. Shakespeare's poems and plays, especially the earliest ones, attest to his acquaintance with the rhetoricians' arguments and his application of many of their specific formulae. Those who wish to examine his reliance on particular schemes and tropes can consult one of the classic studies, such as Sister Miriam Joseph's *Shakespeare's Use of the Arts of Language* (1947), or the work of one of the more recent students of the topic, such as Vickers or Peter G. Platt.[9] Above all, the plays reveal Shakespeare's joy in verbal patterning and poetic artifice.

An overview of Shakespeare's theatrical career implies a shift in his attitude about the rhetorical, but this apparent transformation should be approached cautiously. The apprentice playwright indulges in much verbal display and rhetorical patterning, taking pleasure in the sound and arrangement of words for their own sake; as he gains experience and maturity, we can observe the apparent diminution of such schemes and patterns. This turn away from the superficial attractions of rhetoric has been an axiom of criticism since the beginning of the nineteenth century, when Coleridge complained that 'Sometimes you see this youthful god of poetry connecting disparate thoughts purely by means of resemblances in the words expressing them.[10] The early plays have often suffered condescension from such Romantic and modernist distaste for the 'rhetorical'; such prejudice favours the second half of the career, by which time Shakespeare is supposed to have outgrown his weakness for schemes and patterns.

What must be emphasized, however, is that his dependence on rhetoric never disappears. In one of the mature masterpieces, say *Twelfth Night* or *Macbeth*, the poetic surfaces may seem less formal and artificial than in an earlier text, one of the *Henry VI* plays, for example, but the differences are less substantial than they look. What actually happens, as a brief survey will demonstrate, is that Shakespeare turns his attention from one kind of rhetorical device to another, discarding the more obvious formulae in favour of more subtle manipulations of language. One way of putting the change is to say that the poet internalizes the principles that underlie the obvious figures. In other words, although the verbal manifestations of rhetoric may be less insistent, the principles that animate those forms, ideas such as antithesis or parallelism or irony, are still very much in force.

Pleasure in Patterns

The arrangement of words in some of the early plays is so extravagant that it is sometimes hard to distinguish the serious examples from the parodic. In the first tetralogy (*1, 2, 3 Henry VI* and *Richard III*), for example, the passions of the Wars of the Roses prompt Shakespeare to create some of his most elaborately wrought verse, as in the patterned laments of old Queen Margaret in *Richard III*. In Act 4, with Queen Elizabeth and the Duchess of York for audience, she exults in the fulfilment of her earlier curses on Elizabeth, and the rhetorical excess may be seen partly as a measure of the old woman's madness:

> I called thee then 'vain flourish of my fortune';
> I called thee then, poor shadow, 'painted queen'—
> The presentation of but what I was,
> The flattering index of a direful pageant,
> One heaved a-high to be hurled down below,
> A mother only mocked with two fair babes,
> A dream of what thou wast, a garish flag

To be the aim of every dangerous shot,
A sign of dignity, a breath, a bubble,
A queen in jest, only to fill the scene.
Where is thy husband now? Where be thy brothers?
Where are thy two sons? Wherein dost thou joy?
Who sues, and kneels, and says 'God save the Queen'?
Where be the bending peers that flattered thee?
Where be the thronging troops that followed thee?
Decline all this, and see what now thou art:
For happy wife, a most distressèd widow;
For joyful mother, one that wails the name;
For queen, a very caitiff, crowned with care;
For one being sued to, one that humbly sues;
For she that scorned at me, now scorned of me;
For she being feared of all, now fearing one;
For she commanding all, obeyed of none.
Thus hath the course of justice whirled about,
And left thee but a very prey to time,
Having no more but thought of what thou wert
To torture thee the more, being what thou art.
Thou didst usurp my place, and dost thou not
Usurp the just proportion of my sorrow?

(4.4.82–110)

The passage is a compendium of rhetorical schemes and figures, many of them forms of repetition: alliteration ('caitiff, crowned with care'), anaphora (words repeated at the beginning of successive lines, e.g. 'Where' and 'For'), reiterated words in other positions, repeated questions, isocolonic (identically structured) clauses, the division of successive lines into equivalent parts. The piling up of metaphors in a short space, a favourite means of achieving *copia*, is here so insistent as to seem almost demented: 'a pageant', 'a flag', 'a sign', 'a breath', 'a bubble'. After the string of 'rhetorical' questions concerning the death of her husband and sons, Margaret tears into the series of contrasts between what Elizabeth was and what she has become. The verb that begins the recital of her successor's misfortune, '*Decline* all this', connotes a scholastic exercise, particularly a grammatical recitation, and thus keeps the focus on the topic of rhetoric itself. The exceptional length of the speech—it continues for another five lines—is consistent with the extraordinary length of the scene and with the emotional excess it dramatizes. Shakespeare not only extends the complaints but even calls attention to the three women's volubility: as Queen Margaret exits and Richard approaches, the Duchess of York resolves to meet him and 'Be copious in exclaims' (4.4.135). The formality of these verbal structures is functional, of course: by means of the subtopic of rhetoric the play-wright questions the adequacy of language to define the nature of human suffering and the capacities of evil. But at the same time the young Shakespeare is showing off, indulging his talent for virtuosity and his attraction to the incantatory power of highly wrought language.

Most of the early plays contain similarly flamboyant speeches. The histories are full of verbal fireworks, as is his first tragedy, *Titus Andronicus*. The novice playwright seems to be pursuing to the letter the Erasmian sense of eloquence outlined in the first chapter: abundance, amplification, variety, *copia*. Speakers in plays such as *The Taming of the Shrew* and *The Comedy of Errors* also express themselves by means of such patterns, although the comic context can frequently alter the effect of the arranged language, tipping it over into absurdity. The components of many of the lovers' speeches in *Love's Labour's Lost*, for example, are not too far removed from those of a Queen Margaret or one of the other voluble Plantagenets.

> This wimpled, whining, purblind, wayward boy,
> This Signor Junior, giant dwarf, Dan Cupid,
> Regent of love-rhymes, lord of folded arms,
> Th'anointed sovereign of sighs and groans,
> Liege of all loiterers and malcontents,
> Dread prince of plackets, king of codpieces,
> Sole imperator and great general
> Of trotting paritors—O my little heart!
> And I to be a corporal of his field,
> And wear his colours like a tumbler's hoop?
>
> (3.1.174–83)

Biron's dilated list of synonyms for the god of love is typical of the lovers' discourse in *Love's Labour's Lost*, which consists of frequent rhyming, inventive rhythms, witty wordplay, paradoxes, chiasmic structures, and multiple forms of repetition. Significantly, however, there is little difference between the language of characters with whom we are engaged—the lovers—and that of those from whom we are ironically detached—the buffoons. The best gloss on Biron's description of Cupid is the ridiculous Holofernes' blind assessment of himself: 'This is a gift that I have, simple, simple—a foolish extravagant spirit, full of forms, figures, shapes, objects, ideas, apprehensions, motions, revolutions. These are begot in the ventricle of memory, nourished in the womb of *pia mater*, and delivered upon the mellowing of occasion' (4.2.66–71). *Love's Labour's Lost* is perhaps the most extreme case, but it is not different in kind from the other early plays, such as *The Two Gentlemen of Verona* or the first tetralogy of history plays (1, 2, 3 *Henry VI* and *Richard III*). All of them display what Keir Elam has called 'a devotion to conspicuous verbal forms designed to foreground the linguistic signifier'.[11]

Richard II signals the beginning of Shakespeare's rhetorical maturation; it is one of the works in which we can observe the apprentice becoming a master. (The contemporaneous *Romeo and Juliet* might serve a similar function.) The move towards maturity involves the playwright's learning to subordinate his enthusiasm for the material attractions of patterned speech in favour of a more disciplined recognition of its uses, what Wayne Rebhorn describes as an 'enlarged view of rhetoric'. Henry Bolingbroke is arguably the most effective rhetorician in *Richard II*, even though he ostensibly refuses the polished eloquence of Richard and of his own father, John of Gaunt. As Rebhorn points out, 'the laconic Henry recognizes that if he is to maintain his "name," he must defend it by the rhetorical manipulation of the world, including, of course, the rhetorical manipulation involved in staging silent spectacles of force'.[12] In this respect King Richard embodies the early rhetorical stance that Shakespeare will, in his mature works, transform into a more sophisticated attitude, one in which obvious figures give way to embedded ones, ostentation yields to subtlety, and the rejection of the rhetorical reveals itself as merely another form of rhetoric.

Verbally vain and besotted with the sound and shape of his own reflections, Richard often seems more attached to the form than to the substance of words. After young Bolingbroke's passionate denunciation of Thomas Mowbray (and implicitly, of Richard himself), the King responds to the polemic with a single line, a comment on the accuser's rhetorical style: 'How high a pitch his resolution soars!' (1.1.109). Several of Richard's own speeches might illustrate this dangerous formalism, one of the most poignant occurring at the moment when he physically transfers the crown to Henry Bolingbroke.

> BOLINGBROKE Are you contented to resign the crown?   190
> RICHARD Ay, no; no, ay; for I must nothing be;
> Therefore no, no, for I resign to thee.
> Now mark me how I will undo myself.
> I give this heavy weight from off my head,
>   [*Bolingbroke accepts the crown*]
> And this unwieldy sceptre from my hand,   195
>   [*Bolingbroke accepts the sceptre*]
> The pride of kingly sway from out my heart.
> With mine own tears I wash away my balm,
> With mine own hands I give away my crown,
> With mine own tongue deny my sacred state,
> With mine own breath release all duteous oaths.   200
> All pomp and majesty I do forswear.
> My manors, rents, revenues I forgo.
> My acts, decrees, and statutes I deny.
> God pardon all oaths that are broke to me.
> God keep all vows unbroke are made to thee.   205
> Make me, that nothing have, with nothing grieved,
> And thou with all pleased, that hast all achieved.
> Long mayst thou live in Richard's seat to sit,
> And soon lie Richard in an earthy pit.
> 'God save King Henry,' unkinged Richard says,   210
> 'And send him many years of sunshine days.'
>
>   (4.1.190–211)

At this crux in the action—and in the history of Britain—the King's rhetorical structures imperil the gravity and significance of the act itself, and Shakespeare makes the audience aware that this is so. A cursory analysis of the passage reveals the multiple quibbles in the first two lines ('ay, no; no, ay', 'I', 'no-thing', 'no no'), the *epistrophe* in lines 194–6 ('from off my head', 'from my hand', 'from out my heart'), the *anaphora* in the clauses that begin lines 197–200 (as well as 'My' in 202–3 and 'God' in 204–5), the similarly reversed syntax in lines 201–3, the antitheses in lines 204–5 and lines 206–7, and the outbreak of rhyme from the middle to the end of the lament. The deposition seems to imply an imbalance between signifier and signified: it is as if the speaker devotes more attention to the manner of his utterance than to its tragic meaning.

One of the great themes of *Richard II* is the passing of the old feudal order and the emergence of the world of practical politics, and rhetoric is one of the victims in this transition. John of Gaunt, with his famous hymn to England ('This royal throne of kings, this sceptred isle'; 2.1.40–68); the Bishop of Carlisle, with his oracular indictment of usurpation (culminating in 'The blood of English shall manure the ground'; 4.1.105–40); Richard himself—the brilliant rhetoricians in this world are the political losers. The title of the 1597 quarto text advertises *The Tragedy of Richard II*, and the language that best captures its tragic meaning is found in Richard's great prison soliloquy (5.5.1–66), the speech in which he movingly recognizes his waste of talent:

> But whate'er I be
> Nor I, nor any man that but man is,
> With nothing shall be pleased till he be eased
> With being nothing.
>
> (5.5.38–41)

Defeated and reduced though he is, Richard has suffered no diminution of poetic power. The speech is as rhetorically brilliant as his earlier performances, resounding with assonance and lexical repetition and the familiar sorts of wordplay. But it also attests to a new conception of the value of verbal ornament. Language now serves Richard as an instrument for understanding the self and acknowledging error; the colours of rhetoric no longer insistently call attention to themselves; a mutuality of form and meaning has been achieved. Through this transvaluation of language Shakespeare magnifies Richard's tragic stature, elevating him from verbal dandy to suffering hero. And like Richard, Shakespeare himself seems to acquire a new discipline in the deployment of rhetorical formulae. After 1595–6, that is, about the time he wrote *Richard II*, Shakespeare rarely indulges in the extravagant patterning of the early years. The later plays demonstrate that the playwright is master of rhetoric, not vice versa.

Rhetoric Revised

Convincing proof that Shakespeare's view of rhetoric undergoes a metamorphosis is that, in the tragedies from *Julius Caesar* (1599) onward, the obviously 'rhetorical' speakers are usually either fools or villains. The most comically notorious is Polonius, particularly in his allegation of Hamlet's 'madness'. When the Queen, impatient with the minister's roundabout speech, requests that he use 'More matter with less art', Polonius replies:

> Madam, I swear I use no art at all.
> That he is mad, 'tis true; 'tis true 'tis pity,
> And pity 'tis 'tis true—a foolish figure,
> But farewell it, for I will use no art.
> Mad let us grant him, then; and now remains
> That we find out the cause of this effect—
> Or rather say 'the cause of this *defect*',
> For this effect defective comes by cause.
> Thus it remains, and the remainder thus.
>
> (*Hamlet*, 2.2.97–105)

Captive to the surface of language, Polonius proves the opposite of what he intends, that he 'use[s] no art at all'. Pretensions to logical process ('Mad let us grant him, then; and now remains') combine with the unnecessary reliance on rhetorical forms (the *epanorthosis* of 'Or rather say') and a good deal of verbal trifling ('effect defective') to make the speaker ridiculous. Gertrude is right to object that the 'matter' is entirely obscured by its means of delivery.

Claudius deliberately seeks to obscure the 'matter' of his conduct when in the second scene he publicly announces his marriage:

> Therefore our sometime sister, now our queen,
> Th'imperial jointress of this warlike state,
> Have we as 'twere with a defeated joy,
> With one auspicious and one dropping eye,
> With mirth in funeral and with dirge in marriage,
> In equal scale weighing delight and dole,
> Taken to wife.
>
> (1.2.8–14)

This might have been a simple statement—'I have married my sister-in-law'—but the ugliness of the truth leads Claudius to prolong and contort the expression of it. As Stephen Booth puts it, 'The excessively lubricated rhetoric by which Claudius makes unnatural connections between moral contraries is as gross and sweaty as the incestuous marriage itself."[13] The speaker calculates his balances, contrasts, pairings, rhythmic alignments, and aural polish to make his questionable marriage more acceptable to the Danish court. But the playwright asks us to see through these effects. Later Claudius confesses this linguistic dishonesty in an aside, equating his 'most painted word' with 'the harlot's cheek'. It is this characterization of 'the harlot rhetoric' that many thinkers of the seventeenth and eighteenth centuries would come to fear and that has given verbal ornament the bad name from which, in some quarters, it still suffers.

These two instances, trivial and vile as they are, should not be taken as proof that Shakespeare has rejected rhetoric entirely. On the contrary, they provide further evidence of an expanded and more subtle view of the art. The passionate utterances of the tragic heroes and heroines may not be as conspicuously patterned as those of Henry VI, old Queen Margaret, or Richard II, but they are no less dependent on the canons of rhetorical theory.

> She swore in faith 'twas strange, 'twas passing strange.
> 'Twas pitiful, 'twas wondrous pitiful.
>> (*Othello*, 1.3.159–60)

> Yet I'll not shed her blood,
> Nor scar that whiter skin of hers than snow,
> And smooth as monumental alabaster.
>> (*Othello*, 5.2.3–5)

> This supernatural soliciting
> Cannot be ill, cannot be good.
>> (*Macbeth*, 1.3.129–30)

> I am a man more sinned against than sinning.
>> (*King Lear*, 3.2.60)

> Come night, come Romeo; come, thou day in night,
> For thou wilt lie upon the wings of night
> Whiter than new snow on a raven's back.
>> (*Romeo and Juliet*, 3.2.17–19)

> What's Hecuba to him, or he to Hecuba,
> That he should weep for her?
>> (*Hamlet*, 2.2.561–2)

> Nor th'imperious show
> Of the full-fortuned Caesar ever shall

> Be brooched with me, if knife, drugs, serpents, have
> Edge, sting, or operation.
>
> (*Antony and Cleopatra*, 4.16.24–7)

All of these passages rely upon rhetorical turns to which the Renaissance theorists had assigned specific names and functions: *anastrophe*,
abnormal word order, in Othello's contemplation of murder; *antime-
tabole*, 'turning about', in Hamlet's play on 'Hecuba'; *conduplicatio*,
doubling, in Juliet's *apostrophe* to night; and *metaphor*, of course,
everywhere. But the listener's attention is fixed mainly on their function, not mainly on their sound. The difference between Shakespeare's
early and later practice is that experience fosters a more judicious and
especially a more varied use of schemes and tropes and figures. And
many of these turns are so memorable because they are used with
relative infrequency.

Somewhere along the way Shakespeare discovered that the most
effective form of rhetoric is that which conceals itself. If, as Cicero and
his Renaissance disciples argued, the chief aim of rhetoric is to move
others through speech, then Shakespeare's tragic heroes must be
accounted among his greatest rhetorical successes. The critical tradition, not to mention the history of performance, makes it clear that for
many people over the centuries Shakespeare's greatest achievement is
his creation of such speakers as Hamlet, Othello, Falstaff, Cleopatra,
and Prospero. Othello disclaims rhetorical ability—'Rude am I in my
speech'—but this pose, of course, is one of the oldest of the rhetoricians'
tricks. From a strictly rhetorical point of view, it can be argued that the
triumph is not only Shakespeare's depiction of such persuasive speakers
but his scrutiny of the sources and implications of their verbal power.
The mature dramatist is always alert to the doubleness of rhetoric, and
he keeps his audience aware of its pleasures and its potential dangers.
Even those characters who, like Coriolanus, decry the specious attractions of eloquence can be heard to employ it, sometimes even in the act of
scorning it: 'Must I go show them my unbarbèd sconce? | Must I with my
base tongue give to my noble heart | A lie that it must bear?' (*Coriolanus*,
3.2.99–101). Hotspur is another such contradictory case, lamenting the
need to use language while holding centre-stage to proclaim at length
his aversion to words. This immense and complex topic will be addressed
more directly and comprehensively in the final chapter.

Artifice Again

At the very end of his career Shakespeare's view of rhetoric seems to undergo another turn, a renewed commitment to the pleasure of unconcealed artifice. Beginning with the late tragedies, *Macbeth*, *Coriolanus*, and *Antony and Cleopatra*, and continuing with *Pericles* and the other late romances or tragicomedies, the poet in Shakespeare appears to succumb once more to the temptations of pattern, especially the satisfactions of auricular arrangement. Here is a representative passage from the third act of *Cymbeline*, marked in different typefaces to suggest some of the many aural relationships:

> Where is Posthumus? What is in thy mind
> That makes thee stare thus? Wherefore breaks that sigh
> From th'inward of thee? One but painted thus
> Would *be* interpreted a thing perplexed
> *Be*yond self-explication. Put thyself
> Into a haviour of less fear, ere wildness
> Vanquish my staider senses.

> (3.4.4–10)

Technically, this passage illustrates the scheme known as *parimion*, in which many (or, in its pure form, all) words in a line begin with the same letter. But what is important is the representative quality of the excerpt, the fact that it typifies the elaborate, almost overwrought texture of the poetic surface in the late plays. Consonants and vowels are multiplied to such an extent that, paradoxically, they do not demand our notice as insistently as do the earlier patterns of words and syntax. So it is with other textural and auricular properties—metaphor, rhyme, wordplay, metrical irregularity.

The subtle and yet pervasive deployment of poetic schemes and figures at the end of his career signifies a profound change in Shakespeare's view of rhetorical forms, poetic surfaces, language in general, and even of the theatre itself. He seems to have transcended the doubts about the duplicities of speech, the harlotry of words, that had occupied him so thoroughly in plays like *King Lear* and *Macbeth* and *Coriolanus*. In fact, the late plays, particularly *The Winter's Tale*, *Cymbeline*, and *The Tempest*, may be said to indicate a rhetorical turn—

a renewed faith in the theatrical enterprise, a devotion to the surface, a commitment to the material value of the medium, a positive assessment of such potentially dubious phenomena as illusion, ornament, and the signifier as signifier. This submission to the frankly rhetorical is especially meaningful because it reminds us that Shakespeare was very much a Renaissance playwright, as much as we might like to make him, in Ben Jonson's words, 'not of an age, but for all time'. His embrace of the artificial in a late play like *The Tempest* gives the lie to the tidy but misleading narrative by which Shakespeare presciently enacts the course of intellectual history from the Renaissance to the Enlightenment and beyond: this is how the great Romantic critics, notably Coleridge, liked to see his career, as a Shakespearian progress towards their own reverence for authenticity and distrust of artifice, their own distaste for 'mere rhetoric'. His mature devotion to poetic surfaces and ornamentation reveals that what may have appeared to be a transcendence of the rhetorical in mid-career was in fact an absorption of its principles, a more sophisticated approach to a system he never forsook.

Shakespeare and the Principles of Rhetoric

It is worth returning, by way of summation, to my earlier suggestion that Shakespeare can be regarded as the ideal student of Renaissance rhetoric. The statement applies in the specific sense, in that he enthusiastically and brilliantly adapted for the stage the schemes and tropes of the humanist masters. But his place in the rhetorical tradition is most profitably considered in more liberal terms. To the greatest of the humanist teachers such as Erasmus, rhetoric was substantially more than the systems of figures, and so it was for Shakespeare. Of much greater significance are the principles that animate these rhetorical forms, the Aristotelian argument that eloquent speech leads to the discovery of truth, and the Ciceronian refinement of this view, that the instruments of rhetoric prompt us to recognize the complexity of identifying the nature of truth.[14] A single example from the history of rhetorical pedagogy will illustrate the legacy that Shakespeare received and exploited. English grammar school pupils were taught to practise the *disputatio in utramque partem*, a Ciceronian exercise requiring the writer both to promote and deny a political or philosophical position derived from history. Calculated to give students practice at expressing different and even contradictory ideas as persuasively as possible, this pedagogical assignment forced them to search out the most effective verbal means available, regardless of the merit of the argument or their own opinions about it. To one with a theatrical bent, the value of such an activity, putting appropriate words into the mouths of disparate speakers, can hardly be overestimated.

I refer to this exercise in argumentation as a kind of synecdoche for rhetoric in general, as an illustration of how the study of expression exposes the framework of any kind of thought. Learning to promote opposing positions in equally convincing terms appears to have generated in the apt pupil a kind of perspectival understanding of the world, a consciousness of the provisional nature of all philosophical positions and of the contribution of rhetoric to the validity of all ideas. Recent students of rhetoric in early modern Europe have identified 'its connection to skepticism, its sense of the contingency and uncertainty of the world of experience, its recognition of the gap between language and reality, and its reassuring commitment to dialogue and debate rather than dogmatic assertion'.[15] The ultimate effect of rhetorical training, in other words, must have been not only verbal but also philosophical.

Such perspectivism, it is generally agreed, is a defining feature of Shakespearian drama. Throughout his career—tentatively in the early works, and then wholeheartedly—the dramatist encourages in his audience a receptiveness to multiple points of view, a refusal of absolutes, an awareness of the competing claims of incompatible interpretations. His cultivation of such interpretative complexity accounts for our divided response to a character like Shylock: whether he is regarded as a hateful usurer or as victim of a smug Christian community (and the history of the play's reception attests to the appeal of both), *The Merchant of Venice* impels its audience to entertain both positions and to acknowledge that both contain elements of truth. Such perspectivism also asks the auditor to scrutinize and admire the verbal means by which these contrary positions are established. Watching Iago persuade Othello to accept a horrible lie is both a fearful and a beautiful thing. In all the great tragedies, Shakespeare encourages in each sensitive spectator a kind of internal disputation. It is the source of our struggle, in *Romeo and Juliet*, with the attractiveness and foolishness of the title characters, or, more abstractly, with the beauty and danger of passion. It causes us to feel both scorn and pity for King Lear, sympathy and disgust for Antony and Cleopatra. It is the quality that makes the plays endlessly fascinating, debatable, and—what would have meant most to Shakespeare the theatrical shareholder—revivable. The mixed response may be the most valuable product of Shakespeare's engagement with the rhetorical tradition.

cf   PROSPERO, specific
       or
       WINTER'S TALE, general.

3

What is the Figure?

John Keats's copy of *A Midsummer Night's Dream* contains, after the play-text, a printed excerpt from the commentary of Dr Johnson, who manages to hold his enthusiasm in check:

Wild and fantastical as this play is, all the parts in their various modes are well written, and give the kind of pleasure which the author designed. Fairies in his time were much in fashion; common tradition had made them familiar, and Spencer's poem had made them great.

Keats has scribbled over the entire passage so as to mark it out, written 'Tie' in front of the printed 'JOHNSON', and beneath it inscribed in ink four quotations (or misquotations) from the play:

> Such tricks hath *weak* imagination
> To kill cankers in the Musk rose buds.
> The clamorous Owl that hoots at our quaint Spirits
> Newts and blind worms do no wrong
> Come not near our faery queen.'

Thus Keats mocks the sober neoclassical response to the enchantments of Shakespeare's supernatural comedy. He metaphorically transforms Johnson, he of the '*weak* imagination', into a canker in a Shakespearian rose, an owl hooting at spirits, and a newt and blind worm that should keep their distance from the imperial Shakespeare. The appropriation of these figures suggests that what appealed to Keats above all things in Shakespeare's work was its wealth of imagery. He exclaims in a letter over the 'beauties in the Sonnets—they seem to be full of fine things said unintentionally—in the intensity of working out conceits'.[2] Thus, his Romantic reading forecasts the twentieth century's fascination with Shakespeare's figurative language.

But up to that point in literary history, Keats was an exception. John Dryden, for all his admiration, thought that Shakespeare's devotion to imagery sometimes made his plays unnatural and confusing, objecting that 'his whole style is so pestered with figurative expressions that it is as affected as it is obscure', and when adapting Shakespeare's plays for the Restoration stage Dryden eliminated images and systematically reduced the metaphoric quality of the lines.[3] His suspicion of the poetic figure is seconded by Dr Johnson, who believed that 'the force of metaphors is lost, when the mind, by the mention of particulars, is turned more upon the original than the secondary sense, more upon that from which the illustration is drawn than that to which it is applied'.[4] What troubles Johnson is the errancy of metaphor, its tendency to fly from its principal subject and lose the reader in the vague precincts of its 'illustration'. Neoclassical poetics, in other words, considered the figure to be an excrescence, something added, an ornament that should not be allowed to get in the way. By contrast, many nineteenth-century poets and critics shared Keats's attraction to Shakespearian imagery and metaphor, and they are largely responsible for teaching the twentieth century to revere the image. That formidable topic, modern interpretation of Shakespearian imagery, will be taken up in the next chapter.

Whatever value we assign it, figurative language is everywhere in Shakespeare's plays. It is chiefly this feature that leads new readers and spectators, those unfamiliar with the conventions of early modern drama, to describe the language—figuratively, by the way—as unnecessarily 'flowery' or 'elaborate' or 'high-flown'. To ignore or avoid the poetic properties of a play by Shakespeare, to 'read over' or 'read through' the figurative language, is spectacularly to miss the point. If poetic devices are regarded as unnecessary, then poetry itself must be regarded as unnecessary, a judgement that history prohibits. This is because poetry—or poetic language in drama—offers benefits unavailable in plain speech: insight, emotional experience, the condensation of complex ideas, memorability, pleasure. But readers unaccustomed to early modern language and to Shakespeare's poetic use of it may need some help in confronting the images, similes, metaphors, and other tropes on which he and his contemporaries heavily (and happily) depend.

Vocabulary is a problem. The English word 'image'—I here post the required caveat about the difficulty of defining it adequately—derives from the Latin root for 'copy' or 'likeness' (*imago*), itself a derivative of the verb 'to imitate' (*imitare*). Awareness of that etymology can be helpful in thinking about poetic and especially dramatic imagery because a play is a theatrical image of the world: Aristotle famously defined 'plot' as the 'imitation of an action'. Since the playwright's task is to re-produce or re-present experience on the stage, what the audience sees is a 'picture', a 'likeness', a secondary reality constructed to delight the spectator with its correspondence to the material world. In language, an image is a verbal copy of a thing, a word calculated to produce a likeness of an object in the mind of the receiver. Except for function words such as articles, prepositions, and conjunctions, most words are images of some sort: in the sentence 'The smiling baby gobbled the birthday cake', each of the five principal words produces an image which the mind then amalgamates into a larger picture. Most recent writers on figurative language have cautioned against the older tendency to stress the visual qualities of the term 'image'. In the sentence just cited, the effect of the verb 'gobbled' would seem to be kinetic as much as visual, although here the distinctions become very subtle, and almost no two people will agree on exactly what an image is and how it works in the mind. Indeed, even 'works in the mind' is a problematic phrase, since minds apparently process stimuli in different ways, and one person's perception of an image may differ from another's. To complicate the problem even more, some linguists and critics contend that all language is entirely metaphoric, that the use of any word or verbal sign 'essentially involves "getting at" one kind of reality "through" another. The process is fundamentally one of "transference".'[5]

Rather than labour over precise definitions of 'image', 'metaphor', and other such terms, my procedure will be practical. By examining some particularly vivid and memorable Shakespearian figures, I hope to introduce the reader to the technique and to ways of talking about it, even if definition remains elusive. Accordingly, this chapter will first take up some cases of sensuous imagery, figures employed to a great extent for their pictures and sounds. Moving then to the operation of metaphor, it looks at both early modern and twentieth-century descriptions of how metaphor is thought to work. It then considers the semantic functions of imagery and metaphor on a limited scale, confining the discussion to short pieces of text and then to some longer passages. The following chapter will attempt a more comprehensive analysis of what these devices contribute to the passages and plays in which they appear. Of course the split between operation and contribution is arbitrary and almost impossible to sustain, and I propose it reluctantly as the least unsatisfactory way of managing a very large topic. In both chapters, my aim is to persuade readers that figurative language is among the most valuable tools in the Shakespearian kit.

Images and metaphors may be grouped together with rhyme, metre, puns, and other such verbal features essential to poetry. Some of these features are known as *tropes*, from the Latin word for 'turn', since they turn a word away from its literal or everyday meaning, turn it to some extra-literal or figurative task. Ordinary speech aims at transparency, at clarity: the purpose of the verbal medium is to disappear, giving the listener—at least hypothetically—unmediated access to the speaker's meaning. In everyday conversation, as a consequence, speakers tend to avoid conscious use of figurative language in favour of a plain, unornamented form. Metaphors are constantly employed in ordinary speech, most often to clarify abstract ideas, but their value in such cases is almost entirely functional. Poets, on the other hand, are committed not only to meanings but to the pleasures of the verbal medium by which those meanings are conveyed. Poetic language differs from ordinary speech to the extent that it is concerned with more than meaning, and figurative language is one reliable signal of that concern. Sigurd Burckhardt brilliantly captures the value, to a poet, of figures of speech and other such formal properties in the following passage, an expansion of a phrase quoted in my introduction:

the nature and primary function of the most important poetic devices—especially rhyme, meter, and metaphor—is to release words in some measure from their bondage to meaning, their purely referential role, and to give or restore to them the corporeality which a true medium needs.... [The poet] can—and that is his first task—drive a wedge between words and their meanings, lessen as much as possible their designatory force and thereby inhibit our all too ready flight from them to the things they point to. Briefly put, the function of poetic devices is dissociative, or divestive.[6]

It may seem paradoxical or inconsistent to argue that a word is chosen to forestall understanding, to delay the listener's semantic apprehension of the word. But in that delay, that distraction from purpose, is the essence of poetry.

The Pleasures of the Picture

Cleopatra, Queen of Egypt, to her attendants:

> Give me mine angle. We'll to th'river. There,
> My music playing far off, I will betray
> Tawny-finned fishes. My bended hook shall pierce
> Their slimy jaws, and as I draw them up
> I'll think them every one an Antony,
> And say, 'Ah ha, you're caught!'

(Antony and Cleopatra, 2.5.10–15)

Antony and Cleopatra is famous for its exotic and colourful patterns of imagery, and here the quality that demands immediate notice is the appeal to the senses. Sight, sound, and touch are engaged by the concrete and sensuous nouns. The 'angle', or fishing tackle, the 'bended hook', the 'tawny' colour of the fish's fins, the 'pierc[ing]' of 'Their slimy jaws' are only the particular elements of the picture: the larger scene is set by 'th'river' and 'My music'. In this passage 'music' may be an image both aural, as in 'melody', and visual, since the word could also refer to the Egyptian queen's 'band of musicians'. The music adds to the sensuousness of the recollection, and the image is supplemented by the auditory pleasures of Cleopatra's speech, not only the assonance and consonance of 'Tawny-finned fishes' but also the lush verbal music of the scene's opening lines: 'Give me some music—music, m<u>oo</u>dy f<u>oo</u>d | *Of* us that trade in *love*'. The passage further illustrates the problem of separating image and metaphor. Cleopatra deftly exploits the metaphoric uses of the image as she turns the fish into figures for Antony, her choice of 'betray' as a synonym for 'catch', for example, carrying a powerful charge. It suggests the deceptiveness of the angler with baited hook, but it also prepares for the metaphoric equation of fish and man. The verb reminds us that Plutarch and the Roman historians depicted Cleopatra as an enchantress and Antony as her victim, and even though Shakespeare challenges the orthodox portrait of both figures, still the great problem of the play is the exact nature of

Antony's betrayal—of duty, of nation, of spouse, of lover, of self. But I am getting ahead of myself.

It is difficult to keep from getting ahead of oneself when discussing imagery because it is almost impossible to treat images in isolation. Poetic diction is always performing semantic work, no matter how much it justifies itself by virtue of its visual or aural beauty. An especially striking image may serve as the illustrative part of a metaphor, or very often the image itself contains an embedded metaphor. Even when the image is more or less 'pure', i.e. does not obviously function in another figure of speech, it undertakes a task of some kind, and sometimes more than one. Consider Falstaff's assessment of Justice Shallow in the soliloquy that concludes his visit to Gloucestershire in *2 Henry IV*. After summarizing Shallow's youthful follies and elderly lies, Falstaff finishes by remarking that despite these fictions, and despite his friend's former thinness, 'now has he land and beeves' (3.2.318–19). The final noun, meaning 'beefs' or cattle, appears to be a straightforward image, and yet it reveals much, both about the wealth of Justice Shallow and the greed of Falstaff, who plans to take advantage of him. That simple word also offers an instantaneous glimpse at the placid country life that the military rebellion threatens to disrupt. A slightly more ample instance from the same play is Doll Tearsheet's outrage at Pistol's assuming the title of 'Captain':

You a captain? You slave! For what? For tearing a poor whore's ruff in a bawdy-house! He a captain? Hang him, rogue, he lives upon mouldy stewed prunes and dried cakes.   (2.4.139–42)

The specificity of Doll Tearsheet's images ('poor whore's ruff', 'mouldy stewed prunes', 'dried cakes') makes her derogatory point with great economy, sketching a character of desperation and cowardice. Both Doll's and Falstaff's lines are in prose, not poetry, and yet the images are memorable and functional. And the audience should be accustomed to such language because the play is full of similar images of appetite and petty crime.

What such images reveal is that passage upon passage is profoundly nuanced and connotative. Virtually every word, even those without obvious metaphorical duty, is embedded in discursive networks that contribute texture and complexity to the phrase or passage or play. Memorable instances of such interlocking images might be the 'plumèd troops', the 'neighing steed and the shrill trump, | The spirit-stirring drum, th'ear-piercing fife, | The royal banner' from Othello's lament about the loss of his military 'occupation'; or Prospero's 'Ye elves of hills, brooks, standing lakes and groves'. One of the most extensive of such imagistic passages is Romeo's recollection of the apothecary's shop where he will buy poison.

> I do remember an apothecary,
> And hereabouts a dwells, which late I noted,
> In tattered weeds, with overwhelming brows,
> Culling of simples. Meagre were his looks.
> Sharp misery had worn him to the bones,
> And in his needy shop a tortoise hung,
> An alligator stuffed, and other skins
> Of ill-shaped fishes; and about his shelves
> A beggarly account of empty boxes,
> Green earthen pots, bladders, and musty seeds,
> Remnants of packthread, and old cakes of roses
> Were thinly scattered to make up a show.
>
> (*Romeo and Juliet*, 5.1.37–48)

Romeo's speech is not noticeably metaphorical in its details, although the whole episode arguably functions as a metaphor, the shop substituting for the tomb where Juliet has just been put to rest. The fiction of legal commerce ('to make up a show') resonates with the fiction that Friar Laurence has devised for Juliet and that will kill Romeo. But what is immediately arresting is the abundance and colour of the images, those visual elements from which Shakespeare fabricates the sinister interior of the shop. The power resides in the connotation of the nouns: the stuffed creatures, the nearly empty shelves and stale contents, the 'tattered weeds' and 'overwhelming brows' of the apothecary himself. The shop of the poison-seller makes mortality vivid, creating an ominous mood consistent with Romeo's desperate state of mind (he has just learned of Juliet's 'death') and forecasting the fatal end of their story. Its function is affective—to trouble the audience with gloomy pictures.

Image as Metaphor

Having so far resisted assigning extra-literal duty to imagery in order to stress its pictorial value, I should now acknowledge frankly that its role in the creation of metaphor is probably the chief contribution of the Shakespearian image. 'Metaphor' derives from the Greek word *metaphora*, meaning 'to carry over'. To borrow the definition from Aristotle: 'Metaphor is the application to one thing of a name belonging to another thing.' In the broadest sense, a metaphor is an act of substitution: one word (B) is used in place of another word (A) to clarify the nature or function of A. When Romeo says to Juliet at her window 'speak again, bright angel', he metaphorically substitutes one noun for another, 'angel' for 'Juliet'. The effect of this transference is to 'apply' or 'carry over' to Juliet the properties of the angel, and in this case, the particular purpose is not only to clarify what she is but also to glorify her.

Early modern poetics provides a context for understanding Shakespeare's way with metaphor. George Puttenham, John Hoskins, and other such cataloguers and theorists conceive of the metaphor as a fairly simple figure—nobody frets over the subtleties of definition or function—but they use some terms that are unfamiliar and therefore instructive for the modern reader.[7] Here is Hoskins, from the *Directions for Speech and Style* (1599): 'A METAPHOR, or TRANSLATION, is the friendly and neighborly borrowing of one word to express a thing with more light and better note.'[8] This sentence is the first entry under the larger heading 'FOR VARYING'. Like Hoskins, many of Shakespeare's contemporaries regularly describe the metaphor as an act of 'translation', a term that had not yet assumed its invariable modern meaning, to convert a text from one language to another. 'Translation' derives from the Latin for 'crossing from one side to another', implying motion and easy correspondence. Hoskins's other term, 'a borrowing', or a temporary removal of a word from one context to another, is also meaningful. For many sixteenth-century writers, using a metaphor involved no more than a simple exchange of one word for another, since literary culture offered a set of conventional comparisons from which it was not necessary to stray. As Anne Ferry puts it, 'some sixteenth-century formations of metaphor were dominated by a fundamental assumption that language somehow preexists outside the mind of the poet or the actual lines of his verse, in some place from which it may be borrowed word by word'.[9] Wherever the metaphor comes from, its main purpose is indicated in Hoskins's reference to illumination ('to express a thing with more light'), its making the original object easier to see ('better note'). And Hoskins's remarks are representative of his colleagues' views: discussion of metaphor in the late sixteenth century was simpler than it would become.

For both sixteenth-century commentators and their twentieth-century descendants, whatever their analytical differences, the basic principle governing metaphor is the perception of resemblance. The poet, wishing to characterize or elucidate his subject, or *tenor*, chooses a second image as a *vehicle* for doing so. Thus, in 'speak again, bright angel', Juliet is the tenor and 'angel' the vehicle. Usually in the metaphor, as this example reveals, the tenor is unnamed but clearly indicated. In the simile, on the other hand, the tenor is specified, as in Helena's 'I am as ugly as a bear' (*Dream*, 2.2.100), where 'I' is the tenor and 'bear' the vehicle. Proposed originally by I. A. Richards in the 1930s, these terms have proved themselves, despite occasional objection, to be durable instruments for analysing the operation of imagery.[10] Recently George Lakoff and Mark Turner have devised alternatives, referring to the main subject as the 'target domain' and to the image that describes it as the 'source domain'.[11] Pictures or ideas taken from the source domain ('bright angel', with all the celestial glory that phrase implies) are aimed at the target domain (Juliet), the topic that wants definition or illumination. A third set of definitions involves the 'recipient field' (tenor) and the 'donor field' (vehicle), the second bestowing clarification on the first.

Whatever we call the two parts, twentieth-century literary criticism has concentrated on this duality in the structure of the metaphor. Interestingly, the difference between the two parts seems not to have interested early commentators, who saw the metaphor as a case of efficient verbal substitution, usually one word for one word. Guides designed to help aspiring writers began to appear, not just rhetorical handbooks like *The Art of English Poesy* but even collections of words and phrases from which choice examples might be selected. One of the most impressive of these was assembled by the inveterate compiler Robert Cawdrey, he of the first English dictionary. Published in 1600, its full title is *A Treasurie or Storehouse of Similies: Both Pleasaunt, Delightfull, and Profitable, for All Estates of Men in General. Newly Collected into Heades and Common Places*. Cawdrey's compendium runs to 860 pages of dense text and even provides an index of categories or topics for which similes are listed ('Abilitie, Accusation, Adams disobedience and fall'). A needy author was welcome to borrow one of these ready-made figures to enrich the meaning of his own text. Such an attitude toward figuration exemplifies the tendency of theory to lag behind practice: to Puttenham and his colleagues, metaphors were easily chosen from storehouses such as Cawdrey had provided, whereas for Shakespeare and many of his fellow dramatists and poets, the rhetorical notion of 'invention' was being expanded to something like its modern meaning. The figurative language of Marlowe and Shakespeare and Webster, in moving far beyond the conventional and familiar, begins to display something of the originality that the Romantics and the moderns would come to prize.

The pleasure a listener takes in perceiving the resemblance between tenor and vehicle helps to account for the prominence of metaphor, not only in Shakespeare's language but in poetry generally. This pleasure is difficult to describe, but the effort is worth making because to understand the process by which the image is perceived is to acquire the means of appreciating Shakespeare's other poetic devices— wordplay, rhymes, metrical patterns, repetition and variation. As I have indicated, Shakespeare's contemporaries are not especially help-ful in analysing the way the metaphor works, but occasionally one of the handbooks will acknowledge the complexities attendant upon the metaphoric transfer. Henry Peacham, in describing the figure known as metalepsis, where a word stands in for a larger idea, traces the workings of the perceiver's intelligence as it effects the figurative substitution, and in so doing discloses the mental rewards produced:

This figure is a kind of *metonymy*, signifying by the effect a cause far off by an effect nigh at hand: yet it is a form of speech seldom used of Orators and not oft of Poets, yet is it not void of profit and utility, *for it teacheth the understanding to dive down to the bottom of the sense, and instructeth the eye of the wit, to discern a meaning far off.* For which property it may well be compared to an high prospect, which presenteth to the view of the beholder an object far distant by leading the eye from one mark to another by a lineal direction, till it discerneth the thing that is looked for.[12]   (italics mine)

The crux of this description, as my emphasis suggests, is its tracking the route of the mind through the process of apprehending the metonymy. Peacham's two clauses suggest the twin pleasures of figur-ative language: first, the mental exercise involved in working out the specific terms of the comparison, that is, the excitement of the search; and second, the triumph of having made the identification, of having seen the object from a great distance. In short, the pleasure of seeking, and the pleasure of finding. Or the delight of not knowing, quickly followed by the delight of knowing.

Later commentators have amplified our sense of what we feel in grasping the poet's substitution of one object for another. Wordsworth speaks of 'the pleasure which the mind derives from the perception of similitude in dissimilitude. This principle is the great spring of the activity of our minds, and their chief feeder.' In the lines following these, where he treats the alternations of metre, Wordsworth expands the principle to insist on the vital relation between likeness and difference: central to all art, he says, is 'similitude in dissimilitude, and dissimilitude in similitude'.[13] We take pleasure in noticing that Juliet is like an angel, and we take pleasure in noticing that she is mortal, not like an angel, even though Romeo thinks so.

The richness of this relation is demonstrable in hundreds of Shakespearian metaphors, but I have chosen a single line from *Pericles*: 'I am great with woe, and shall deliver weeping' (5.1.106). It is spoken by the despairing King just before he recognizes and is reunited with the daughter he thought dead. Examined strictly, the line figures Pericles (the tenor) as a pregnant woman (the vehicle) ready to give birth. The verb 'deliver' serves for both speaking and childbirth. 'Weeping' may be taken as an adverb describing the manner of expressing woe, or it may be the object of the verb 'deliver', i.e. the thing delivered. In either case, Pericles has been carrying the burden like an expectant mother, but for some sixteen years. The dissimilarity between tenor and vehicle, the improbability of comparing a desiccated old man to a fertile mother, reminds the listener of the play's constant concern with youth and age, birth and death, and mortality generally. The similarities, however, are numerous. Pericles is going to be 'deliver[ed]' not only *of* his grief but also *from* his grief (a third sense of the word), in more ways than he knows. He is in fact about to regain his lost daughter and wife. The unlikely image of pregnancy extends not only forward to his welcoming his child and to the emotional rebirth of Pericles himself, but also backward to the birth of Marina in the midst of the storm and the woeful 'death' of her mother at sea. And in a play that begins with incest, Pericles as mother is one more instance of topsy-turvy sexual relations.

The interaction of tenor and vehicle sets off a series of connotative charges, a burst of semantic electricity running back and forth between the two terms of the metaphor, as the associations of one move quickly back to the other, and vice versa. When Lady Macbeth says to her husband, 'Look like the innocent flower, | But be the serpent under't' (1.5.64–5), the command is based on two metaphors. In the first, the tenor is Macbeth's mild and loving appearance towards his king; the flower is the vehicle, connoting beauty and benevolent nature. (It might be pointed out, parenthetically, that the vehicle 'innocent flower' is itself a metaphor, since 'innocent' is an adjective drawn from the human—or at least the animal—domain, and flowers are not usually assigned moral valences.) In the second metaphor, where the tenor is Macbeth's murderous self, the serpent is the vehicle, connoting guile and venom. In both of these, the vehicle initially amplifies our understanding of Macbeth's nature, but what we know of that nature, Macbeth's conscience and his ambition, sends us back to the flower and the serpent, drawing from them the further connotations of fragility ('innocent flower'), fertility (Duncan's garden metaphors), and even the associations of the Garden of Eden, of Satan's taking the form of a serpent to entrap Eve, and thus of original sin. In other words, it is the particularity of the tenor *in its dramatic context* that determines the operation and ultimate effect of the metaphor: if 'flower' and 'serpent' were applied to another character in another play, the particular connotations would be altered even if the general sense remained the same. It is this semantic and imaginative circuit that excites the mind and makes appreciation of the Shakespearian poetic text such a challenging and rewarding activity.

So vital is the role of connotation in figurative language that it deserves further development. When image follows image in a passage unusually dense with figures, the imaginative exercise required of the perceiver can be quite exhilarating. The 'closet scene' of *Hamlet* is one such episode: the Prince mistakenly murders Polonius and then berates his mother for her union with Claudius, at which point the play—along with and by means of its language—seems to spin out of control. Multiple images fill the speeches of Hamlet, who does most of the talking, and when Gertrude attempts to console herself by attributing her son's words to mental illness, he graphically objects:

> Mother, for love of grace
> Lay not a flattering unction to your soul
> That not your trespass but my madness speaks.
> It will but skin and film the ulcerous place
> Whilst rank corruption, mining all within,
> Infects unseen.
>
> (3.4.135–40)

This passage brilliantly establishes the difference between the paraphrasable content of a statement and the effect of its figuration. The literal meaning is fairly simple: don't comfort yourself with the excuse that I'm mad and you're not guilty; to do that will make the sin even worse.

The metaphoric expression is not simple at all, but adds nuance and colour, mostly dark, to the semantic sense of Hamlet's words. An 'unction' is an ointment, a healing cream, and the noun can be used physically or figuratively. Here it is figurative: 'unction' is the vehicle for an excuse, a lie that Gertrude tells herself to evade responsibility. In the next act Laertes tells Claudius that he 'bought an unction of a mountebank': this usage is literal, but his unction is poison. Medicine and poison are often indistinguishable in *Hamlet*, and elsewhere Shakespeare seems to have used the two nouns synonymously. (In the 1608 quarto text of *King Lear*, when Regan complains that she is ill, Goneril responds with a sly aside: 'If not, I'll ne'er trust poison' (sc. 23, l. 94); in the Folio, on the other hand, she'll 'ne'er trust medicine' (5.3.90).) The adjective 'flattering', a loaded word in a drama set at court, where polite lies and empty words are a major concern, reinforces the danger of the 'unction': it makes you feel better, but it is worthless, and in fact toxic. Neither 'trespass' nor 'madness' actually 'speaks', of course: Hamlet here personifies the two nouns, with the Queen's 'trespass' as the eloquent expositor of her tainted soul. The convenient fiction ('unction') that Hamlet is insane will 'skin and film the ulcerous place': the verbs ('skin and film') are vehicles for 'cover up' or 'hide', while the 'ulcerous place', or open sore, represents the lustful and incestuous union that Hamlet deplores, or perhaps Gertrude's consciousness of it ('soul'). The salve to the soul permits 'rank corruption', some raging disease, to 'mine' (or undermine, dig into) the already dangerous wound and to 'infect' it even further. And, finally, 'rank' brings multiple connotations to a political drama about illness and rot.

At the risk of the reader's patience, a little more detail will illustrate how figuration helps to make this passage as colourful as it is. The several vehicles—disease, a greasy cream, a scab or viscous layer covering the wound, the suppurating inner part of it—all convey a feeling of mortality and sickness. The nominative 'corruption' is a very active vehicle, setting mines and stealthily contaminating. 'Mining' is secondarily a metaphor: although its primary sense is 'undermining' or subverting, it also imports into the passage the sense of explosives and danger; the same meaning is extended a few lines later in Q2's image of the 'enginer | Hoist with his own petard' and of Hamlet's intention concerning Rosencrantz and Guildenstern, to 'delve one yard below their mines | And blow them at the moon'. The illness metaphors increase the already abundant cluster of disease images for which *Hamlet* is famous. And if this excerpt is unusually vivid, it differs from most of Shakespeare's poetry only in degree, not in kind.

Figuration is a potent affective device, not only describing the world but also shaping the audience's feelings about characters, events, and arguments. The poet asks us to see one object or idea as if it were another so that we may employ that perception to evaluate the original object. The vehicle of a metaphor may magnify, or minimize, or mock the tenor; it may help us to reconsider or even reverse our opinion of the subject; it may introduce an ironic counter-current that contradicts or modifies other dramatic stimuli. The process of evaluation, moreover, is difficult and intricate, including as it does the subject, the metaphoric substitute for it, the several connotations of that vehicle, the speaker, the dramatic context, and the perceiver. A usefully ambiguous figure concludes the very first speech of *Antony and Cleopatra*, in Philo's metaphoric judgement on Antony. His 'captain's heart', according to the Roman soldier, has

> become the bellows and the fan
>   To cool a gipsy's lust.
> *Flourish. Enter Antony, Cleopatra, her ladies, the train,*
>   *with eunuchs fanning her*
>   Look where they come.
>   (1.1.9–10)

Philo's verbal trope precedes its visual equivalent, as his image of Antony's heart as 'the bellows and the fan' is transmuted theatrically into that of the *eunuchs fanning* Cleopatra. (The stage direction implies that the sexlessness of the fanners would be apparent.) In the convergence of the two images, Antony, figuratively speaking, becomes a eunuch, a man emasculated in the service of the Egyptian Queen. This critique represents the masculine view, the Roman argument found in Shakespeare's source, North's translation of Plutarch, but it is not the only available opinion. The critical history of *Antony and Cleopatra* discloses a series of antithetical readings: to some, it is a negative portrait of potential greatness wasted in sensuality; to others, a sympathetic picture of passion destroyed by earthly limits. Both positions can be supported by a host of metaphoric evidence. The play's oscillation between these two poles is reflected in the vehicles applied to Cleopatra herself: 'gipsy', 'Rare Egyptian', 'wonderful piece of work', 'serpent of old Nile', 'great fairy', 'a most triumphant lady', 'strumpet', 'witch', 'morsel', 'eastern star', 'nag' [horse], 'nightingale', 'Egyptian dish', 'a cow in June', 'a boggler', 'a whore', 'Triple-turn'd whore', 'a trull' [slut], 'Empress', 'lass unparalleled'. *Antony and Cleopatra* is one of Shakespeare's most richly figurative plays, and its metaphors and similes and other tropes supply the atmosphere of extravagance, exoticism, and cosmic scope that make it what it is.

Figures and Fiction

Sometimes an entire play, but more often a particular passage, will strike the listener as especially 'rich', and that term invites interrogation. What does it mean to speak of the 'richness' of lines of verse? What is a 'wealth' of colourful images? These terms themselves are metaphors. And what are the larger implications of such figurative density and fullness? To ask such questions is to consider the nature of poetry itself, to wonder what leads a writer to call an object, one which already has a 'proper' name, by another term, one which is obviously fanciful, stretched, in some sense inappropriate. To ask such questions is also to consider the nature of drama, since the playwright undertakes a similar re-presentation of persons and events. Metaphor, in other words, is fundamental to the making of fiction. It is also a crucial element in the Platonic suspicion of and the Puritan outrage at the theatre. To make the transfer from one name to another is to stretch the mind and, strictly speaking, to stretch the truth. We might recall Huckleberry Finn's term for the tales he narrates—'stretchers'.

One passage hospitable to the analysis of metaphor, taken from a play almost uniformly abundant in figuration, is Juliet's outburst on learning that Romeo has killed Tybalt in the street brawl.

> O serpent heart hid with a flow'ring face!
> Did ever dragon keep so fair a cave?
> Beautiful tyrant, fiend angelical!
> Dove-feathered raven, wolvish-ravening lamb!
> Despisèd substance of divinest show!
> Just opposite to what thou justly seem'st—
> A damnèd saint, an honourable villain.
> O nature, what hadst thou to do in hell
> When thou didst bower the spirit of a fiend
> In mortal paradise of such sweet flesh?
> Was ever book containing such vile matter
> So fairly bound? O, that deceit should dwell
> In such a gorgeous palace!
>
> (*Romeo and Juliet*, 3.2.73–85)

First, the entire speech is a kind of trope, an elaborate apostrophe addressed to the absent Romeo. Second, it contains an extraordinary number of figures, extraordinary even for this play—practically one in every line and in some lines more than one. Third, and this is the critical point, the passage is built on a series of contradictory images, or oxymorons. Recording Juliet's discovery of an apparent inconsistency in her husband, a malicious inner self in an attractive exterior, the speech moves rapidly from one antithesis to another, occasionally expanding a pair of contrasting images, more often compressing them into a short phrase and then moving on to the next. This twelve-line speech abounds with paired metaphors, all with a single tenor: Romeo.

The epitome of this method occurs in the third and fourth lines, packed as they are with oxymoronic phrases:

> Beautiful tyrant, fiend angelical!
> Dove-feathered raven, wolvish-ravening lamb!

It is worth inspecting the arrangement of these metaphors, the substance of which is identical—evil interior, lovely exterior. In the first line, both the adjectives are positive, both the nouns negative, but the structure of the line is a *chiasmus*, or criss-cross: adjective, noun / noun, adjective; positive, negative / negative, positive. The second line complicates the pattern. Still there are two phrases, but this time each comprises a compound adjective and then a one-word noun. Although the distribution of the two pairs of terms here is identical rather than chiastic—i.e. adjective, noun / adjective, noun—one of the nouns is negative and the other positive, and so with the adjectives. In other words, not only are there contradictions within the phrases, but the structures of the matching phrases contradict each other. Such formal details are meaningful because they permit us to chart the way the listener's mind bounces between the opposite poles. The process of comprehension creates a state of imaginative hyperactivity that excites the listener's intelligence, directing it to mimic the motion of Juliet's mind and thus to participate in her anguish. Moreover, her repetitions accustom the listener to the pattern of contradiction, and familiarity with that shape is helpful in apprehending the content of the multiple images. So quickly does Juliet move through the list of antithetical metaphors that the mind barely has time to process the connotative details of each; knowing the pattern affords a firmer purchase on the sense of the speech.

The concentration of figures and the speed of their delivery make Juliet's speech especially illuminating as we think about the motive for metaphor. Juliet uses language as most poets do, even though her words come forth in a manic rush: she is attempting to apprehend an unthinkable subject, to grasp at its essence by naming and renaming it, to hurl forth a series of oxymoronic and hyperbolic vehicles in an attempt to get it right. Her effort is self-conscious and even ostentatious, but it is only an exaggerated form of what every speaker does in the act of communication. Some characters are less apt to use figurative language, others more inclined to, and there are many different reasons for doing so. Within about two minutes of their first entrance in *1 Henry IV*, Falstaff and the Prince engage in a contest of similes. It begins with Falstaff's claim that he is 'as melancholy as a gib cat, or a lugged bear', continues with two alternative vehicles suggested by the Prince ('Or an old lion, or a lover's lute'), and proceeds through more possible comparisons from Falstaff and then again from the Prince. The simile game is recreational in two senses: it amuses the participants, of course, but it also represents their various efforts to make their conversation and their days and nights more vivid, less conventional and humdrum. Such verbal games keep the Prince from thinking about his courtly responsibilities and keep Falstaff from facing the truth about himself, a truth he knows but prefers not to contemplate. For Hal and Falstaff, the vehicles are what matter, since they delight in spinning out the comparisons. The inevitable errancy of the metaphoric transfer takes them out of themselves. For Juliet, on the other hand, the vehicles are mainly instruments for comprehending the all-important tenor.

The density of figuration in Juliet's exclamation and many other passages in the plays raises the question of reception. How can the listener be expected to absorb and come to terms with a blizzard of images in such a brief period of time? The process I described earlier, in which the mind recognizes the substituted noun, appreciates its aptness to the principal subject, and then ponders the connotations evoked by the comparison, would seem almost impossible to experience when metaphors follow metaphors as quickly as they do in Juliet's speech. It is tempting to conclude that the Elizabethans were more adept than we at comprehending such highly figurative speech, and it may be true that the oral culture that helped to produce the public-theatre plays allowed listeners to process poetic information with unusual rapidity. But in this case history is less helpful than histrionics and psychology for explaining the power of figures, especially this capacity to stimulate the mind and influence the emotions or judgement.

In the first place, there are too many words to be processed because the rush of events often seems to require an extra-verbal effect. Juliet's verbal eruption signifies that her world is crashing down on her, and while each metaphor is functional and carefully shaped, what is immediately striking is their plenitude and their explosive effect. One critic suggests that we may not be expected to process every metaphorical transaction:

[i]n the swift passage of the scene on the stage the audience has no time to register ambiguities or nuances, or perhaps even any 'sense' at all in the form of an extractable meaning.... Like Desdemona in the brothel scene in *Othello* (IV,ii), we understand the passion but not the words.[14]

Imagery functions subliminally as well, and we may well be absorbing more than we know. As one expert puts it, speaking of poetic language in general, 'Figures convince . . . not by a strictly logical presentation but by an appeal to the irrational, the part of the mind that delights in their multiple meanings and deep reassurances.'[15] These conjectures may seem to discredit the foregoing analysis: if the audience cannot assimilate much of Shakespeare's figurative language, then what is the point of dwelling so specifically on the structure of a metaphor or the nuances of an image? But the force of association and connotation should not be undervalued, particularly when images group them-selves into clusters or families, as Juliet's do in the speech just exam-ined. Moreover, in the theatrical moment there are other pointers, such as Juliet's pattern of oxymorons, or the speaker's tone, or other contextual clues that reinforce the listener's associative understanding of particular figures.

Near the beginning of *1 Henry IV*, as the Percys begin to plot their rebellion, Hotspur delivers a stirring speech about honour (1.3.201–8). It is full of memorable images: 'an easy leap' to 'the pale-faced moon', a 'dive into the bottom of the deep' to 'pluck up drownèd honour by the locks'. When he finishes, his uncle Worcester turns to Hotspur's father and remarks: 'He apprehends a world of figures here, | But not the form of what he should attend' (1.3.209–10). What Worcester means is that the impetuous Hotspur, caught up in the beguiling images and metaphors for glorious action, has forgotten the point of the discus-sion. Lest I make the same mistake, I now turn to the larger formal and semantic functions of figurative language, the subject of the next chapter.

A World of Figures

Image and metaphor came into their own in the first half of the twentieth century, entering and for a time dominating the critical discourse; by the close of the century, however, they found themselves neglected and even dispossessed. Having begun the last chapter with a glance back at Dryden's and Johnson's views of the Shakespearian figure, I should like to supplement that survey with a quick review of the latter end of the critical tradition. Neoclassical distrust of the poetic vehicle yielded to its opposite in the modern era, as twentieth-century critics came to fetishize the Shakespearian metaphor. In so doing they emulated the leading contemporary poets. To reflect even briefly on modernist poetry is to recognize that its aesthetic exalted the image as the governing element: Eliot's coffee spoons, Pound's 'petals on a wet, black bough', William Carlos Williams's red wheelbarrow, or indeed the wasteland itself. Accordingly, critics of Shakespeare favoured a similar emphasis, prizing his imagery in a way that not even the Romantics (and certainly not the Augustans) had done. Modern study of imagery and metaphor took a variety of forms, from the discovery of patterns by Caroline Spurgeon and Wolfgang Clemen to the isolation of the image by the descendants of the New Critics, and so compelling was their work that at mid-century the study of figuration occupied the centre of the critical enterprise. But by about 1980 these methods of enquiry, more or less exhausted, had yielded to the energies of New Historicism and other contextual modes, and the image was dismissed from the critical scene.

The work of Spurgeon and Clemen contributed much to twentieth-century thinking about Shakespearian drama. Conceived partly as a linguistic, quasi-scientific alternative to the character criticism of the previous century, image study began its occupation of the field with Spurgeon's *Shakespeare's Imagery and What it Tells Us* (1935). Her passions for inclusiveness and for taxonomy led her to collect hundreds of images, to group them into categories, to identify the patterns into which they seemed to arrange themselves, and to abstract from these observations a psychological profile of the author. Along with lists of examples and multi-coloured charts, she offered surmises about the biographical ramifications of repeated images, most notoriously the suggestion that Shakespeare the man loved most animals 'except spaniels and house dogs [which] he disliked probably because his fastidious senses revolted from the dirty way they were kept and fed at table'.[1] In the chapter entitled 'Shakespeare's Tastes and Interests', one of the running heads is 'His Sympathy for Snails'. For all the quaintness of her method, however, Spurgeon added the helpful concept of 'iterative imagery' to the critical vocabulary. At almost the same time, the German scholar Wolfgang Clemen was also examining repeated images with an eye for their semantic functions and their affinities with other images and themes. He avoided, happily, Spurgeon's tendency to ignore dramatic context and to attribute characters' opinions to their creator. Instead, he used such patterns to postulate the thematic coherence of a play and to trace changes in Shakespeare's metaphoric practice over the course of his career.[2]

This promotion of the poetic image led the New Critics of the 1940s and 1950s to take up the same subject but to try to refine the method. In one of the classic examples of New Critical practice, an essay on the imagery of *Macbeth* from 1944, Cleanth Brooks asserted the need to 'free ourselves of Miss Spurgeon's rather mechanical scheme of classification'. At the same time, however, he attested to the relatively undeveloped state of image study at the date of his writing: 'Indeed, for the average reader the connection between spontaneity and seriously imaginative poetry is so strong that he will probably reject as preposterous any account of Shakespeare's poetry which sees an elaborate pattern in the imagery.'[3] Within a very few years, and owing partly to Brooks's brilliant example, everyone was seeing patterns everywhere— and seeing little else. The work of Spurgeon and Clemen and Brooks generated, in the prime of the New Criticism and then in its late phases (*c.*1955–75), a host of similar studies, each declaring that a certain strain of imagery was the key to unlocking the (previously unnoticed) meaning of a particular play. Not only was the text removed from the early modern culture that produced it, but oftentimes the images themselves were extracted from the play, to be dissected and admired and displayed in the appropriate thematic cases. Such isolation of a figure risks diminishing the play to a single dominant theme. It also obscures those counter-currents that create semantic and poetic multiplicity, qualities which more recent critics have seen as vital to Shakespeare's work.

Objections to the excesses of image study, particularly its reductiveness, were posted even in its day of success. In a sensible book entitled *Style in Hamlet* (1969), Maurice Charney cautioned about the exclusiveness of image study and lamented the way it had been performed over the previous decades. Pointing out, for example, that Spurgeon's narrow concentration on images of disease and corruption in *Hamlet* derived from the nineteenth-century Romantic conception of the melancholic Prince, Charney countered by demonstrating that the play contains just as many images of war and armaments as those of pollution. He concluded that such 'imagery forces us to see the action of the play as a relation between antagonist and protagonist, "the pass and fell incensèd points / Of mighty opposites" (5.2.61–2), and not as a dramatized projection of a single character'. He showed that the kind of imagery a critic elects to notice determines and is determined by the way the critic regards all the other elements of the drama. Insisting on critical attention to the theatrical origins of the play, Charney warned that 'one cannot separate the image from what it images, the vehicle from the tenor. To claim otherwise would be to give the image a spuriously autonomous status'.[4] Such critical balance was difficult for most practitioners to maintain, however, and so the study of imagery and its role in thematic coherence fell quickly out of favour, done in by its own narrow scope. Awareness of this critical history can perhaps keep us from repeating some of our predecessors' errors as we think about the larger semantic effects of figurative language.

Networks of Images

The place to begin such analysis is with a sustained passage. At certain crucial moments in many of the plays the attentive mind begins to perceive a distinct semantic coherence among images. Such aggregation of related figures is one of Shakespeare's preferred means of securing the thematic or emotional effect of a speech or episode. Important examples would include the images of light and dark that crowd into Romeo's final speech in Juliet's tomb (5.3.73–120), the metaphors of the stage that Coriolanus summons when urged to 'act' in a humble manner before the citizens of Rome (3.2.99–137), or the images of poison and corruption in the Ghost's appearance to Hamlet (1.5.32–91). The linkage between figuration and the meaning of a dramatic moment is clearly discernible in Prince Hal's crucial interview with his father in the centre of *1 Henry IV.*

The King's denunciation of his son for neglecting his royal duty dominates the scene: in a not-unfamiliar parental move, the gruff parent spends most of the time talking about himself, positing his own youthful behaviour as a model for his son's. His speeches are exceptionally figurative, relying much more heavily on metaphors than his earlier language, particularly that in *Richard II*, has led us to expect. He selects images of clothing to describe his regal conduct ('dressed myself in...humility', 'My presence like a robe pontifical'); refers repeatedly to eyes and visibility in asserting the effects of royal appearance on the populace; and links Hal's social promiscuity to that of Richard II, with whom the people were quickly 'glutted, gorged, and full'. In this lengthy self-justification the alert listener will have noticed that the King repeats the metaphor of the wished-for sun employed by the Prince in his first soliloquy (1.2.194–200). Shakespeare's return to the figure in this crucial encounter suggests that father and son are not as far apart as King Henry believes.

But it is Hal's retort to his father's hectoring that illustrates most convincingly the semantic affinity of a group of metaphors:

> for the time will come
> That I shall make this northern youth *exchange*
> His glorious deeds for my *indignities*.
> Percy is but my *factor*, good my lord,
> To *engross* up glorious deeds on *my behalf*;
> And I will *call* him to so strict *account*
> That he shall *render* every glory up,
> Yea, even the slightest worship of his time,
> Or I will tear the *reckoning* from his heart.
> This, in the name of God, I *promise* here,

> The which if he be pleased I shall perform,
> I do beseech your majesty may salve
> The long-grown wounds of my intemperature;
> If not, the end of life *cancels* all *bonds*,
> And I will die a hundred thousand deaths
> Ere *break* the smallest *parcel* of this *vow*.
>
> (3.2.144–59; my italics)

As the emphasized words indicate, the common strand among the Prince's metaphoric vehicles is commerce. The governing metaphor figures the Prince as master or overlord, with Hotspur as his agent, or 'factor'. The verbs and nouns that forecast the Prince's defeat of his competitor evoke the world of business, of capital and interest, of contracts. The noun 'reckoning', or counting up, even looks back two scenes to the 'parcel of a reckoning' that is the extent of young Francis the waiter's conversation, and to the bill of reckoning found in the sleeping Falstaff's pocket; it also points forward to the day of reckoning, the duel between Hal and Hotspur at Shrewsbury. Words that we might not immediately connect with the discourse of business turn out to have such roots: 'indignities', for example, derives from the Latin for 'worth'. Although other metaphors are at work as well, notably the image of Hal's behaviour as an illness ('intemperature') and his father's pardon as a 'salve', the mercantile images saturate the defence almost to the exclusion of other figures and ideas. The quoted lines are even framed by appropriate images. Preceded by a calculation of Hotspur's honours ('multitudes') and a statement of the Prince's desire that his own disgrace be 'redoubled', they are followed by the King's borrowing of his son's imagery: 'Our hands are full of business; let's away' (3.2.179). Shakespeare thus signifies the reversal in the Prince's behaviour, his forsaking the realm of the tavern and turning towards the court. The responsibilities of adulthood and royal duty are represented by this cluster of commercial metaphors because, finally, the Prince is getting down to business: his language certifies that he has joined the family firm.

The coherence apparent in a single dense passage may also extend to larger units, indeed to entire plays. Unfortunately our thinking about such consistency has been tainted by overstated arguments promoting this or that strain of imagery as *the* unifying thread in a given play. In fact, abuse of the principle of organic unity was one of the critical errors that has led to the defamation of poetic analysis and makes it necessary still to defend close reading. But the misapplication of a critical method does not invalidate the practice altogether or outlaw the insights it produces. On the contrary, hyperbolic claims should teach us to read more prudently and self-consciously: in this case, we ought to recognize that while groups of metaphors make a genuine contribution to the semantic effect of a play, they coexist with other metaphoric strains, and that all of these constitute only one of many formal and theatrical instruments at the dramatist's disposal.

Having become alert to imagery and its functions, one can scarcely pick up one of Shakespeare's plays without being struck by its pictorial and metaphoric density, consistency, and multiplicity. For the moment, I should like to concentrate on consistency. *Macbeth* might be expected to form the centrepiece of an argument about the unifying value of metaphor, but Brooks provides such a detailed analysis of plant and clothing imagery that it seems prudent simply to recommend his famous essay and turn to other plays.[5] But which, and how to choose? As indicated earlier, *Hamlet* exhibits several major metaphoric veins, notably illness (Spurgeon's favourite), military discourse (Charney's alternative), and parts of the body. Further, Shakespeare returns almost obsessively to the ear in that play, introducing it as a receptacle for poison (in the death of Old Hamlet), associating it with slander and rumour, and connecting it with the problem of how humans receive and act upon information, the central questions of epistemology and the relation of knowledge to action. *Troilus and Cressida* and *Measure for Measure* teem with images of appetite, disease, and bodily failure, *Romeo and Juliet* exploits contrasts between day and night, youth and age, and male and female, and *Antony and Cleopatra* situates its title characters in a cosmic context. Admitting the attraction of all these texts, and asking the reader's indulgence if my choice is too familiar, I shall examine some of the metaphoric through-lines developed in *King Lear*.

If the ear is the primary organ in *Hamlet*, the eye tends to dominate *Lear*. Other senses are not neglected—smell, for example, arises frequently—and it is worth noting that allusions to the eye are almost as numerous in *Hamlet* as in *Lear*. But from the very first scene of *King Lear* characters revert again and again to the organ of sight. Goneril's first lines describe her father as 'dearer than eyesight' (1.1.56). The old King orders Kent 'out of [his] sight' (1.1.157), to which the candid earl replies, 'See better, Lear, and let me still remain | The true blank of thine eye' (1.1.158–9). Cordelia bids her sisters farewell 'with washed eyes' (1.1.268). These early, explicit references to eyesight and vision are supplemented by the more or less metaphoric use of 'look', 'appear', and 'see': combined with the ocular images, such apparently innocent verbs reinforce the theme of visual perception. The image of the eye returns immediately in the second scene when Gloucester demands to read the letter that Edmund has hidden and dismissed as 'nothing': 'Let's see. Come, if it be nothing, I shall not need spectacles' (1.2.34–5). Shakespeare's constant reiteration of these images lays the ground-work for what may be the most barbarous act depicted in any of his plays, the blinding of Gloucester by Cornwall and Regan. He must have wanted us to recall Goneril's earlier line ('dearer than eyesight') when he makes her propose the punishment for Gloucester's loyalty to Lear: 'Pluck out his eyes' (3.7.5). After this episode, all the references to 'seeing' (most of them metaphors for the process of understanding) become even more poignant as Gloucester roams the countryside with 'bleeding rings' instead of eyes. This extensive network of ocular images conveys Shakespeare's anxiety over the forms of non-literal blindness common to humans: the inability to penetrate obvious deception, the inescapable tendency to see what one wants to see, the consequences of self-delusion, wilfulness, and insensitivity. Evil is invisible when, as in *Lear*, it disguises itself as filial affection, good manners, or common sense.

The problem of dissimulation is further articulated through the many references to clothing, but that theme is by no means the limit of their semantic contribution. The sartorial images remind us con-stantly of the distance between outward show and inner truth, the gap that spoils the love test in the first scene. Some of these establish the drama's suspicion of financial and sexual 'luxury', particularly those that mention the wicked daughters' clothing ('what thou, gorgeous, wear'st | Which scarcely keeps thee warm') but also mad Tom's recol-lection of his discarded courtly apparel ('gloves in my cap' and 'the rustling of silks'). Such images proclaim that power tends to conceal its ambitions and operations, that 'robes and furred gowns hide all' (4.5.161). Characteristically, Shakespeare throughout the action of

King Lear supplements this verbal motif with stage pictures: Edgar's bare blanket when he plays the vagrant lunatic, Lear's attempt to disrobe on the heath ('Off, off, you lendings!' (3.4.102)), the parodically regal crown of weeds in Act 4, Kent's disguise as Caius through most of the play, and the dressing of Lear in 'fresh garments' as part of his rehabilitation. Images of eyes and of clothing are not the defining techniques of *King Lear* but function as part of an ensemble of verbal and theatrical cues. Moreover, they are hardly unique to this play: years before, Shakespeare had used images of clothing with great comic success in *The Taming of the Shrew*, and the emphasis on vision (and understanding what one sees) can probably be found in every play he wrote. But in certain cases, as in his tragic version of the self-satisfied, foolish old King, clusters of poetic images lend unusual force and colour to the telling of the story.

Image and Symbol

Even casual acquaintance with Shakespeare's plays discloses that certain figures are regularly associated with certain topics. Caroline Spurgeon doubtless drew some bizarre conclusions, but her statistics themselves are sound, and they establish the poet's tendency to return to a few prominent discursive fields as sources of figuration. A brief mention of some of those areas will prepare for a study of the uses of the image for symbolic purposes. The natural world, of course, provided Shakespeare with an extremely fertile matrix. Savage animals, particularly wild dogs, wolves, and tigers, are summoned to represent personal and civil disorder. Throughout the histories such images enliven the presentation of political rebellion or familial treachery, as when Henry IV fears that after his death England 'wilt be a wilderness again, | Peopled with wolves, thy old inhabitants' (*2 Henry IV*, 4.3.265–6). At the other extreme, perfect social order seems to call for images of bees, most famously in Ulysses' lengthy speech on degree from *Troilus and Cressida*, but other places as well, because they are 'Creatures that by a rule in nature teach | The act of order to a peopled kingdom' (*Henry V*, 1.2.188–9). (For all the tidiness of such metaphors, however, interpretative caution is required. In both these instances the speaker's dubious motives should colour the listener's response to the poetic figure and should thus unsettle the tidy picture of order.) Birds appear with great frequency, often as a kind of counter-example to the beast imagery, bearing connotations of freedom and perhaps transcendence. Vegetation, also, is everywhere: the tree represents royal lineage in the histories; weeds indicate opportunism and disorder; flowers are employed for their delicacy, scent, and colour; the ripeness of fruit serves repeatedly as a reminder of mortality. To move from the natural to the artificial, we find music to be one of Shakespeare's most familiar and suggestive images: the musical scale, from which notes are selected for their relation to one another and are played in proper time, connotes social harmony, emotional balance, and a life in tune with nature. This is only the barest sketch of some of Shakespeare's favourite veins or clusters. In fact, so common and persuasive are the figures borrowed from this or that discourse that fanciful readers over the centuries have decided that Shakespeare must have been a lawyer, that he had surely spent years at sea, that certainly he had had medical training, or that the many credible references to monarchy and courtly matters meant that the provincial William Shakespeare could not have written the plays at all.

Some of these images and metaphors are used so frequently and so multifariously—the mention of music provides an entryway to the topic—that we are obliged to describe them as symbols. The imprecision and confusion surrounding the terms 'symbol' and 'symbolism' are very great, and yet the method is so vital to Shakespeare's style that it demands exploration. The key in such cases is to prevent ourselves from becoming mired in subtlety and to find a workable definition that points to the essential meaning or contribution of the symbol. According to *The Princeton Encyclopedia of Poetry and Poetics*,

symbolism resembles figures of speech in having a basic doubleness of meaning between what is meant and what is said . . . , but it differs in that what is said is *also* what is meant. The 'vehicle' is also a 'tenor', and so a symbol may be said to be a metaphor in reverse, where the vehicle has been expanded and put in place of the tenor, while the tenor has been left to implication.

This is a useful statement, building as it does upon I. A. Richards's familiar terms. An alternative formulation sees the symbol, unlike the metaphor, as investing both terms with equal value. The red and white roses in the Temple Garden scene of *1 Henry VI* constitute a fairly rudimentary symbol, since the audience can both see the object and contemplate its referent. But as Shakespeare develops his poetic skills he begins to augment the semantic possibilities of certain images so that they evoke a profound range of potential meanings. Three of the most suggestive Shakespearian symbols are the garden, the sea, and the stage.

The garden makes for an apt beginning because it can be both straightforward and complex. Its most elaborate appearance comes in the third act of *Richard II*, when the caretaker and his man explicitly and extensively compare the strife-torn kingdom to a garden neglected by its overseer. The scene seems to exist almost entirely for the development of this symbol: King Richard is the derelict gardener, Henry Bolingbroke and his henchmen the 'fast-growing sprays | That look too lofty in our commonwealth' (3.4.35–6). The specificity of the correspondences and the quantity of detail give extraordinary force to this symbolic matrix. The 'fruit trees | ... over-proud in sap and blood', the 'Superfluous branches', the 'bearing boughs', the 'wholesome herbs | Swarming with caterpillars'—all these images suggest political equivalents. As the gardener completes his list of analogies, the Queen steps forward to rebuke the speakers for contemplating the deposition of the King, referring to the gardener as 'old Adam's likeness' and asking, 'What Eve, what serpent hath suggested thee | To make a second fall of cursèd man?' (3.4.76–7). Her elaboration of the metaphor to include the loss of Eden points the way towards the later uses of this fundamental and polysemous trope, and Shakespeare carries it through to the very end of the tetralogy. The Epilogue to *Henry V*, speaking of the triumphant King, declares that 'the world's best garden he achieved', but in this instance the audience is well aware of the lurking serpent, the ruination of Paradise by his heirs in the Wars of the Roses.

Not only in the remainder of the *Henriad*, but throughout the tragedies and most memorably in *Hamlet*, Shakespeare identifies the garden with evil, particularly with original sin. To the Prince, mourning his father's death and mother's unseemly marriage, the world is 'an unweeded garden | That grows to seed' (1.2.158–59). Thoughts of Eden often return Shakespeare to the story of Cain and Abel, the crime with 'the primal eldest curse upon't, | A brother's murder' (3.3.37–8). These words are spoken by Claudius, perhaps the boldest of Shakespeare's brother-killers, but they apply beyond *Hamlet*—to virtually all of the history plays (the first tetralogy as well as the second) and also to dramas of perverted kinship, e.g. *Macbeth*. Sometimes the extremes of fratricide and original sin are absent, and the garden is merely a garden, an uncomplicated symbol of order, fertility, and beauty. Elizabethan woodcuts and paintings of gardens—whether herb or flower or vegetable gardens—are so symmetrical and enchanting that the symbolic appeal of the image is easy to grasp. We see such spaces in *The Winter's Tale* (Perdita's pure garden, with hybrids forbidden), *The Taming of the Shrew* ('fruitful Lombardy, | The pleasant garden of great Italy'), and *The Two Noble Kinsmen* (the charmed garden in which Palamon and Arcite first see Emilia). The green worlds of *A Midsummer Night's Dream* and *As You Like It* might be considered variations on this image. And, predictably, Shakespeare may elect to invert the positive connotations. Iago develops a detailed metaphor of the body as a garden, one in which the owner-gardener sows what he likes and reaps what he sows (*Othello*, 1.3). But in the mouth of this psychopath the usual ideas of fertility, order, and logical yield are vitiated by the malicious intent that generates the figure.

The sea is almost infinitely suggestive, from the earliest plays to *The Tempest*. It can act as a destructive force, as in *The Comedy of Errors*, splitting the family and separating brother from brother, child from parent. With the passage of time, however, it also reunites the same family by bringing Antipholus of Syracuse to the city of Ephesus, where his father has landed and where his lost twin resides. Even as an apprentice, Shakespeare recognizes and evokes symbolically the uncertainty, the danger, and the promise of the sea. The questing Antipholus sounds a note of melancholy when he describes himself as 'like a drop of water | That in the ocean seeks another drop' (1.2.35–6) and losing his identity in the vastness of the sea. Such an identification is familiar: in 'Dover Beach' Matthew Arnold evokes the mystery of the sea and recalls that long ago Sophocles had heard its 'eternal note of sadness'. And this tradition should remind us of the phenomenon described in the previous chapter, the tendency of Renaissance poets to select from a set of conventional images. As symbolic instruments, these three Shakespearian favourites were familiar not only to Renaissance dramatists but to poets in many different cultures and ages.

The ocean seems to have been an especially appealing symbol to Shakespeare because of its paradoxical status: constant yet always changing, threatening and life-giving, salty and fresh. In at least a third of the plays it serves the narrative, returning Antonio's ships in *The Merchant of Venice*, separating and then uniting Viola and Sebastian in *Twelfth Night*, aiding the defeat of the Turks in *Othello*, protecting the island nation in the history plays. Most of the late works, particularly those sometimes called the romances, depend heavily upon the ancient parallel between seafaring and the journey of a human life. *Pericles*, the first of these late plays, presents a daughter named Marina, born in a storm at sea, and her name is only the most obvious of the several ways the sea shapes the action and ideas of the play. Even when it is not physically present the sea is available for symbolic reference. What Viola says about the salvation of her brother applies generally: 'O, if it prove, | Tempests are kind, and salt waves fresh in love' (*Twelfth Night*, 3.4.375–6).

The stage is probably the most pervasive and meaningful of all Shakespeare's symbols. Considering the gallons of ink devoted to this single trope, I can do no more than gesture at its most obvious functions.[6] To begin with, theatrical metaphor permeates the language of many characters, even those who have no histrionic affiliations at all. 'Cue', 'scene', 'act', 'pageant', 'show', 'prompt', 'perform', 'present'— these nouns and verbs are unacknowledged figures that have become a part of common speech.[7] Hamlet offers a triple metaphoric pun when he refers to 'this distracted globe': his head, the theatre, the world. Shakespeare frequently exploits the etymological implications of the Greek word for actor—*hypokrit*—and makes some of his most charismatic persons self-conscious theatrical performers. Many of the wicked, such as Richard III, Iago, and Edmund, beguile their victims with histrionic manœuvres, and even those who may not seem like performers speak frankly of their need to 'disguise' their criminal behaviour.

The most meaningful symbolic exploitation of the stage is the play-within-the-play, a device to which Shakespeare frequently returns. Several works (*A Midsummer Night's Dream*, *Love's Labour's Lost*, *Hamlet*, and *The Tempest*) contain a full-dress play-within-the-play, others (*1 Henry IV*, *Timon of Athens*, and *Pericles*) offer skits or pageants that function similarly, and many demand at least some form of dress-up. The play-within-the-play becomes a theatrical symbol that alters the audience's perspective and affects their view of the theatre and themselves. By framing the inner play with the main theatrical action, the playwright constructs a series of receding stages. In *Hamlet*, for example, 'The Murder of Gonzago' is a theatrical entertainment performed for the characters in *Hamlet*, which is a theatrical production performed for spectators in 'the real world', whose actions may be (so the series would imply) an entertainment performed for a celestial audience. Such semantic possibilities were available in the symbolic structure of the theatre, as Anne Righter's study of this topic demonstrates. The metaphor underlying Jaques's 'All the world's a stage, | And all the men and women merely players' was hardly new, but Shakespeare amplified it into a sophisticated investigation of the power and the limits of illusion.

Representing and Misrepresenting the World

The poetic figure is an instrument for apprehending and remaking the world. Othello describes the Muslim he killed in Aleppo as 'the circumcisèd dog'; the awakened lovers in *A Midsummer Night's Dream* find that the nocturnal events now seem 'small and indistinguishable, | Like far-off mountains turnèd into clouds'; Goneril responds to her husband's censure with 'No more. The text is foolish', as if he were a fatuous clergyman preaching an ineffectual sermon; Lady Percy mocks Hotspur's singlemindedness by calling him a 'paraquito'. When these speakers select or invent such metaphors and analogues for their experience, they attempt to capture the event or feeling or idea, and to fix it in illuminating and memorable form. Robert Weimann summarizes this effort when he says that metaphor

forms the very core and center of that creative and receptive activity by which, through poetry, man as a social being imaginatively comprehends his relation to time and space and, above all, to the world around him. The essence of metaphor is to connect; to interrelate ideas, the concrete and the abstract, but also the general and the particular, the social and the individual.[8]

Figuration in general, as Weimann goes on to suggest about metaphor, also serves to connect the imagination of the poet with the mind of the listener. Characters trope on a plain word or phrase so that, as we might say, they can put a spin on an idea, and by means of such tropes they create imaginative substitutes for the ordinary elements of experience. Shakespeare thus figuratively transmutes the raw material of existence into an artistic shape so that it can be observed and assessed.

This is an artistic act that not only represents the world but also refashions it poetically.

Sometimes, however, the re-creation fails; that is, the substituted figure may be incongruent with the original term, or the gap between tenor and vehicle is so great that it exposes the impropriety of the comparison. Certain instances of this technique are instantly discernible. When Claudius attempts to talk Hamlet out of his grief by insisting that death is natural and that all men have lost their fathers, 'from the first corpse to he that died today', the ironic gap is glaring: the 'first corpse' was Abel, murdered by his brother, and (figuratively speaking) 'he that died today' would be Old Hamlet, murdered by his brother. Either Claudius' figurative language is lazy and ill considered, or it is stunning in its audacious allusion to murder. A much more brutal example occurs in the blinding scene of *King Lear*, when just before the horrific act the tortured Gloucester comforts himself by personifying divine retribution:

> GLOUCESTER   But I shall see
> The wingèd vengeance overtake such children.
> CORNWALL See't shalt thou never.—Fellows, hold the
>   chair.—
> Upon those eyes of thine I'll set my foot.
>
> (*The Tragedy of King Lear*, 3.7.63–6)

Here Cornwall brutally literalizes Gloucester's figurative phrase, troping physically on the abstract 'see', so that the shift from figurative to literal triggers the blinding of the old man.

At times a metaphor or figure may sound plausible in context but will still imply an inconsistency. In *The Merchant of Venice*, when Bassanio goes to make his choice among the caskets, Portia is left alone to reflect on the significance of the moment. In doing so, she appeals to the realm of myth:

>   Now he goes,
> With no less presence but with much more love
> Than young Alcides when he did redeem
> The virgin tribute paid by howling Troy
> To the sea-monster. I stand for sacrifice.
>
> (*The Merchant of Venice*, 3.2.53–7)

Bassanio may be a genuine lover and suitor, but he is scarcely a Hercules risking all to save the captive Hesione. Or he may be an adventurer in quest mainly of Portia's fortune, the earlier scenes having raised some doubts about his motives. In the latter case the metaphor is perhaps ironically apt: upon rescuing Laomedon's daughter, Hercules demanded as his reward not the maiden herself but her father's famous horses. With figures like this one, the metaphoric act diminishes the object of comparison while at the same time uncovering the bias or delusion of the image-maker. Portia is caught up in the music and exhilaration of the moment, and her ecstasy calls attention to the indecorum of her language. Allusions such as this one from the immense source-field of classical myth and history remind us of Shakespeare's plundering the works of Ovid and Plutarch for figurative material. Although I have not given them much attention, allusions are uncommonly meaningful figures because their connotative associations are definite and immediate. They represent what one critic refers to as verbal terms with histories attached to them.[9]

A huge gap between image and referent opens in Brutus' soliloquy in the second act of *Julius Caesar*, as he confesses his fears about Caesar's ambition and rationalizes the conspiracy to stop him:

> It must be by his death. And for my part   10
> I know no personal cause to spurn at him,
> But for the general. He would be crowned.
> How that might change his nature, there's the question.
> It is the bright day that brings forth the adder,
> And that craves wary walking. Crown him: that!
> And then I grant we put a sting in him
> That at his will he may do danger with.
> Th'abuse of greatness is when it disjoins
> Remorse from power. And to speak truth of Caesar,
> I have not known when his affections swayed   20
> More than his reason. But 'tis a common proof
> That lowliness is young ambition's ladder,
> Whereto the climber-upward turns his face;
> But when he once attains the upmost round,
> He then unto the ladder turns his back,
> Looks in the clouds, scorning the base degrees
> By which he did ascend. So Caesar may.
> Then lest he may, prevent. And since the quarrel

> Will bear no colour for the thing he is,
> Fashion it thus: that what he is, augmented,   30
> Would run to these and these extremities;
> And therefore think him as a serpent's egg,
> Which, hatched, would as his kind grow mischievous,
> And kill him in the shell.

(2.1.10–34)

This is an especially complex episode because it depends upon Brutus' ineptitude at making metaphors. Sincerely and patriotically troubled that Caesar might prove a tyrant, he clutches at figures that will justify the assassination first to himself and later to the people of Rome. Brutus is determined to find danger in the sunshine—hence the image of the adder—even though he has no evidence, as he admits in lines 19–21. The conclusion of the speech, especially the logical route to it, confirms our sense of Brutus' moral fallacy: since what Caesar 'is' is blameless, the speaker must 'fashion' (l. 30) an argument. His proposal for making the case remains vague ('run to *these* and *these* extremities') until he imagines a menacing picture. Repeating the earlier image, he decides to 'think him as a serpent's egg   and kill him in the shell'. Ironically, it is not Caesar's but Brutus' own 'affection' or desire that has overcome his 'reason', and his language reveals his fault. The vehicle of the simile grossly misrepresents the tenor, and clearly Shakespeare expects the audience to notice and to deplore the distortion. *Julius Caesar* brilliantly exemplifies the suggestion that 'the plays evidence an acute awareness of this human longing for significance and configuration, but there is also evident in them a desire to allow incongruity just enough voice to trouble an otherwise satisfied sleep'.[10]

Imagery and Culture

'This human longing for significance and configuration' is the impulse that poetry and drama were created to satisfy, and their figurative components are among the artist's most effective tools for delivering that satisfaction. Many of Shakespeare's contemporaries—and possibly the playwright himself—also satisfied that same longing through religious faith. In both arenas, the theatre and the church, access to this sense of pattern was dependent on various forms of visual representation—icons, stage pictures, ceremony, poetic images. At the same time, however, a primary feature of the Reformation in England was its iconoclasm, that process by which Protestants cleansed their church of 'graven images' and other 'idolatrous' material representations of divinity. The reformers loudly objected to the veneration of icons and other physical symbols associated with the excesses of Rome.

These same Protestants, however, embraced a complex system of spiritual symbolism, most notably their figurative interpretation of Christ's injunction to partake of his 'body'. 'Calvin's explanation of the Eucharist grounds it in a real correspondence whereby "physical signs ... represent to us, according to our feeble capacity, things invisible; and spiritual truth, which is at the same time represented and displayed through the symbols themselves." '[11] John Calvin, the Protestant theologian whose pronouncements from Geneva reverberated through Europe, here identifies imagery or 'typology' as an essential property of reformed Christianity, just as it was of Catholicism. The fierceness of the religious disputes about representation is one proof that the early modern mind was extremely sensitive to figuration, whether verbal or visual, religious or secular. Another indication is Queen Elizabeth I's brilliant manipulation of the symbolism of virginity and majesty.[12] Most of Shakespeare's contemporaries would have agreed with Fluellen, the Welsh Captain in *Henry V*, that 'there is figures in all things'.

Awareness of this historical phenomenon reminds us that Shakespeare's imagery, brilliant as it is in his artistic hands, must be seen also as a cultural product. In other words, the theological controversies of his age leave no doubt that a Shakespearian image often meant different things to the original audience from what it does to the modern playgoer or reader. To return to *King Lear* for a moment, images of eyes and clothes can be found throughout the various discourses of the period, from sermons to conduct books to other forms of historical, political, and imaginative writing. Garden imagery was also a favourite of religious commentators. Both apparel and the garden appear in an astonishing sermon delivered by Richard Crosse and printed in 1603, in which the Puritan polemicist figuratively attacks poetic figuration: 'fine phrases ... swelling words, bombasted out [i.e. stuffed with cotton] ... with much polished and new-made eloquence: ... many [preachers] become affected to their phrases, Metaphors, Allegories, and such figurative and superlative terms, and so much vain eloquence, as they yield no fruit at all to their auditors, but drive them to amazement."[3] So ingrained is the habit that the preacher cannot express himself without metaphors.

Certain kinds of imagery may have led the audience beyond the text and playhouse and into the social or political realm, and the modern reader should be alert to such historical or topical resonance. *Coriolanus*, for example, displays an imagistic concentration on the body, its needs, and the effects of privation. The tragedy thus rehearses a Shakespearian trope familiar from the history plays, the equation of the body politic with the physical body: government of the self corresponds to government of the state. The crucial instance of this strain in *Coriolanus* is Menenius' famous 'fable of the belly', an elaborate socio-political metaphor appropriated from classical and humanist sources and designed to establish the proper relation between rulers and populace concerning the appropriate distribution of goods. The metaphor and its variations have been related to the Jacobean controversy over the enforcement of enclosure laws, a governmental policy that threatened farmers and led to civil unrest in the Midlands.[14] Moreover, as recent criticism has helpfully shown, the somatic imagery that pervades the history plays in particular can also be found in the work of many early modern political theorists, from Sir Thomas Elyot and Sir Thomas Smith up to King James himself.

The topicality of the fable in *Coriolanus* is unusual: unlike many of his contemporaries, Shakespeare rarely refers to current events. Ben Jonson's comedy *The Alchemist*, on the contrary, takes place in the district of Blackfriars in the late summer of 1610, exactly where and when the play was being performed. It depends upon references to the recent depredations of the plague, to well-known local personalities, to radical Protestant sects, as well as to various urban types such as ambitious London merchants and smug law clerks. Shakespeare usually avoids such specificity, although there is the occasional dig—for example, the suggestion that the priggish Malvolio is a Puritan. Nonetheless, much of his figurative language must have been enriched by the audience's familiarity with local geography, civic controversies, and other such pages from what we call the social text. For instance, the appetitive images associated with Falstaff would have had a special kind of power in the licentious district of Shoreditch, the 'liberty' where The Theatre was located and the *Henry IV* plays were performed.

More generally, it is vital that we historicize Shakespeare's figurative vocabulary if we are to feel the affective charge that certain images are calculated to produce. Consider the orange, for a final instance. Citrus fruits were rare and precious in Elizabethan England because they were perishable and had to be imported, normally from Spain or Africa. Consciousness of this fact clarifies the emotional apex of the wedding scene in *Much Ado About Nothing*, when Claudio says contemptuously to the father of the bride he is spurning, 'Give not this rotten orange to your friend' (4.1.32). Heard with our own cultural assumptions, the figure, particularly the relation of vehicle to tenor— orange for bride—seems extremely peculiar. It would not have seemed so in 1599. Another striking instance is Hamlet's sardonic demonstration that a king can 'go a progress through the guts of a beggar'. The noun 'progress' had a particular meaning to the Elizabethan ear, an extravagant ceremonial journey taken by the monarch and retinue through the realm. Lodging with important aristocratic families, often for an extended stay, the sovereign enjoyed celebrations of majesty and demonstrations of popular affection. Elizabeth I's royal progresses were famous for their opulence and enormous expense. Her subjects would have caught the gross impropriety of Hamlet's image, which the passage of time has softened.

Although twentieth-century critics devoted substantial energy to the analysis of metaphor, the topic is scarcely exhausted. I have reserved some of these historically significant figures until the end of my discussion in order to suggest one path that analysis may profitably take. The abuses of image study left many with a distaste for poetics, and in recent years little attention has been paid to the visual properties of the language. We have much to learn about the cultural contexts of Shakespeare's figurative vocabulary.

Loosening the Line

Shakespeare's Metrical Development

Hamlet, at the end of the verses he sends to Ophelia, laments his poetic inadequacy: 'O dear Ophelia, I am ill at these numbers.' His creator had no such problem. As might be expected, Shakespeare's technical skills grew prodigiously as he gained experience at composing verse for speaking characters, and this chapter attempts to trace the development of his blank verse from the beginning of the career to the end. Gifted from the first with a keen ear, he found himself adept at imitating the verse style of contemporary dramatists, whereupon he quickly began to modify the established metrical conventions to suit the particular demands of the stories he chose to dramatize. Shakespeare's blank verse develops over the course of his career from regular to irregular, from smooth to rough, from rhythmically simple to rhythmically various. This development from metrical simplicity to sophistication recapitulates aurally the thematic and tonal complication detectable in his passage from, say, the first to the second tetralogy, or from *The Comedy of Errors* to *Twelfth Night*. Moreover, it is not too much to say that the complication of the pentameter not only reflects but also *promotes* the thematic density of the later plays. In other, blunter words, *Hamlet* is richer than *Titus Andronicus* in part because the sound of its verse is more various and complex. The following outline must be done in broad strokes, given the limitations of space, but readers will be able to fill in gaps and recognize those moments where greater subtlety and qualification might be in order.

Early Verse

I begin with part of a long speech from *3 Henry VI* (first printed as *Richard, Duke of York*), Clifford's plea to King Henry to resist the aggression of the Yorkist faction.

> CLIFFORD My gracious liege, this too much lenity
> And harmful pity must be laid aside.   10
> To whom do lions cast their gentle looks?
> Not to the beast that would usurp their den.
> Whose hand is that the forest bear doth lick?
> Not his that spoils her young before her face.
> Who scapes the lurking serpent's mortal sting?
> Not he that sets his foot upon her back.
> The smallest worm will turn, being trodden on,
> And doves will peck in safeguard of their brood.
> Ambitious York did level at thy crown,   20
> Thou smiling while he knit his angry brows.
> He, but a duke, would have his son a king,
> And raise his issue like a loving sire;
> Thou, being a king, blest with a goodly son,
> Didst yield consent to disinherit him,
> Which argued thee a most unloving father.
> Unreasonable creatures feed their young,
> And though man's face be fearful to their eyes,
> Yet, in protection of their tender ones,
> Who hath not seen them, even with those wings
> Which sometime they have used with fearful flight,   30
> Make war with him that climbed unto their nest,
> Offering their own lives in their young's defence?
> For shame, my liege, make them your precedent!
>
> (*3 Henry VI*, 2.2.9–33)

The structure of this verse fairly represents Shakespeare's early— though perhaps not his earliest—practice. The organization of thought is artificial and highly structured without being excessively or amateurishly stiff. Near the beginning of the plea (ll. 11–16), the three questions and answers take almost identical form, each query occupying a full line followed by the negative response as the next full line. Similar structural patterns emerge as Clifford continues, particularly in his formulation of the contrasts between Henry and York, some of them oppositions of single lines, some of pairs.

The organizing principle that guarantees the regularity of the passage is the correspondence between the main grammatical unit, the independent clause, and the chief poetic unit, the pentameter line. To say this is only to say, of course, that the lines are mostly end-stopped, that some form of terminal punctuation ends the line. This property is most obvious in the series of interrogatives just mentioned: six discrete sentences (three questions and three answers) set forth in six pentameter lines, each question and each answer ending at the terminus of the poetic line. Such an arrangement at such a moment serves to encapsulate and thus to emphasize the political urgency of Clifford's claims. But it is vital to recognize that the entire speech is similarly if less obviously organized—regular, metrically balanced, and with very little deviation from the pattern of endstopped lines.

The more significant conclusion is that throughout this passage, and throughout the early plays in general, the poet seems to be thinking in ten-syllable units. Although the punctuation of Renaissance printed texts is a complex issue—much of the pointing may have been done by scribes or compositors—the several kinds of stops in this passage are revealing. Of the twenty-four lines quoted, only two are printed without some kind of terminal punctuation, and half are given a full stop. The commas at the ends of lines are pertinent in this context because they indicate, almost as well as a full stop or a question mark, the normal congruence between the semantic and the poetic unit. Even when the sentence is longer than a pentameter line, the grammatical segments tend to correspond to the poetic joints. In the pair of lines that follows the questions, for example, 'The smallest worm will turn, being trodden on, | And doves will peck in safeguard of their brood', the compound sentence splits into two separate units divided equally between two lines. Although the first line is broken by a comma to accommodate 'being turned upon', the two parts of the sentence nevertheless match each other: each contains a subject, a verb, and then a conditional phrase modifying the verb, the first one participial, the second prepositional.

The freestanding line in these early plays, unbroken and endstopped though it may be, is never a seamless whole. The grammatical components of the sentence, such as prepositional phrases or objective clauses, break the pentameter line, however subtly, into smaller segments; and Shakespeare's poetic development may be charted partly by his manipulation of these midline breaks. At this early stage, the poet deliberately seeks to mask the effect of such interruptors. The general impression that the ear receives during the course of a full-length play—some 3,000 lines, the majority endstopped—is one of congruity and equivalence. In other words, the similar length of each poetic unit, about ten syllables, imparts to the work a sense of aural uniformity. Virtually all the verse in the early comedies and histories exhibits exactly this kind of lineal regularity. Sometimes it is more audible, sometimes less, and variations deriving from particular narrative or theatrical requirements occasionally present themselves. In Clifford's speech, for example, the trochees that begin the alternating lines answering his rhetorical questions ('Not to the beast', 'Not his that spoils', 'Not he that sets his foot') break the iambic rhythm, but they establish instead a complementary aural pattern. For the most part, as Clifford's speech demonstrates, the poetic line rules.

To examine Shakespeare's beginnings as a poet is to wonder about the sources of and influences on his approach to blank verse. The initial problem the young poet faced was the sovereignty of the ten-syllable line, the challenge of fitting English sentences into decasyllabic units.[1] We should recall, while noting Shakespeare's youth and inexperience, the relative youth of the medium itself. Owing to the comparative novelty of dramatic blank verse, the custom among its practitioners was to make the fit between sentence and line as smooth as possible. That the line and the phrase were identified with each other at this point in literary history is most readily apparent in the work of Christopher Marlowe. Surely the most stimulating model for an ambitious young playwright at the end of the century, Marlowe wrote verse in which, according to George Saintsbury, '[t]he lines are not merely stopped at the end, but they are constructed to stop at the end. They are moulded individually, not collectively.'[2] For English dramatic poets at this period, the endstopped line was expected, and Shakespeare would have been abnormal had he flouted that convention in his apprentice work.

Such regularity was hospitable to Shakespeare's own theatrical and narrative inclinations, particularly the dramatic subjects to which he was initially attracted. The division of poetic speech into roughly equal poetic lines reflects the highly formalized action in Shakespeare's early drama, helping to create what G. R. Hibbard describes as a 'pattern of total opposition and balanced confrontation'.[3] The fundamental narrative conflict in the first tetralogy, York versus Lancaster, dictates an oscillation between leaders, camps, groups of characters, and political claims. At times the artifice of this antithetical method becomes noticeably bald, or, more neutrally, emblematic. The Temple Garden scene (2.4) of *1 Henry VI* in particular is famously schematic, with Richard Plantagenet and the Earl of Somerset urging the assembled gentlemen to pluck white and red roses respectively, thus declaring their allegiance in the struggle for the crown. It is understandable that, as a novice playwright, Shakespeare would be drawn to historical sources providing a clear conflict between parties and ideas, and the multiple balances and oppositions arise from the choice of the historical subject. This kind of parallel also marks the symbolic stage directions in *3 Henry VI*: '*Alarum. Enter a Sonne that hath kill'd his Father, at one door: and a Father that hath kill'd his Sonne, at another doore*' (Folio text). Here the dramatist enlists even the physical properties of the theatre itself, the two doors at either end of the upstage wall, to depict symmetrically the devastating effects of political strife.

Even in his earliest plays Shakespeare exploits the aural conventions of metrical symmetry and equivalence to produce meaning. Specifically, the various balances serve to represent one of the main political problems of the first history cycle, the competing claims of the factions vying for the English throne after the death of Henry V. Such rhythmic contention structures the dialogue in the fourth act of *Richard III*, as King Richard sues to his sister-in-law for the hand of her daughter, his own niece, in marriage.

> KING RICHARD Say I will love her everlastingly.   280
> QUEEN ELIZABETH But how long shall that title 'ever' last?
> KING RICHARD Sweetly in force unto her fair life's end.
> QUEEN ELIZABETH But how long fairly shall her sweet life last?
> KING RICHARD As long as heaven and nature lengthens it.
> QUEEN ELIZABETH As long as hell and Richard likes of it.
> KING RICHARD Say I, her sovereign, am her subject [low].
> QUEEN ELIZABETH But she, your subject, loathes such sovereignty.
> KING RICHARD Be eloquent in my behalf to her.

> QUEEN ELIZABETH   An honest tale speeds best being
>   plainly told.
> KING RICHARD   Then plainly to her tell my loving tale.   290
> QUEEN ELIZABETH   Plain and not honest is too harsh a
>   style.
> KING RICHARD   Your reasons are too shallow and too
>   quick.
> QUEEN ELIZABETH   O no, my reasons are too deep and
>   dead—
>
> $(4.4.280–93)^4$

The two speakers match each other stychomithically, returning full line
for full line. When one alters the pattern by inserting a midline pause
('Say I, her sovereign'), the other responds in kind ('But she, your
subject'). Throughout the early histories poetic lines oppose each other
in this way—just like scenes, speeches, patriarchs, families, brothers,
queens, regions, roses. And just as the opposing houses make up a larger
national or political unit, so ultimately the poetic lines march together
to create a dramatic whole vivified by their contention.

Such a pattern of opposition obtains in the early comedies as well,
notably *The Comedy of Errors*, with its two sets of twins, complementary sisters, and warring city-states. In all the early comedies, but
particularly in *The Taming of the Shrew, Two Gentlemen of Verona*,
and *Love's Labour's Lost*, the parallel plots yield a similarly balanced
alternation. The blank verse line in these plays is noticeably regular
and relatively simple, although close attention discloses that the young
playwright soon begins to discover and exploit the value of poetic
variation and altered pattern. In composing the dialogue in *Errors*,
for example, he manipulates the pentameter to differentiate between
speakers and to transform the dramatic mood. Consider the juxtaposition of two speeches in the second scene.

> ANTIPHOLUS OF SYRACUSE   He that commends me to
>   mine own content,
> Commends me to the thing I cannot get:
> I to the world am like a drop of water,
> That in the ocean seeks another drop,
> Who, falling there to find his fellow forth,
> Unseen, inquisitive, confounds himself.
> So I, to find a mother and a brother,

In quest of them (unhappy ah) lose myself.
> *Enter Dromio of Ephesus*

Here comes the almanac of my true date:
What now? How chance thou art returned so soon?
DROMIO OF EPHESUS Returned so soon? Rather
   approached too late:
The capon burns, the pig falls from the spit;
The clock hath strucken twelve upon the bell:
My mistress made it one upon my cheek:
She is so hot because the meat is cold:
The meat is cold, because you come not home:
You come not home, because you have no stomach:
You have no stomach, having broke your fast:
But we that know what 'tis to fast and pray,
Are penitent for your default to-day.

> (1.2.33–52; Folio punctuation)[5]

Superficially this is early verse: almost every line is endstopped, and the phrasal repetitions of Dromio's reply resemble the formal patterns of the first tetralogy. Yet the internal variations immediately establish a strong rhythmic opposition between master and servant. Both speak blank verse, but Antipholus' lines are long and leisurely, whereas Dromio's are choppy and urgent. The contrast arises mainly from Shakespeare's exaggeration of the caesura, the midline pause, in Dromio's lines. The servant's parodic logic splits them in half, especially towards the end of the plea, and the irony is intensified by the use of *gradatio*, the rhetorical ladder-figure by which the servant ascends to the long-lined couplet forming the conclusion. It is just such playful variation and exaggeration that Shakespeare will magnify as he gains more experience with the mechanics of iambic pentameter. But variation depends on a firmly established norm, and the metrical uniformity of the apprentice plays gives the early verse, with a noticeable pause at the end of almost every line, an identifiable aural imprint that the poet almost immediately begins to undo.

Metrics in Mid-Career

Shakespeare's metrical development does not merely parallel his thematic evolution; it helps to produce it. Rhythm is intimately related to meaning, as both cause and effect. The transition from the early to the later histories—and from the comedies to the tragedies as well— depends upon a dismantling of antithetical categories, a breaking down of simple oppositions combined with more intense scrutiny of their constituent parts. Robert Y. Turner, charting the movement from the *Henry VI* plays to *Richard II* and from plays like *Two Gentlemen* to *Dream*, describes the maturation this way:

> In Shakespeare's later, more mimetic apprentice plays, the general truths of the sort which govern and shine through episodes of the earlier chronicles are modified by particularities of circumstance and character.... Mimetic drama, far from being without moral purpose, heightens awareness by diminishing the absoluteness of general moral truth. The less certain we are in placing our judgments, the more aware we become of our standards and cautious about simple approval or disapproval of specific behavior.[6]

What Turner says of the metamorphosis in the first ten plays or so is even more evident in Shakespeare's movement from apprenticeship to maturity. By the end of the 1590s, as Norman Rabkin has demonstrated in his famous analysis of *Henry V*, absolute judgements are proscribed. Every conclusion seems to imply its own opposite and then seems paradoxically to reassert itself, and the audience is immersed in an atmosphere of uncertainty and contradiction.[7]

The experience of constant modification is aural as well as hermeneutic, and it is easy to see that interpretation is to some extent a function of metrical destabilization. Turner's comment about 'general truths ... modified by particularities of circumstance and character' applies also to the mature poetic line, complicated as it is by pauses, hesitations, recursions, lunges forward. The overriding fact is that Shakespeare introduces immense variety into the sound of the pentameter. Fewer lines are endstopped than in the early plays, but what is especially telling is that the basic ten-syllable unit has been dismantled. Midline breaks occur frequently, sometimes more than once in a line. At the same time, many phrases run longer than a single line. The texture of the verse is less formal, less artificial, more 'natural', more 'conversational'. We might say that the line has ceded a good deal of its authority to the sentence.

Any number of celebrated speeches from the great tragedies might be cited to illustrate this movement from uniformity to irregularity.

Here is Brutus' passionate rejection of the proposal that the conspirators should swear their commitment to the assassination, from the
second act of *Julius Caesar*:

> No, not an oath. If not the face of men,
> The sufferance of our souls, the time's abuse—
> If these be motives weak, break off betimes,
> And every man hence to his idle bed.
> So let high-sighted tyranny range on
> Till each man drop by lottery. But if these,
> As I am sure they do, bear fire enough
> To kindle cowards and to steel with valour   120
> The melting spirits of women, then, countrymen,
> What need we any spur but our own cause
> To prick us to redress? What other bond
> Than secret Romans, that have spoke the word
> And will not palter? And what other oath
> Than honesty to honesty engaged
> That this shall be or we will fall for it?
> Swear priests and cowards and men cautelous,
> Old feeble carrions, and such suffering souls
> That welcome wrongs; unto bad causes swear   130
> Such creatures as men doubt; but do not stain
> The even virtue of our enterprise,
> Nor th'insuppressive mettle of our spirits,
> To think that or our cause or our performance
> Did need an oath, when every drop of blood
> That every Roman bears, and nobly bears,
> Is guilty of a several bastardy
> If he do break the smallest particle
> Of any promise that hath passed from him.
>
> (2.1.113–39)

This passage is apt because it presents important similarities to Clifford's appeal to Henry VI. Like the earlier speech, this one is a plea, an
effort at persuasion, although in this case Brutus opposes rather than
proposes an action. The Roman's verse is looser than the earlier, his
passion expressed less artificially; and yet the poetry is still carefully
patterned, if much more subtly. The metrical differences between the
two passages help to tell the story of Shakespeare's poetic development.

After a decade of experience the poet has overthrown the tyranny of the ten-syllable segment and replaced it with a productive counterpoint between sentence and line. In the first place, he has discovered the capacity of enjambment to create aural variety and especially to affect the rhythm of a speech. Less than half of Brutus' lines are endstopped, and half of the endstopped lines are split with internal pauses. While it is still true that the end of the line sometimes coincides with the close of a phrase, nevertheless the joints of the sentences are not so exposed, do not declare themselves to the extent that they have done in the earlier passage. In fact, in the mature style the grammar of the sentence often propels the listener into the next line, as when the terminal word is a verb demanding an object: 'unto bad causes swear | Such creatures as men doubt; but do not stain | The even virtue of our enterprise.' Similar momentum arises from a construction such as 'bear fire enough | To kindle cowards'.

The value of enjambment is that it affords the poet greater range in controlling the rhythms and tempo of the speech. For all the vigour and energy of the language in the early histories, the verse can become monotonous because the ear accustoms itself to the predictability of the stops, and thus to the equivalent length and weight of each phrase. By the time he wrote *Julius Caesar*, Shakespeare had learned to defeat that predictability by varying the length of phrases and sentences. In Brutus' speech, the length of the sentences increases from the brief utterance at the beginning ('No, not an oath') to the bravura twelve-line sentence that concludes the passage ('Swear priests and cowards . . . hath passed from him'). The irregularity of the pauses—here their temporary elimination—contributes a propulsive energy as phrases run over the ends of lines and thus convey the passion and inevitability of the speaker's claims. This pace is accelerated by the poet's treatment of the smallest metrical units, particularly his introduction of the pyrrhic foot, a poetic unit composed of two soft syllables, as the argument approaches its climax:

> Thĕ évĕn vírtŭe | ŏf ŏur | éntĕrpríse
> Nŏr th'ínsŭppréssĭve méttlĕ | ŏf ŏur | spírĭts

Such control of tempo is part of the mature poet's skill at manipulating the metre for rhetorical effect.

In the contention between the metrical beat and potential challenges to it, such minute variations create moments of defeat and
recovery, loss and gain, speed and stop, aural conflicts that serve to
invigorate and particularize the poet's representation of human
speech. For example, the pyrrhics substitute for the normal iambs
throughout the passage, and these variants contribute not only velocity
but also a foiling effect that emphasizes what follows. In the first line
just cited, the removal of accent on 'of our' throws the weight onto
'enterprise', an emphasis promoted by the recovery of iambic regularity
at the end of the line. Often the pyrrhic foot is combined with other
metrical tactics to magnify that emphasis. The combination of a
pyrrhic foot with a spondee (two hard syllables), for example, points
the meaning in several of Brutus' lines:

> Whăt néed wĕ ánў spŭr bŭt oŭr own caúse

or

> Thăt wélcŏme wróngs; ŭntŏ bád caúsĕs swéar

Spondees alone can exert such pressure, as in 'Till each man drop by
lottery'. Moreover, the manipulation of caesurae creates a complex and
potentially meaningful aural texture. Sometimes the midline pause
becomes a pivot for an antithetical turn, exaggerating the opposition
between two ideas. The following pair of contiguous lines depends on
such a turn: 'And will not palter? And what other oath | Than honesty
to honesty engaged.' The stop in the centre of the pyrrhic, acting as a
kind of metrical equivocation, underscores the meaning of 'palter';
then, by way of contrast, resolution is re-established with the aggress-
ive regularity of the following line, the certainty of the beat secured
again by the repetition of 'honesty to honesty'.

This kind of auditory recapitulation should alert us to the fact that
Brutus' speech, although an example of the mature style, is still
rigorously formal. It is replete with rhetorical figures, in particular
the multiple instances of repetition: the phonemic ('bear fire'), the
several uses of the series (verbal and clausal), the noticeably dense
alliteration, the reiterated phrases ('What other bond', 'what other
oath'), and the interweaving of words and sounds into large patterns
('To *th*ink *th*at *or our* cause *or our* performance | *Did* need an oath,
when *every d*rop of blood | That *every* Roman *bears*, and nobly *bears*').
Clearly the sense of design and formality is almost as intense as in the

apprentice verse of the early histories. But Shakespeare's devotion to metrical intricacy helps to subordinate such rhetorical patterns: the more that goes on in the line, the less obvious any single trope or characteristic is likely to seem.

The mature Shakespeare's metrical freedom with the poetic line permits him to exploit the sound of verse in the service of various dramatic ends. The most striking use he makes of such variation is to represent character in action, his skill at doing so being most apparent in the major tragedies. In plays like *Hamlet* and *King Lear*, where the dramatic power springs directly from major changes in the tragic figure's sense of self and engagement with others, variations in speech afford an especially economical and effective means of revealing such experience. For example, Othello's psychological disintegration is captured aurally in a major linguistic shift: as Iago's poison works upon him, the eloquent, orotund poetic sentences of the early scenes degenerate into short, monosyllabic outbursts ('O, blood, blood, blood!'), and even into the relatively unstructured medium of prose. In each of the tragedies Shakespeare begins by establishing a poetic baseline for the protagonist and then violating or eroding that norm as the action proceeds.

Such a metrical transformation is vital to the representation of King Lear's tragic arc. In the second act, having arrived at Gloucester's house to meet Regan and Cornwall, Lear finds his daughter and her husband unwilling to greet him or even to acknowledge his desire to see them. As the stubborn old King begins to perceive the devastating consequences of his abdication, the firm metrical patterns of his speech, clearly audible in the opening scene, begin to dissolve.

> The king would speak with Cornwall; the dear father
> Would with his daughter speak, commands, tends service.
> Are they 'informed' of this? My breath and blood—
> 'Fiery'? The 'fiery' Duke—tell the hot Duke that—
> No, but not yet. Maybe he is not well.
>
> (2.2.273–7, Folio text)

The shifts in mood are instantly apparent, and the speech continues with still another reversal into fury, but what is also striking is the way that Shakespeare has manipulated the sound of the lines to magnify those temperamental alterations.

Of the five lines quoted, three are extrametrical, containing eleven syllables instead of ten, and these additional syllables are placed at the end of the line, creating what is known in metrical parlance as a feminine ending. One major characteristic of Shakespeare's prosodic development is that he makes greater use of this extra syllable. The early verse is relatively free of feminine endings: its regularity and endstopped quality necessitate a firm accent at the end of the line. As his approach to metrics begins to relax, the feminine ending begins to appear with much greater frequency. Perhaps surprisingly, Lear's opening speech contains such weak endings: 'Meantime we shall express our darker purpose. | Give me the map there. Know that we have divided | In three our kingdom' (1.2.36–8). But this speech is very much under control, the feminine endings and other rhythmic aberrations perhaps indicative of the divided sense of authority that will plague the King throughout the action. In his outburst against Regan and Cornwall quoted above, the drooping line endings clearly signal the old man's frustration. Indeed, this device is only one of the many metrical variations in which the King's failing sense of power is encoded: trochees ('Fiery?' at the beginning of the line), trochees combined with spondees ('Tell the hot Duke'), caesurae near the end of the line, repeated stops and starts. Emotional volatility generates multiple challenges to the customary beat, and thus the authority of the pentameter is compromised in the same way that Lear's power is diminished by his daughters.

Late Experiments

The metrical range of *King Lear* is typical of Shakespeare's practice in his middle period. As he moves beyond the mature tragedies into the final phase, the years that produced the dramas known as the romances, he permits the metrical frame to become looser and looser, so much so that variation threatens to efface the pentameter altogether. But the poet never forgets—and he demands that the listener remain alert to—the value of the fundamental pattern, no matter how extravagant and playful the departure from it. By means of such tension between line and phrase, the aural experiments in plays such as *Cymbeline*, *The Winter's Tale*, and *The Tempest* become as audacious as the theatrical invention.

So irregular are the rhythms of the late plays that a number of readers, particularly in the first half of the twentieth century, conjectured that Shakespeare had lost his power of concentration, or become bored with his work, or simply failed to revise his initial drafts.[8] Recent study has disputed those conclusions, explaining that the primary cause of this metrical distortion is the radical compression for which the playwright seems to strive. Packing as much thought as possible into the space of the sentence, he often eliminates such potentially superfluous elements as relative pronouns, conjunctions, even verbs. Moreover, he depends heavily and repeatedly on enjambed lines and extrametrical endings. The short phrases he has begun to favour tend to produce segmented lines, some of them divided more than once, as well as frequent trochaic or spondaic feet that disturb the regularity of the line.[9]

The vast difference between the late style and the regular pentameter of the early plays becomes immediately audible in the language of the romances. It is not necessary to seek out passages in which a character suffers emotional pressure—a kind of mad scene—and is therefore inclined to speak rough or distorted verse. On the contrary, virtually any extended speech exhibits the sophisticated sound of the late style. For example, Innogen's first entrance in disguise, in the Welsh scenes of *Cymbeline*, typifies its characteristic metrical variety.

> Two beggars told me
> I could not miss my way. Will poor folks lie,
> That have afflictions on them, knowing 'tis
> A punishment or trial? Yes. No wonder,
> When rich ones scarce tell true. To lapse in fullness
> Is sorer than to lie for need, and falsehood
> Is worse in kings than beggars. My dear lord,
> Thou art one o'th' false ones. Now I think on thee
> My hunger's gone; but even before I was
> At point to sink for food. But what is this?
> Here is a path to't. 'Tis some savage hold.
> I were best not call; I dare not call; yet famine,
> Ere clean it o'erthrow nature, makes it valiant.
> Plenty and peace breeds cowards, hardness ever
> Of hardiness is mother. Ho! Who's here?
> If anything that's civil, speak; if savage,
> Take or lend. Ho! No answer? Then I'll enter.

(3.6.8–24)

Far from the uniformity characteristic of the early pentameter, the rhythmic structure of this late verse seems almost random. The security attendant upon the endstopped line has been withdrawn, and the unreliability of the beat aurally conjures up a world of uncertainty and change. At least half the lines are extrametrical. Sometimes the extra unstressed syllable enfeebles the mood: 'yet famine'; 'if savage'. Sometimes it propels the listener from the end of the line into the beginning of the next: 'I was | At point to sink for food'; 'hardness ever | Of hardiness is mother'. However, when the line is enjambed, as in the last two instances, the poet refuses to create momentum, for as soon as the sense is pushed into the next line there is an abrupt halt: 'Two beggars told me | I could not miss my way'; 'knowing 'tis | A punishment or trial?' Not only is the pattern of the regular beat suppressed, but other kinds of symmetries are twisted as well. For example, parallel phrases just miss: 'I were best not call; I dare not call; yet famine...'[10] The jumpiness of Innogen's last three lines is characteristic, in that Shakespeare seems utterly insouciant about the force of the metrical foundation. He observes its norms, but only just. Variation and playfulness are the ruling impulses.

When characters do speak under the influence of extreme emotion, these metrical variables become especially conspicuous. Surely one of the most expressive speakers is Leontes in the first act of *The Winter's Tale*, as he simultaneously addresses his son and reveals his fears of being a cuckold:

> Inch-thick, knee-deep, o'er head and ears a forked one!—
> Go play, boy, play. Thy mother plays, and I
> Play too; but so disgraced a part, whose issue
> Will hiss me to my grave. Contempt and clamour
> Will be my knell. Go play, boy, play.

(1.2.187–91)

Most of the metrical properties of the late style are audible here: feminine endings, late pauses, short phrases, ellipses, reversed feet, an elusive rhythmic structure. In this instance they serve to characterize the delusional speaker and to convey through the ear the intensity of mood, but they also contribute significantly to the tension between the normative rhythms of verse and the dictates of this speaker's syntax. That tension constitutes one of Shakespeare's primary means for representing the emotional conflicts of the action in *The Winter's Tale* and all the last plays.

A few more passages from the late work will illustrate the extent to which Shakespeare has committed himself to the principle of metrical variety, subordinating the regular beat to the semantic energies of the sentence. These examples do not require extensive commentary, since the features just enumerated can be heard immediately, but it is necessary to quote at some length to provide a sense of the syntactic and metrical range. In the festival in the fourth act of *The Winter's Tale*, Perdita offers to strew her lover with garlands, provoking an ironic question from him followed by a passionate rejoinder from her:

> FLORIZEL   What, like a corpse?
> PERDITA No, like a bank, for love to lie and play on,
>   Not like a corpse—or if, not to be buried,
>   But quick and in mine arms. Come, take your flowers.
>   Methinks I play as I have seen them do
>   In Whitsun pastorals. Sure this robe of mine
>   Does change my disposition.
>
>   (4.4.129–35)

The short phrases, multiply-segmented lines, light endings, and reversed feet are four of the most familiar stylistic traits of the late phase. A similar range is audible throughout *Cymbeline*. In the second act, Posthumus is falsely persuaded of his wife's infidelity, and his rhythms, while perhaps not as violent as Leontes' deformations, are equally irregular.

>   O vengeance, vengeance!
>   Me of my lawful pleasure she restrained,
>   And prayed me oft forbearance; did it with
>   A pudency so rosy the sweet view on't
>   Might well have warmed old Saturn; that I thought her
>   As chaste as unsunned snow. O, all the devils!
>   This yellow Giacomo in an hour—was't not?—
>   Or less—at first?
>
>   (2.5.8–15)

Henry VIII (or *All is True*), written with John Fletcher some year or so after *The Tempest*, is categorized in the Folio as a history play but displays a number of affiliations with the romances. Coleridge perceptively referred to it as 'a sort of historical masque or show-play'. Early in the action, before her divorce trial, Queen Katherine intercedes on behalf of those subjects opposed to Wolsey's commission on taxation. In doing so she wins Henry's approval against the Cardinal, whose scheme is cancelled by the King in forceful verse.

> Things done well,
> And with a care, exempt themselves from fear;
> Things done without example, in their issue
> Are to be feared. Have you a precedent
> Of this commission? I believe not any.
> We must not rend our subjects from our laws
> And stick them in our will. Sixth part of each?
> A trembling contribution! Why, we take
> From every tree lop, bark, and part o'th' timber,
> And, though we leave it with a root, thus hacked
> The air will drink the sap. To every county
> Where this is questioned send our letters with
> Free pardon to each man that has denied
> The force of this commission. Pray look to't—
> I put it to your care.

>   (1.2.89–103)

This last passage is especially useful in a discussion of prosody for at least two reasons. First, its metrical structure contrasts pointedly with the political speech considered at the beginning of this chapter. Lineal equivalence has been deliberately avoided; lines have been broken into two or more parts; ellipsis packs the line with sound; feminine endings are numerous. Second, it exemplifies the conversational, non-rhetorical, irregular verse form which Shakespeare favoured at the end of his career. The emotion is passionate, the King is issuing a command and a rebuke to an overweening prelate, and the speech manages to generate a distinctive kind of poetic force. But it is not poetic in the same way that it would have been had Shakespeare dramatized this conflict in the early 1590s.

In the early verse, strong feeling is represented by a succession of sweeping pentameter lines that come to full and powerful stops, and the sound is usually vigorous and dynamic. Shakespeare is able to

educe different moods and effects from this verse style, but the rhythmic baseline exerts a constant and potentially uniform influence. At
the end of the career, the poet has so substantially enlarged his means
of achieving rhetorical power, as the example from *Henry VIII* abund-
antly reveals, that the range of metrical devices gives the actor much
greater flexibility. The rhythmic complexity of Henry's answer to his
own rhetorical question about precedent—'I believe not any', coming
as it does at the end of the line—suggests a kind of audacity and slyness
deriving from Shakespeare's years of experience at filling poetic con-
tainers with dramatic feeling.

The forceful challenge to the metrical foundation, which effectively
diminishes the regularity and lineal equivalence heard in the earlier
plays, creates a kind of paradox in relation to the other theatrical
characteristics of the romances and late collaborations. The speech
rhythms have become more nearly 'natural' or conversational, and yet
the plays themselves, both the nature of the stories chosen and the
dramatic presentation of them, have become more artificial and
'unrealistic'. Shakespeare has moved, in other words, from the repre-
sentational style of the tragedies to what is known as the presentational
style of the romances. The late plays are exceptionally self-conscious,
insisting on their artificiality and deriving much of their dramatic
power from the playwright's exploitation of their connection with
myth and fairy tale. These plays seem, in other words, deliberately
unreal, much less naturalistic than a play like *King Lear*. How is it,
then, that the poetic language seems less artificial, more 'natural' than
in the earlier works? The answer, at least in part, is that only in his use
of rhythms does the poet seek to conceal evidence of artifice.

Other poetic features rush forward to stand in for the apparently
'unpoetic', irregular beat, suggesting a writer eager to advertise his
poetic ingenuity. Extravagant alliteration, other forms of consonance
and assonance, various forms of lexical and phrasal repetition help to
pull words together, creating a poetic coherence that ameliorates the
loss of iambic consistency.

> *Wh*ere is Posthumus? *Wh*at is in *th*y mind
> *Th*at makes *th*ee stare *th*us? *Wh*erefore breaks *th*at sigh
> From *th*'in*w*ard of *th*ee?
>
> (*Cymbeline*, 3.4.4–6)

to *pur*ge *h*im of that *h*umour
That *p*resses *h*im from sleep
(*The Winter's Tale*, 2.3.38–9)

How *b*ravely *th*ou *b*ecomest *th*y *b*ed
(*Cymbeline*, 2.2.15)

The ear finds comfort less in the pulsation of constantly repeated iambs than in the duplication of consonants and the reiteration of words. The assurances of order arise, in other words, from a greater variety of auditory means. The unseen artificer has expanded his kit of tools.

Here Follows Prose

In the garden scene of *Twelfth Night*, as Malvolio reads aloud and tries to decipher a mysterious love letter found on the walkway, he pauses to register a change in the style of the anonymous author: 'Soft, here follows prose.' His notice of the stylistic shift is telling. The movement from verse to prose denotes a change in mood, a formal relaxation that sets the remainder of the letter apart from its poetic beginning. Especially significant is the fact that Malvolio comments on the change. Since he is reading, his eye immediately notes a difference in lineation. Likewise, in the case of oral discourse, the Elizabethan ear was apparently alert to the change from one form to another. In *As You Like It*, as Jaques and Rosalind converse informally in prose, the love-struck Orlando enters speaking verse, a single line of iambic pentameter: 'Good day and happiness, dear Rosalind.' The wooer's formality is too much for Jaques, who leaves the stage with 'Nay then, God b'wi'you an you talk in blank verse.'

These two episodes constitute historical proof of a major difference between the early modern and the modern ear, specifically that Shakespeare's first audiences seem to have been more sensitive to verbal structures than their modern counterparts. The distinction may also have to do with changes in performance style. Little is known for certain about the style of Elizabethan acting, but some scholars believe that dramatic verse was declaimed in an oratorical and perhaps sing-song manner, thus differentiating it immediately from less rigidly structured prose.[1] Whether this is so or not, we can be sure that Shakespeare counted on his listeners to hear the difference between the structured rhythms of verse and the comparative informality of prose, and that he exploited those differences for theatrical effect.

The most useful definition of prose is that it is not poetry, and the cardinal difference between verse and prose is one of rhythm, or, more specifically, the kind of rhythm. Though Shakespeare uses a variety of verse measures, by far the commonest is blank verse. As indicated in the preceding chapter, blank verse normally consists of lines of ten syllables organized into five beats, each beat constituting an iamb, one unaccented followed by one accented syllable ('Tŏ bé'). Thus, on the printed page, the verse line ends after the tenth syllable (the fifth beat), with a new line beginning at the left-hand margin and signified by a capital letter. Metrical variations often disturb such lines, and many lines consist of more than ten syllables, especially in the later plays, but in general the regular beat is audible and, once we are alert to it, familiar and pleasing. Since prose lacks the regular rhythms of verse, it is printed without such breaks, its lines extending all the way to the right-hand margin and with capital letters used mainly to mark the beginning of a new sentence. But to say that prose is without the uniform beat of verse is not to say that it lacks cadence or harmony. Every competent writer or speaker develops some kind of rhythm in individual sentences and in their combination: several long sentences may be abruptly followed by a short one, for example, or a number of similarly constructed sentences may unfold in sequence. A talented stylist will manipulate these variations so as to affect the ear and guide the mind of the listener. Often the rhythms of prose are situational, developed according to the topic of the speech and the particular impulses or style of the speaker. But superficially speaking, prose is less strictly organized than poetry, less formal and intense. And therein lies its principal dramatic value for Shakespeare. In order to consider that value, I have divided the topic into four main parts: (1) the historical contexts of Elizabethan prose, (2) the established conventions for using dramatic prose and Shakespeare's modification of them over the course of his career, (3) a description of the major syntactical structures and verbal flourishes that the dramatist employs, and (4) a brief survey of some of the most brilliant uses of prose in the mature work. The chapter ends with a coda describing the indescribability of certain memorable passages.

Prose Models *circa* 1590

Shakespeare's skill at writing dramatic prose should be seen in light of the philosophical and pedagogical debates over language occurring at the end of the sixteenth century. The conventions of prose style were much discussed by Tudor rhetoricians, who usually took their arguments and examples from their Latin predecessors, and a non-dramatic writer's stylistic choices were thought to be charged with meaning. Indeed the kind of English prose a writer chose to employ carried intellectual and even moral significance. It is worth reiterating not only that the English language was coming into its own in the early modern age, but that thinkers in the period seem very much aware that it was doing so. The fierce debate over whether the Bible should be translated into the vernacular, one of the major issues of Reformation politics in England and on the Continent, indicates that language itself was a topic of grave concern for many British people. Recognizing the emergence of England as an international force, scholars and courtiers felt the need for a vernacular appropriate to the dignity of a world power. Moreover, since education was a growing concern of the Elizabethans, proper composition was then, as it is today, a central component of the pedagogical conversation.

Familiarity with the prose models Shakespeare inherited will clarify his own practice, particularly the ways in which he took up and varied the prevailing forms of expression. The prevalent view at the middle of the sixteenth century favoured intricate sentences based on parallel clauses, other elaborate rhetorical patterns, and stylistic decoration for its own sake: the Ciceronian style. The competing opinion, which eventually supplanted the older view, regarded style strictly as a means of conveying thought and consequently disapproved of obvious rhetorical patterns: this has come to be known as Senecan prose. Such easy categories are easy to dismiss, and the simplification involved in such division has provoked objection, but the distinctions are nevertheless useful for the writing of the period. The great monuments of late sixteenth- and early seventeenth-century English prose can be divided more or less neatly, according to the stylistic sympathies of their creators, into two main categories: the formal, scrupulously patterned, 'rhetorical' style of John Lyly's *Euphues* (1578) or Richard Hooker's *Laws of Ecclesiastical Polity* (1594) which more or less followed the Ciceronian model; and the loose, asymmetrical, more 'natural' style of Thomas Nashe's *Unfortunate Traveller* (1594) or Francis Bacon's *Essays* (1597–1625), works which conformed to the Senecan model. In practice, of course, the results were never as tidy as the dicta of the rule-givers would imply. Nashe began writing a kind of Ciceronian prose that he eventually transformed into its opposite, and a work like Sidney's *Arcadia* resists classification in such terms.

Nevertheless, such categories help to reveal the controversies about the forms and functions of prose and, what is more, the basis for those differences. The following sentences from *Euphues: The Anatomy of Wit* make for a useful starting point:

The sun shineth upon the dunghill and is not corrupted, the diamond lieth in the fire and is not consumed, the crystal toucheth the toad and is not poisoned, the bird Trochilus liveth by the mouth of the crocodile and is not spoiled, a perfect wit is never bewitched with lewdness, neither enticed with lasciviousness. Is it not common that the holm tree springeth amidst the beech? That the ivy spreadeth upon the hard stones? That the soft featherbed breaketh the hard blade? If experience have not taught you this you have lived long and learned little; or if your moist brain have forgot it you have learned much and profited nothing. But it may be that you measure my affections by your own fancies, and knowing yourself either too simple to raise the siege by policy or too weak to resist the assault by prowess, you deem me of as little wit as yourself or of less force, either of small capacity or of no courage.[2]

Our sense of the symmetrical balances of Lyly's prose may be illuminated and sharpened by a comparison with a passage from one of Bacon's essays.

To pass from theological and philosophical truth to the truth of civil business, it will be acknowledged even by those that practise it not that clear and round dealing is the honour of man's nature; and that mixture of falsehood is like allay in coin of gold and silver, which may make the metal work the better, but it embaseth it. For these winding and crooked courses are the goings of the serpent, which goeth basely upon the belly and not upon the feet. There is no vice that doth so cover a man with shame as to be found false and perfidious. And therefore Montaigne saith prettily, when he enquired the reason why the word of the lie should be such a disgrace and such an odious charge—saith he, 'If it be well weighed, to say that a man lieth is as much to say as that he is brave towards God and a coward towards men'. For a lie faces God and shrinks from man.[3]

These excerpts point the distinction between Ciceronian and anti-Ciceronian prose with particular clarity because Lyly and Bacon rely on many common elements, notably an argumentative thrust and a liberal use of metaphor. The resemblances are overshadowed, however, by the contrasting form of the sentences. Whereas Lyly's words and phrases come in patterns ('is not corrupted . . . is not consumed . . . is not poisoned . . . is not spoiled') and pairs ('*raise* the *siege* by *policy* . . . *resist* the *assault* by *prowess*'), and even exhibit alliteration and assonance within those structural patterns, Bacon resolutely avoids any such arrangement. Even though many of his sentences are long and intricately structured, they lack the ornamentation and stylistic self-regard of the older type.

An analytic description of Shakespeare's prose in relation to contemporary practice requires a multitude of qualifications and caveats. First, Shakespeare's prose is a theatrical instrument, speech written for dramatic characters, and that function makes it qualitatively different from the foregoing models. Second, every major character is given a more or less distinctive voice, and naturally some speakers lean more towards the patterned style than others. Certain gifted speakers, a Hamlet or an Iago, for example, move nimbly from style to style depending on the moment. The most self-conscious may themselves parody a distinctive style, as Falstaff does when he uses Lylyan Euphuism to impersonate the King in the tavern scene of *1 Henry IV*: 'If then thou be son to me, here lies the point: why, being son to me, art thou so pointed at?' (2.5.409–11). Third, the playwright alters and varies his prose speech as his career proceeds, a development that makes critical generalizations about twenty years' worth of 'Shakespearian prose' especially hazardous. Still, the benefits of historical contextualization finally outweigh the risks, and we should probably say that the playwright's prose more nearly resembles the old-fashioned, Lylyan style than it does the Baconian.

The requisite modification to this blunt statement is that Shakespeare transforms the fundamental patterns of Euphuism into a more apparently natural style. Still, the skeleton of Lyly's balanced sentences and his fondness for lexical repetition are never entirely effaced. They are clearly audible in Falstaff's mocking threat to Prince Hal: 'An old lord of the Council rated me the other day in the street about you, sir, but I marked him not; and yet he talked very wisely, but I regarded him not; and yet he talked wisely, and in the street too' (*1 Henry IV*, 1.2.83–7). Falstaff's pride in his verbal invention might lead us to expect such echoing, but even when a speaker is not so playful, the equivalent syntactical shape makes itself felt: 'I cannot be a man with wishing, therefore I will die a woman with grieving' (*Much Ado*, 4.1.323–4). One hears it even in parts of sentences, as in Portia's 'If I live to be as old as Sibylla I will die as chaste as Diana' (*The Merchant of Venice*, 1.2.103–4). Jonas Barish identifies nicely the particular nature of Shakespeare's debt to his Ciceronian predecessors:

> Shakespeare starts with the highly specialized set of expressive devices worked out by Lyly, inflects them variously, fills them with nuance, widens their range, and so finally transcends them, but without departing from the structural principles on which they are based. One tends not to notice the logicality of Shakespeare's prose because it is managed with such virtuosity as to seem as natural as breathing. But by his constant invention of fresh logical formulas, his endless improvising of new patterns, Shakespeare, if anything, carries logical syntax even further than Lyly.[4]

Rarely do Shakespeare's symmetries seem as bald or self-promoting as Lyly's, but as Barish's last clause implies, they are more efficacious in the sense that they are calculated to elucidate contrarieties of meaning. Recognition of the Lylyan precedent leads to the discovery that its traces are everywhere, and having established this lineage, we discover further that Shakespeare's transformation of the model is even more significant than his dependence on it.

Prose, Comic and Tragic

For Shakespeare, verse is the dominant form and prose the subordinate, a relationship consistent with the practice of most early modern dramatists. When Elizabethan playwrights did write dialogue in prose, they tended to employ it for comic scenes, and indeed some playwrights wrote comedies entirely or mainly in prose: George Gascoigne in *Supposes* (1576), his translation of an Italian comedy, John Lyly in his court comedies of the 1580s, and Ben Jonson in his comical satires at the turn of the seventeenth century. Tragedies or chronicle plays, on the other hand, were normally written in verse. This division reflects the persons and milieux considered appropriate for each mode: put in the simplest terms, Elizabethan tragedy dealt with kings, comedy with clowns, or at least with ordinary people. Since the representation of common folk would seem to require the equivalent of everyday language, the characters of comedy were more apt than high-born persons to speak prose. As a beginner, Shakespeare tends to observe this social distinction fairly strictly. His first history plays are composed almost entirely in verse, as is his first tragedy, *Titus Andronicus* (except for one prose exchange between Titus and a rustic messenger); the early comedies offer both verse and prose, with the lords and ladies speaking blank verse and the secondary figures prose. Even in the early plays there are exceptions to these guidelines, but in general Shakespeare's practice as a dramatic apprentice is thoroughly conventional.

In the earliest comedies the stylistic distinctions are socially determined. Upper-class characters tend to speak verse, servants and lower-class figures prose. Love stories, usually involving the high born, are conducted in verse, whereas the more farcical scenes ask for the informality of prose. Thus these first comedies contain much more verse than prose: in *Two Gentlemen of Verona*, *The Taming of the Shrew*, *The Comedy of Errors*, *Love's Labour's Lost*, and *A Midsummer Night's Dream*, the proportion of prose lines is never more than 30 per cent (*Errors* has less than 15 per cent). The connection between rank and speech appears plainly in *A Midsummer Night's Dream*: the members of the Athenian court (not only Theseus and Hippolyta but also the young lovers) and the denizens of the spirit world, including Puck and the attendant fairies, speak verse, whereas the amateur actors, the 'rude mechanicals', speak prose, except in their theatrical performance at court, a tragedy written in execrable rhyme. Although Bottom addresses Titania in prose, she speaks verse to him, a separation which comically sustains the distinction of rank between them. Even in *A Midsummer Night's Dream*, however, exceptions occur, as in the last act, when the courtly figures punctuate the labourers' performance with informal commentary in prose.

From about 1595 the percentages change as Shakespeare begins to devise his own rules for appropriate speech. Although prose is still given to servants and clowns, exceptions become more numerous and more extensive. In the great romantic comedies, the apogee of his work in this mode, the earlier proportion of verse to prose is reversed: over 70 per cent of *Much Ado About Nothing* is written in prose, and the percentages for *As You Like It* and *Twelfth Night* are almost as great. In these plays the alternation between verse and prose is so frequent, so unschematic, and so skilful that it is risky to generalize. The undeniable fact, however, is that theatrical demands tend to overrule the conventions of social class. In *Twelfth Night*, for example, Sir Toby

Belch and Sir Andrew Aguecheek are both knights, but as agents of low comedy they speak only prose.

A similar flexibility marks the dramatist's movement from the earlier to the later histories. The first tetralogy (*1, 2, 3 Henry VI* and *Richard III*), consisting of plays which are more conventional than those that will follow, contains mostly verse. In the later cycle (*Richard II, 1* and *2 Henry IV,* and *Henry V*), however, a great deal of prose is spoken, mostly in the tavern and on the battlefield among non-ranking soldiers.[5] Royal characters often use prose to answer prose-speaking servants or messengers, and sometimes kings in private moments will descend to prose, as Henry V does in wooing Princess Catherine. Sir John Falstaff, although he can speak verse and does so in the company of the King, speaks mostly prose. His inventive locutions are supplemented by various forms of prose: the confused speech of Mistress Quickly, the nattering of Justice Shallow, and the sober lectures administered to Falstaff by the Lord Chief Justice (who addresses the new King in verse, of course). A full 40 per cent of *Henry V* is written in prose, not only the royal wooing but the frivolous chat of the French courtier-soldiers and the variously inflected speech of the English, Welsh, Irish, and Scottish soldiers who make up the British force at Agincourt.

One of the mature comedies, *The Merry Wives of Windsor* (c.1597), is written almost entirely in prose, and in this respect it stands as a notable exception in the Shakespearian canon. It differs from the norm in other ways as well. The relative emphasis of the two plots inverts Shakespeare's normal practice: typically he foregrounds the romantic plot and subordinates the farcical or satiric story, emotionally, if not statistically. Here, however, he focuses on Falstaff's ludicrous seduction schemes, glancing only briefly at young Fenton's attempts to marry Anne Page against the wishes of her father and mother. Consequently, the verse of the two lovers, the only verse speakers in the play, accounts for only 5 per cent of the lines. A legend first recorded in the eighteenth century holds that the playwright concocted *The Merry Wives* because Queen Elizabeth desired to see Falstaff in love, and such a theory of origin might help to account for the local setting: this is the only Shakespearian comedy set in England. Whether the legend is true or not, it seems clear that the bourgeois nature of the setting—no kings or princesses here—dictated the choice of medium.

When Shakespeare turned to tragedy around 1599–1600, he began to create some of the most memorable blank verse in the canon, but the contribution of prose to plays such as *Hamlet* and *Othello* is hardly negligible. The most productive way of thinking about its role in Shakespearian tragedy is to revert to the simple negative definition: prose is not poetry. Since verse is the dominant form, he employs prose precisely because it is not poetry, because it makes a change. In other words, the introduction of a speech or scene in prose signals an alteration of mood, a relaxation of tension, a tonal variation that influences the audience whether or not they are conscious of the shift. Prose can also signal reversals in character, indicating for example the onset of madness or a loss of control: familiar instances include Ophelia's mad scenes in the second half of *Hamlet*; Othello's psychological disintegration, represented by his epileptic seizure, in Act 4; and Lady Macbeth's sleepwalking scene.

Usually, however, the shift into prose is less obvious, its effect primarily tonal. The transition may occur in the midst of a scene, and only for a moment. A compelling example is the conversation between Lady Macduff and her son, in the scene which ends with their murder (*Macbeth*, 4.2). The episode divides into three parts: Ross's justification of Macduff's flight to England; the Lady's falsely telling her son that his father is dead and was a traitor; and the murder itself. The first and third sections are in verse. The second divides stylistically into two parts: it begins in verse, but as the conversation becomes more intimate and even comic—e.g. the boy's claim that if her husband were dead Lady Macduff would be looking for a new one—mother and son relax into the private form of prose banter. This stylistic informality ironically prepares for the entrance of the murderers. Sometimes the shift from verse to prose is more pointed. In the third scene of *Othello*, after the formal and public defence of his marriage, Othello and Desdemona exit the stage with the Venetian grandees, leaving Iago and Roderigo to converse privately and lengthily in the more informal style. Here the privacy of the encounter and the malignity of Iago's words emphasize the sinister strain that will later infect and destroy the hero. In the fourth act prose works differently: the touching nocturnal conversation as Emilia helps Desdemona prepare for bed is mostly in verse, but it dips briefly into prose when Emilia playfully confesses her casual views of female adultery. Again, what is most important about many of these moments is the shift itself from one medium to another, and most of the remainder of this chapter will be concerned with the theatrical effect of such transitions. First, however, it will be worthwhile to examine the shapes and colours of some typical sentences.

Logic and the Shape of the Sentence

When the young Shakespeare began to write dramatic prose, he found in the Ciceronian stylists a syntactical shape hospitable to his most profound habit of mind. This way of looking at the world, noticed by everyone from critics to actors to acute listeners, may be described as an unfailing passion for antithesis. The taste for opposition, for comparison and contrast, for juxtaposition, helps to explain the forms adopted by his prose speakers, but it accounts for considerably more than that. It determines the word choices that fill those forms, the construction of his verse sentences, the pairing of characters, the alternation of scenes, the blending of modes (as in tragicomedy), the complementarity of ideas. We might expect, given such an antithetical approach to experience, that Shakespeare's prose would conform to the pattern known as parataxis, a term connoting the equal disposition of clauses and phrases. And to some extent this is true. In the paratactic style, elements are linked with conjunctions, 'and' or 'but' or 'neither... nor', and compound sentences tend to predominate, frequently with clauses of relatively equal length. Hypotaxis, its opposite number, lends itself more readily to a hierarchical arrangement of ideas and entails a high quotient of complex sentences, introductory clauses, and other such subordinated elements. In light of the complex demands of dramatic context, it is probably vain to try to designate Shakespeare's style as predominantly paratactic or hypotactic, as can be done with those of his non-dramatic predecessors and contemporaries. The prevailing effect is more apt to be paratactic than hypotactic since prose is often used for informal conversation rather than for carefully structured argument, and since hypotaxis tends to require extended speech and lengthy sentences. For the most part, however, Shakespeare combines the two kinds of syntactical arrangement.

To describe the structure of Shakespearian prose, I return briefly to Barish's identification of the insistent logicality of the Shakespearian prose sentence: its argumentative movement, its division into constitutive parts, its accentuation of that division, its dependence on 'if... then' clauses, its fondness for syllogism, its symmetrical comparisons and demarcation of segments, its intricate but palpable counterbalances. A few examples will reveal the outlines of the formal structures that Shakespeare favours. In *The Taming of the Shrew*, Petruccio's servant describes the journey of his master and Katherine to his country home:

> GRUMIO But hadst thou not crossed me thou shouldst have heard how her horse fell and she under her horse; thou shouldst have heard in how miry a place, how she was bemoiled, how he left her with the horse upon her, how he beat me because her horse stumbled, how she waded through the dirt to pluck him off me, how he swore, how she prayed that never prayed before, how I cried, how the horses ran away, how her bridle was burst, how I lost my crupper, with many things of worthy memory which now shall die in oblivion, and thou return unexperienced to thy grave. (4.1.64–75)

Here, Henry V woos the French princess:

> KING HENRY What! A speaker is but a prater, a rhyme is but a ballad; a good leg will fall, a straight back will stoop, a black beard will turn white, a curled pate will grow bald, a fair face will wither, a full eye will wax hollow, but a good heart, Kate, is the sun and the moon—or rather the sun and not the moon, for it shines bright and never changes, but keeps his course truly. If thou would have such a one, take me; and take me, take a soldier; take a soldier, take a king. And what sayst thou then to my love? Speak, my fair—and fairly, I pray thee.
>
> (*Henry V*, 5.2.158–68)

In *Twelfth Night*, the Clown displays his mental agility for the Duke, Orsino:

> FESTE Now my foes tell me plainly I am an ass, so that by my foes, sir, I profit in the knowledge of myself, and by my friends I am abused; so that, conclusions to be as kisses, if your four negatives make your two affirma-

tives, why then the worse for my friends and the better
for my foes. (5.1.16–21)

In *Othello*, Iago begins his scheme against his master by enlisting the
aid of Roderigo, love-sick for Desdemona:

> IAGO I have told thee often, and I re-tell thee again and
> again, I hate the Moor. My cause is hearted, thine hath
> no less reason. Let us be conjunctive in our revenge
> against him. If thou canst cuckold him, thou dost
> thyself a pleasure, me a sport. (1.3.363–8)

It might be objected that some of these passages represent special
cases, King Henry's a persuasive brief for marriage, Feste's a virtuoso
analysis of a paradox. Even so, in their logical connectives and
balanced phrases ('thyself a pleasure, me a sport'), they are only slightly
magnified versions of the syntactical shapes audible in almost every
prose passage. Syllogistic organization is especially serviceable because
Shakespeare often employs prose as a vehicle for comic interplay, and
such dialogue often depends on specious logic and rhetorical pretension. Yet even in the most serious passages, the same framework can be
discerned beneath the embellishments, permitting 'the utmost freedom and flexibility, like a ground bass on which an infinite number of
variations may be played'.[6]

Shakespeare fleshes out the syntactical bones of his prose with an
array of verbal flourishes to individuate his various speakers. Such
effects, which might be grouped under the category of 'coloration',
include malapropism, eccentric pronunciation, extravagant repetition,
peculiar diction, and other linguistic idiosyncrasies. Perhaps the
informality of the medium encourages the development of peculiar-
ities not so often found or so extravagantly set forth in verse: this is not
to say that such effects are unavailable to the poetic speaker, but they
seem to be more frequent in prose. And since prose is frequently
spoken in comic situations, verbal tics and extravagant stylistic turns
seem much more prominent.

Certain characters, for example, seem uncommonly devoted to the
making of lists. This serializing impulse represents a specific man-
ifestation of the generally paratactic structure of Shakespearian prose,
with clauses strung together by means of conjunctions or linked by

nothing more than parallel structure. Pompey in *Measure for Measure*, former pimp and now assistant to the Viennese executioner, describes various customers from the brothel he encounters in the prison: 'young Dizzy, and young Master Deepvow, and Master Copperspur and Master Starve-lackey the rapier and dagger man, and young Drophair that killed lusty Pudding, and Master Forthright the tilter, and brave Master Shoe-tie the great traveller, and wild Half-can that stabbed Pots, and I think forty more' (4.3.12–17). This familiar comic turn also animates Biondello's recitation of Petruccio's wedding costume and his pitiful horse in *The Taming of the Shrew*:

hipped, with an old mothy saddle and stirrups of no kindred, besides, possessed with the glanders and like to mose in the chine, troubled with the lampass, infected with the fashions, full of windgalls, sped with spavins, rayed with the yellows, past cure of the fives, stark spoiled with the staggers, begnawn with the bots, weighed in the back and shoulder-shotten, near-legged before and with a half-cheeked bit and a headstall of sheep's leather which, being restrained to keep him from stumbling, hath been often burst and now repaired with knots, one girth six times pieced, and a woman's crupper of velour which hath two letters for her name fairly set down in studs, and here and there pieced with packthread.   (3.2.48–61)

Many other instances of such series might be cited, such as Edgar's (Mad Tom's) list of demons (*King Lear*, 3.4), or the Clown's grocery list in *The Winter's Tale* (4.3). And occasionally the series is inflated into sentences and paragraphs, as in Falstaff's description of Justice Shallow as a youth at the end of the Gloucestershire visit in *2 Henry IV* (3.2.297–323). The sequence is not entirely unknown in verse passages: Hamlet's 'For who would bear the whips and scorns of time, | Th'oppressor's wrong...' (3.1.72–8) is a well-known example. Still, it seems more common and useful in prose.

Enumeration of this kind is a subspecies of another consistently productive verbal strategy—repetition. George Puttenham and the other cataloguers prescribe several repetitive poetic schemes, such as *epizeuxis* and *ploce* (the repetition of words and phrases with little or no break), and many of these are heard in Shakespeare's verse. But comic, colloquial prose affords him the liberty for the prodigal doubling and tripling of words and phrases. In fact, sometimes he indulges in precisely the kind of excessive repetition that Puttenham specifically condemns.[7] The touchstone for such excess is the voluble Robert Shallow, the country justice of the peace in *2 Henry IV*, who never says anything once.

> Come on, come on, come on! Give me your hand, sir, give me your hand, sir. (3.2.1–2)

> Where's the roll, where's the roll, where's the roll? Let me see, let me see, let me see; so, so, so, so, so. Yea, marry, sir. 'Ralph Mouldy'. [*To Silence*] Let them appear as I call, let them do so, let them do so. Let me see, (*calls*) where is Mouldy? (3.2.95–9)

> SIR JOHN You must excuse me, Master Robert Shallow.
> SHALLOW I will not excuse you; you shall not be excused;
> excuses shall not be admitted; there is no excuse shall
> serve; you shall not be excused.—Why, Davy!
> *Enter Davy*
> DAVY Here, sir.
> SHALLOW Davy, Davy, Davy; let me see, Davy, let me see,
> Davy; let me see. (5.1.3–9)

This is *epizeuxis* if there ever was *epizeuxis*, and the incessant repetition is a brilliant trick of characterization: it identifies a new character, confers immediate theatrical authority, and distinguishes him from his partner, Justice Silence, who, until he gets drunk, does not say anything, even once. It does considerably more than characterize, however, raising important questions about the truth of historical re-creation. Shallow spends virtually all his stage time talking about the past, repeating for us and his companions his glory days at the Inns of Court five and a half decades before, reminiscing—in another list—about friends and foes such as Jane Nightwork, Francis Pickbone, Samson Stockfish, John of Gaunt, and, most notably, the now deceased Old Double.[8] The dramatist, by associating a recalling of the past with the re-calling of words and phrases, is beginning to generate meaning out of the homeliest stylistic materials.

Verbal duplication makes Shallow one of Shakespeare's most memorable and endearing prose speakers. Misnomer, or what would later come to be called malapropism (after Sheridan's Mrs Malaprop), does the same for Dogberry: 'O villain! Thou wilt be condemned into everlasting redemption for this' (*Much Ado About Nothing*, 4.2.54–5). Here as elsewhere the Constable's errors offer a brilliant comic turn and simultaneously promote Shakespeare's themes. A play in which the innocent heroine is a victim of slander, and in which Beatrice and Benedick protect their vulnerable hearts with sharp and witty words, *Much Ado* explores the human damage that language can do. As Hero says in pretending to censure Beatrice's acidic tongue, 'One doth not know | How much an ill word may empoison liking' (3.1.85–6). Dogberry's words are 'ill' in another sense, and his confusion supplies an additional and important strand in the web of ideas about the connection between words and things. His struggles with vocabulary give him a distinctive voice that makes him one of Shakespeare's most popular verbal buffoons.

One of his near relations is the 'fantastical' Spaniard from *Love's Labour's Lost*, Don Adriano de Armado. Armado specializes in fancy diction, driven as he is by the irrepressible need to call a spade anything but a spade. Elaborate, pleonastic, and ridiculous, his astonishing style of speech is captured in the love letter he sends to Jaquenetta, the country girl with whom he is besotted. When the letter is misdelivered, Boyet reads it aloud to the Princess of France and her ladies.

'By heaven, that thou art fair is most infallible, true that thou art beauteous, truth itself that thou art lovely. More fairer than fair, beautiful than beauteous, truer than truth itself, have commiseration on thy heroical vassal. The magnanimous and most illustrate King Cophetua set's eye upon the penurious and indubitate beggar Zenelophon, and he it was that might rightly say *"Veni, vidi, vici"*, which to annothanize in the vulgar—O base and obscure vulgar!— *videlicet* "He came, see, and overcame." He came, one; see, two; overcame, three. Who came? The King. Why did he come? To see. Why did he see? To overcome. To whom came he? To the beggar. What saw he? The beggar. Who overcame he? The beggar. The conclusion is victory. On whose side? The King's. The captive is enriched. On whose side? The beggar's. The catastrophe is a nuptial. On whose side? The King's—no, on both in one, or one in both. I am the King—for so stands the comparison—thou the beggar, for so witnesseth thy lowliness. Shall I command thy love? I may. Shall I enforce thy love? I could. Shall I entreat thy love? I will. What shalt thou exchange for rags? Robes. For tittles? Titles. For thyself? Me.

Thus, expecting thy reply, I profane my lips on thy foot, my eyes on thy picture, and my heart on thy every part.

Thine in the dearest design of industry,
Don Adriano de Armado.'
(4.1.60–86)

A thorough analysis of the comic felicities displayed here practically warrants its own chapter, but a brief analysis will have to suffice instead.

The letter represents one of the most tempting dishes in this 'great feast of languages', to borrow an ironic phrase from one of the play's clowns, offering the most concentrated example of Armado's self-absorption and pretension. Since one of the general concerns of the play is the discrepancy between pretence and truth, particularly in the linguistic register, the posturing Spaniard's affected phrases and overwrought locutions radiate into other corners of the play-world. Moreover, Armado's prose supplies an early look at Shakespeare's own discovery of what he could do with language, particularly his command of prose rhythm, aural patterning, syntactical contrast, and rhetorical schematization. The basis of the plea to Jaquenetta is the antithesis between high and low—King Cophetua and the beggar maid—and that opposition shapes much of the speaker's rhetoric: 'heroical vassal', 'magnanimous and illustrate King . . . penurious and indubitate beggar', 'For rags? Robes. For tittles? Titles. For thyself? Me.' Shakespeare tickles the listener's ear with the extravagance and variety of the many syntactical structures, and he dramatizes that variety by emphasizing the shift from one to another. The long and graceful sentences at the beginning, for example, are supplanted by the choppy rhythms of the questions and answers near the end of the letter. That interrogative pattern even gives an aural dimension to the high–low antithesis, with the speaker's voice rising in the question and falling in the reply.

Armado's prose is also culturally determined, in that much of it is specifically parodic. The elaborate ornamentation may refer mockingly to the celebrated splendour of the Spanish Armada, the defeat of which (1588) still occupied the English imagination. More specifically, however, his mannerisms seem to burlesque the elaborate styles of a number of well-known Elizabethan writers. To mention only the most obvious cases, the ostentatious wordplay at the beginning ('More fairer than fair, beautiful than beauteous . . .') mimics a favourite trick of Sir Philip Sidney in the *Arcadia*; the conspicuously balanced and stylized clauses sound like imitations of John Lyly's Euphuistic sentences; and the articulated series of questions and answers mocks the well-known style of the Cambridge don Gabriel Harvey. The coining of words ('annothanize') and the contrast between Latin and the vernacular

('O base and obscure vulgar') allude to the linguistic controversies over English and Latin discussed in Chapter 1.[9] Other speakers approach Armado's heights of linguistic folly, notably the pedantic Holofernes, who describes Armado as 'too picked, too spruce, too affected, too odd, as it were, too peregrinate, as I may call it' (5.1.12–14). But Armado is the greatest comic speaker in this early play, mostly because his prose stimulates in the audience the kind of mixed response—comic delight and melancholy together—that will distinguish some of Shakespeare's greatest creations.

Another form of coloration is the use of accents and other tricks of speech. These also constitute a form of repetition, a technique of coherence by which the playwright marks a character, often a minor figure whose special characteristic separates him or her from the rest of the cast. Here the pertinent text is the other play in which Justice Shallow appears, *The Merry Wives of Windsor*. In this comedy Shallow's repetitions are still a part of his manner, but they seem less blatant than in *2 Henry IV*, partly because they are surrounded by the idiosyncrasies of other secondary figures, particularly Doctor Caius, Parson Evans, the Host of the Garter Inn, and Mistress Quickly. As in *Much Ado About Nothing*, their different verbal profiles contribute to a symbolic study of the positive and negative possibilities of language. And the potential monotony of a nearly all-prose play is variegated by foreign accents (French and Welsh), manic repetitions of a single phrase, outrageous malapropisms, and many other such deviations. Doctor Caius, the most obvious deformer of standard English, specializes in obvious but amusing errors:

> EVANS If there is one, I shall make two in the company.
> CAIUS If there be one or two, I shall make-a the turd.
>
> (3.3.224–5)

Parson Evans speaks the Welsh equivalent of Caius's stage Franglais, substituting 'p' for 'b', 't' for 'd', often dropping initial consonants (*'oman*), adding an erroneous 's' to singular terms, arranging his thoughts into a simplified, childlike pattern, and often correcting the verbal errors of others. As Master Page puts it, the Parson 'makes fritters of English'. Quickly's speciality, carried over from her speech in the *Henry* plays, is malapropism: 'rushling' for 'rustling', 'infection' for 'affection', 'Ginny's case' for 'genitive case' (a bawdy joke, since 'case' could mean 'vagina'), and, funniest of all, describing the 'virtuous' Mrs Ford as 'fartuous'. Since prose is designed to seem more 'natural', it is not surprising that it often seems connected with the body, both in its subjects and in its relatively loose construction.

Shakespeare does more with prose than cultivate speakers' tics, however, and one benefit of its informality is that prose permits a quick tempo. In conversations requiring rapidity, such as the banter of Petruccio's household servants in *The Taming of the Shrew* (4.1), prose permits quick exchanges without the stiffness sometimes attendant on verse. This scene in particular offers a moment of release, placed as it is immediately after the comic tension of the wedding scene:

> GRUMIO Call them forth.
> CURTIS (*calling*) Do you hear, ho? You must meet my
>   master to countenance my mistress.
> GRUMIO Why, she hath a face of her own.
> CURTIS Who knows not that?
> GRUMIO Thou, it seems, that calls for company to coun-
>   tenance her.
> CURTIS   I call them forth to credit her.   (4.1.86–93)

Prose not only sets this episode apart from those involving the principal characters but also provides a 'natural' atmosphere for the trading of silly witticisms. Were it spoken in verse—we might compare the matching trimetre lines of Richard III and Lady Anne in *Richard III*, 1.2—the feeling of the dialogue would be considerably different.

So it is with two interludes in *The Comedy of Errors*, those scenes in which the pair of foreigners, Antipholus and Dromio of Syracuse, forsake their usual verse and relax into lengthy comic dialogue in prose. Frustrated and confused at being mistaken for their Ephesian twins, all this taking place in the street in a strange city, master and servant take temporary comfort in the security of each other's presence and delight in the exercise of verbal contests. The first (2.2.35–111) turns on a lengthy series of jokes about time and hair (the mock-disputation ends with 'a bald conclusion'), while the second (3.1.71–152) prompts Dromio of Syracuse to an elaborate figurative description of the fat serving maid who pursues him ('She is spherical, like a globe. I could find out countries in her'). The more relaxed medium of prose under-writes the digressive, self-generating quality of these conversations, setting them apart from the more intense and comically manic exchanges of verse. Shakespeare replays this distinctive effect when in mid-career he moves into the tragic mode: the quicksilver repartee between Hamlet and the Gravedigger, for example, depends upon the relative freedom that prose affords.

Most of the properties illustrated so far cohere in the language of Shakespeare's greatest prose speaker, Sir John Falstaff. That a knight of the realm should be the most accomplished speaker of low-life language is an essential element of Shakespeare's design in the two *Henry IV* plays. Prose scenes often, especially in history plays, specifically burlesque the serious topics set forth in the verse of the court, and Falstaff is the mouthpiece for such mockery. His keen ear serves him most obviously in the play-within-the-play of the great tavern scene (*1 Henry IV*, 2.5), in his prose parodies of both Prince Hal and King Henry. These are party-pieces, but even in his less theatrical moments Falstaff's speech beguiles the audience with the familiar elements of Shakespearian prose: logical structure, repetitive patterns, rhythms both familiar and surprising, a distinctive vocabulary including biblical allusions and striking similes, and, perhaps above all, the unfailing knack for surprise. What is more, all these components are overlaid with a heavy coating of irony, for no one takes as much pleasure in Falstaff's verbal gifts as Falstaff himself.

Any of his virtuoso speeches might serve as illustration, the disquisition on honour (*1 Henry IV*, 5.1.127–40), or the defence of sherry-sack (*2 Henry IV*, 4.3.83–121): in both he addresses the audience in soliloquy. A less familiar excerpt, however, catches him in a less obviously performative mode.

> DOLL TEARSHEET They say Poins has a good wit.
> SIR JOHN He a good wit? Hang him, baboon! His wit's as thick as Tewkesbury mustard; there's no more conceit in him than is in a mallet.
> DOLL TEARSHEET Why does the Prince love him so, then?
> SIR JOHN Because their legs are both of a bigness, and a plays at quoits well, and eats conger and fennel, and drinks off candles' ends for flap-dragons [i.e. a bar trick], and rides the wild mare with the boys, and jumps upon joint-stools, and swears with a good grace, and wears his boot very smooth like unto the sign of the leg,

> and breeds no bate with telling of discreet stories, and
> such other gambol faculties a has that show a weak
> mind and an able body. (2.4.241–54)

Even when not delivering one of his star turns, Falstaff is always
performing, as the exorbitant parataxis implies. Such histrionic, self-
conscious rhetoric bespeaks an imaginative impulse. Falstaff has just
explicitly turned the conversation away from mortality, and his sketch
of Poins thus constitutes an assertion of vigour and a strategy for
chasing away the blues.

The Making of Meaning

The brief treatment of Falstaffian eloquence having edged the discussion into the realm of character, I want now to consider the extraordinary utility of Shakespeare's prose. It would be easy to study
various instances of characterization by means of prose, but a more
efficient way of demonstrating Shakespeare's craft is to subordinate
dramatic portraiture to the larger rubric of juxtaposition. Falstaff, for
example, owes much of his eloquence to the contrary voices of King
Henry and Hotspur. Quite early in his career Shakespeare discovered
the value of prose as an alternative medium, specifically the expressive
power of its simplicity relative to verse. Usually it is this relation that
matters. And it is worth restating the rule established earlier, that
many of Shakespeare's most startling effects derive from his productive
breaking of rules, particularly the introduction of prose in unexpected
places. Such artistic independence helps to account for the semantic
possibilities of everyday language.

Even in its title, *Romeo and Juliet* is built on opposition, a principle
that manifests itself in the alternation between verse and prose. The
street scene (2.3), after the nocturnal meeting of the two lovers and
before the deadly swordfight, produces a palpable decrease in tension,
although the feeling of relaxation is still ominous and deceptive, given
the tragic context. Romeo enters to the mockery of his fellows and
responds playfully to their jests:

> MERCUTIO . . . I am the very pink of courtesy.
> ROMEO Pink for flower.
> MERCUTIO Right.

> ROMEO Why, then is my pump well flowered.
>
> MERCUTIO Sure wit, follow me this jest now till thou hast worn out thy pump, that when the single sole of it is worn, the jest may remain, after the wearing, solely singular.
>
> ROMEO O single-soled jest, solely singular for the single-ness!
>
> MERCUTIO Come between us, good Benvolio. My wits faints.
>
> ROMEO Switch and spurs, switch and spurs, or I'll cry a match.   (2.3.54–65)

Such byplay diverts the audience from the suspenseful intensity of the love story, and Mercutio even comments on this distraction:

Why, is this not better now than groaning for love? Now art thou sociable, now art thou Romeo, now art thou what thou art by art as well as by nature, for this drivelling love is like a great natural [idiot] that runs lolling up and down to hide his bauble in a hole.   (3.2.81–5)

Elsewhere such verbal games are conducted in verse, but at this crucial point in the action, with the audience conscious of Romeo's emotional transformation and anxious about the progress of the lovers' clandestine plans, prose helps to ensure an altered mood, briefly slackening the tension and thereby, paradoxically, helping to magnify the tragic anxiety.

Shakespeare's gift for such formal alternation is especially apparent in *Much Ado About Nothing*, a play which fairly represents the prose of the mature comedies. To begin with, the distinction between verse and prose sometimes reflects social difference and sometimes does not. The highest ranking characters, Don Pedro, Don John, and Claudio, speak both verse and prose; the division sometimes corresponds to amatory scenes and sometimes not. In these cases Shakespeare delicately adjusts the language according to the tone he seeks to achieve, and as indicated earlier, tone is often determined by the need for contrast with what comes before or after. The romantic intrigue in *Much Ado* involves two parallel overhearing scenes (2.3 and 3.1): in the first, the male characters promulgate a fiction contrived to make the eavesdropping Benedick think that Beatrice loves him; in the second, the females put a similar trick over on Beatrice. The first of these juxtaposed scenes is in prose, the second in verse. Evidently Shakespeare has altered the language for the purpose of variety, to keep the analogous actions from becoming too repetitious and formulaic.

The climactic church scene, in which Claudio sarcastically rejects his innocent bride, begins in genial prose, although its jocular informality is overshadowed by the audience's ironic awareness of impending disaster. As Claudio announces his 'discovery' of Hero's infidelity, he shifts into the formal register of verse, and the characters continue to speak verse for over 200 lines while a plot is hatched to restore Hero's honour. The scene concludes, however, with the private conversation of Benedick and Beatrice, a kind of coda in which, as he attempts to comfort her for her cousin's misfortune, they finally confess their affection for each other. Here prose seems the appropriate medium: the two wits have resisted and sparred with each other in prose from the opening scene, and their attraction and self-revelations are thus made to seem 'natural' and clear-sighted. Such a tonal relaxation is especially meaningful following the formality of Claudio's ugly charge, an artificial (i.e. false) accusation delivered in a relatively artificial form. This devotion to multiplicity also governs the distribution of verbal forms in *Twelfth Night*: since Shakespeare's dominant consideration is the tonal mixture of high and low comedy, he mingles verse and prose to heighten the dramatic effect of each.

Shakespeare subtly exploits the perceived differences between verse and prose to deepen the audience's engagement with his comic stories and thus to magnify their delight in shift and reversal, both narrative and linguistic. *As You Like It*, composed between *Much Ado* and *Twelfth Night*, owes much of its comic sparkle to such differences. As in *Much Ado*, the integration of the two forms subtly enriches the meaning of the action. While Shakespeare might have chosen simply to link the artificiality of the court with the structure of verse and allow prose to dominate the simple world of the forest of Arden, his actual practice is much more complex, chiefly because one of the foundational themes of the comedy is that the difference between court and country is by no means as clear as we might believe. The complexity of the linguistic palette is further enriched, as in the other romantic comedies, by the extraordinary number of songs and poems and outbreaks of rhyme. Here, however, we can discern with unusual clarity Shakespeare's availing himself of the *ordinariness* of prose. By this point in his career language itself has become one of his chief pre-occupations. He seems particularly fascinated with the human propensity to deceive ourselves with fancy speech, especially in matters of the heart.

Prose thus becomes an instrument for exposing such perilous illusions. In the great wooing scene (4.1), Rosalind, disguised as the experienced shepherd Ganymede, agrees to enact 'Rosalind' so that Orlando can rehearse his love-making. Their discourse is conducted, at the teacher's insistence, entirely in prose. Her aim is to deconstruct Orlando's conventional and derived efforts at courtship, to reveal to him that genuine love consists of more than mooning over the image of a distant female and pinning poems on trees. Consequently their flirtation often reverts to a concern with words, what a lover should say.

> ROSALIND ... Am I not your Rosalind?
> ORLANDO I take some joy to say you are because I would be talking of her.
> ROSALIND Well, in her person I say I will not have you.
> ORLANDO Then in mine own person I die.
> ROSALIND No, faith; die by attorney. The poor world is almost six thousand years old, and in all this time there was not any man died in his own person, videlicet, in a love-cause. Troilus had his brains dashed out with a Grecian club, yet he did what he could to die before, and he is one of the patterns of love. Leander, he would have lived many a fair year though Hero had turned nun if it had not been for a hot midsummer night, for, good youth, he went but forth to wash him in the Hellespont and, being taken with the cramp, was drowned; and the foolish chroniclers of that age found it was Hero of Sestos. But these are all lies. Men have died from time to time, and worms have eaten them, but not for love.   (4.1.83–101)

Orlando and Rosalind both play roles, she consciously, he consciously (in wooing a stand-in) and unconsciously (as the naive courtly lover). 'Ganymede' is the proxy for Rosalind; Orlando is urged to 'die by attorney'. The scraps of legal discourse that creep into the dialogue ('videlicet', 'love-cause') remind us of the logical foundations of

Shakespeare's prose. Speaking disputatiously, Rosalind moves rationally through a list of mythical lovers and debunks the romance of each legend.

This passage illustrates Shakespeare's ability to make the prose part of the meaning. Rosalind's last two sentences—at once flat, rhythmic, ironic, affectionate, sardonic—conclude her proof, clinching the argument for clear-sighted, genuine affection. A further irony attends this dismantling of the clichés and illusions of conventional romantic love, however. Rosalind's role as instructor is a pose, an artificial performance that paradoxically leads her pupil to truth and stimulates his genuine affection for him/her. By the same token, she presses the case for 'authentic' affection in prose that, while putatively more 'genuine' and 'natural' than the rhymes and ornaments of poetry, is itself highly artificial and structured. The language sounds ordinary only because Shakespeare has carefully counterposed it against its opposite. And so the medium in which Rosalind tells the story, a roster of reversals and false appearances and paradoxical discoveries, becomes part of the story.

The worth of prose as a foil to verse is evident in these comedies, but this complementary function is also essential to the effect of the tragedies. The shattering effect of the opening scene of *King Lear* owes much to Shakespeare's instinct for surrounding verse with prose to enhance dramatic tension. Over the course of 300 lines the dramatic intensity takes the shape of a pyramid: (1) a quiet prelude, the conversation among Gloucester, Kent, and Edmund, (2) a heightening of anxiety, as the love test unfolds and Cordelia objects, (3) an outburst of royal anger ending in banishment, (4) a degree of relaxation as Kent exits and Cordelia's marriage to France is arranged, and (5) a quiet coda, in which Goneril and Regan confidentially look to the future. This pattern of heightening and diminishing is underscored by the outbreak of couplets, spoken mostly by Kent, in the central panel (part 3). Sections (2) and (4) are mostly in blank verse, while the opening and closing movements are both in prose. The intimacy and informality of the opening lines communicate a deceptive sense of calm soon displaced by the formality of the ceremony, which is then exploded by the failure of Lear's scheme for dividing the kingdom. Likewise, the closing *tête-à-tête* between Goneril and Regan (5) is quiet and ominous, a moment of sinister calm after the tempestuous events preceding it. At this stage of artistic maturity, Shakespeare is able to manipulate the contrasting verbal forms with extraordinary subtlety and so to control the audience's responses in ways that they may not consciously recognize.

Occasionally the dramatist seems to place prose in competition with verse and to make it obvious that he does so. Such stylistic self-consciousness serves the larger thematic contest between form and substance. To some extent Rosalind's puncturing of Orlando's illusions exemplifies this practice, and the tragic counterpart of that treatment of prose is found in *Julius Caesar*, written probably in the same year as *As You Like It*. One of the most famous passages in the play is Brutus' lament over the body of Caesar, in which 'public reasons' are offered as justification for the conspiracy. Only about 6 per cent of *Caesar* is in prose, most of it spoken by the plebeians; except for a handful of brief prose replies (and these could be regarded as short verse lines), Brutus adheres stoutly to verse, even when those around him are speaking prose. His reversion to prose for the oration is ideological, expressive of his idealistic commitment to undecorated truth. His absolute belief in the sacrificial nature of the assassination dictates his prohibition of oaths for the conspirators (2.1). And over Caesar's body, before the citizens, he insists that the deed be judged dispassionately, that it be described rationally and straightforwardly, without poetic flourish.

Romans, countrymen, and lovers, hear me for my cause, and be silent that you may hear. Believe me for mine honour, and have respect to mine honour, that you may believe. Censure me in your wisdom, and awake your senses, that you may the better judge. If there be any in this assembly, any dear friend of Caesar's, to him I say that Brutus' love to Caesar was no less than his. If then that friend demand why Brutus rose against Caesar, this is my answer: not that I loved Caesar less, but that I loved Rome more. Had you rather Caesar were living, and die all slaves, than that Caesar were dead, to live all free men? As Caesar loved me, I weep for him. As he was fortunate, I rejoice at it. As he was valiant, I honour him. But as he was ambitious, I slew him. There is tears for his love, joy for his fortune, honour for his valour, and death for his ambition.

(3.1.13–29)

It is surely meaningful that the plea lacks imagery.[10] The powerful irony at work here is that while the speech is not poetic, it is nevertheless manifestly rhetorical, so intricately organized and so thoroughly dependent on schemes of equivalence and repetition that it seems calculated and even manipulative. It offers perhaps the clearest demonstration in the canon that prose is never artless, that in the mouths of certain speakers it can be as highly structured, if by different means, as verse is. Famously, of course, Shakespeare juxtaposes Brutus' defence with Antony's emotional and poetic condemnation of the murder. Brutus speaks in prose because he wishes to seem sincere; Antony *is* sincere, and his poetic passion exposes the aridity and speciousness of Brutus' calculated prose.

Rarely are prose and poetry so starkly opposed as in *Measure for Measure*, a dark comedy written during the tragic phase and a play vitally concerned with the meretriciousness of surfaces. Here the conflict between control and disorder in both the body politic and the body personal is expressed in the juxtaposition—we might even say the competition—between poetry and prose. The most passionate verse speaker in the play is the self-deluding Angelo, whose false commitment to 'seeming' leads first to his self-discovery (in his soliloquy, 2.4.1–17) and ultimately to his comic exposure. The conventional and rarely examined axiom that the difference between prose and verse is socially determined is indeed applicable in this play, but Shakespeare uses that contrast in subtle and meaningful ways and asks the audience to be sensitive to the differences. The realm of the court, of which Angelo is the representative—Shakespeare makes much of his status as 'deputy'—is placed in direct competition with the world of the street, the brothel, and the prison. In fact, the main problem of this problem comedy, that the boisterous underworld is in danger of fatally contaminating the entire civic structure of Vienna, is aurally suggested by the tendency of verse to yield to the more urgent and earthy claims of prose. In the very centre of the play (3.1), when the action reaches what looks like an impasse—Claudio is to be executed because Isabella refuses to save him by submitting to Angelo's sexual demands—the play notoriously shifts into prose as the Duke scrambles to salvage his plot to test Angelo and remedy the corruption of the city.

Throughout the fourth act, most pointedly in the prison scene with the Provost, the Duke's attempts to maintain the dignity of verse are thwarted by the unpredictable and uncontrollable impulses of disorderly humanity, such as Barnadine's refusal to be executed as a substitute for Claudio. At one point the Duke, in what seems like a desperate effort to encapsulate and emphasize the ironic justice of his scheme, even ventures into rhymed couplets: 'This is his pardon, purchased by such sin | For which the pardoner himself is in' (4.2.110–11). But of course the message—delivered in cold and unmistakable prose—does not bring the pardon and forces the Duke to new shifts. The lengthy prose trial scene (2.1), in which Escalus patiently attempts to decipher Elbow's errors and Pompey's evasions, helps to clarify the difference between the two realms; Angelo can hold out (and speak their language) only so long, shortly leaving the stage in disgust. Of all the colourful speakers in this play, it is Lucio who, from his entrance in 1.2 until his numerous prose intrusions in the final scene, stands for the undeniability of the physical, the everyday, the prosaic.

Many other functions might be described and examples summoned to illustrate the range and utility of Shakespeare's prose. For example, prose is usually the medium for letters (although they sometimes contain poems). Lady Macbeth makes a memorable entrance reading a prose letter from her husband describing his 'day of success'. *The Winter's Tale,* one of his last plays, contains some brilliantly inventive prose. The long and wrenching trial of the innocent Hermione is conducted almost entirely in passionate verse, but it is resolved instantaneously by the flat prose of an oracular pronouncement: 'Hermione is chaste, Polixenes blameless, Camillo a true subject, Leontes a jealous tyrant, his innocent babe truly begotten, and the King shall live without an heir if that which is lost be not found' (3.2.132–5). The play's penultimate scene is one of the most original Shakespeare wrote. Expecting to see the resolution of the action—the tender reunion of the King and his daughter—we are confronted instead with a long prose discussion in which three unknown gentlemen *narrate* the climax that we have been hoping for. The prosaic quality of this episode is a foil, a preparation for the moving and poetic surprise ending that Shakespeare has in store.

Ineffable Power

I have postponed until last a difficult topic, one that might be called the indefinable affective power of prose. Although it lacks the patterned sound of poetry, prose can be arranged into musical schemes, and since the writer is not confined to the framework of iambic pentameter, words and phrases can be employed in more various and sometimes more intricate combinations. It is also possible that the absence of the poetic beat invites the writer to seek out other forms of rhythm in composing crucial lines. Such rhythmic distinction is audible in the moving phrases Hamlet uses to confide to Horatio his altered attitude about death and his belief in the 'special providence' that determines human events: 'If it be now, 'tis not to come. If it be not to come, it will be now. If it be not now, yet it will come. The readiness is all' (5.2.166–8). These lines can virtually be scanned, although exactly where the emphases fall is up to the actor. I believe that the accent ought probably to fall on the last word of each clause 'now', 'come', 'come', 'now', 'now', 'come'. Alternatively, an actor might do much with the repeated 'not' in each sentence. However the lines are spoken, the repeated 'now' at the end of the first, fourth, and fifth clauses offers speaker and listener ominous confirmation of what we suspect awaits Hamlet at the hands of Claudius and Laertes. And the triply repeated and subtly varied phrases prepare for the moving conclusion, the iambic phrase, 'The readiness is all.' Some of Shakespeare's most memorable lines are written in prose, and as in this case, it is often the rhythmic pattern, especially when based on one of the rhetorical schemes of repetition, that accounts for the incantatory power of the passage.

Readers can readily supply their favourite excerpts: Shylock's 'Hath not a Jew eyes?'; Lance's narrative about his dog Crab in *The Two Gentlemen of Verona*; the Porter's drunken bit in *Macbeth*; several of Falstaff's virtuoso pieces; Iago's 'Put money in thy purse'; some of Autolycus' clever self-justifications. Dogberry's great defence of himself against Conrad's insult ('Away, you are an ass, you are an ass') makes use of most of the rhythmic effects and tonal complexity that the mature Shakespeare is able to achieve with 'ordinary' speech.

Dost thou not suspect my place? Dost thou not suspect my years? O that he were here to write me down an ass. But masters, remember that I am an ass. Though it be not written down, yet forget not that I am an ass. No, thou villain, thou art full of piety, as shall be proved upon thee by good witness. I am a wise fellow, and which is more, an officer, and which is more, a householder, and which is more, as pretty a piece of flesh as any is in Messina, and one that knows the law, go to, and a rich fellow enough, go to, and a fellow that hath had losses, and one that hath two gowns, and everything handsome about him. Bring him away. O that I had been writ down an ass! (4.2.72–84)

This outburst displays the familiar technical tricks: malapropism, reiterated words and phrases, clauses linked paratactically, contrasts in sentence length, the speaker's unsuccessful efforts at irony set against the playwright's skill at it. The lines also benefit from their location, at the end of a comic episode immediately following the wedding scene; thus they lighten the tonal gloom that the shaming of Hero has generated. Thanks also to its comic specificity, the speech is a triumph of tonal complexity. Of course Dogberry's proud self-assessment is ludicrous, and yet Shakespeare has managed by the judicious introduction of detail ('and one that hath had losses') to complicate our feelings of scornful delight, revealing briefly the vulnerable human beneath the foolish exterior and then swiftly pulling back to the boastful surface ('and one that hath two gowns'). And it is also helpful to remember that this passage, like virtually all the others examined in this chapter and many that perhaps should have been included, benefits from what Brian Vickers refers to as 'Shakespeare's gift of phrasing which defies analysis'.[11]

Double Talk

In Sonnet 138, that brilliant and rueful meditation on the incompatibility of truth and passion, the ageing speaker confesses his willingness to accept his lover's infidelity and acknowledges her tolerance for his deceptions.

> When my love swears that she is made of truth
> I do believe her though I know she lies,
> That she might think me some untutored youth
> Unlearnèd in the world's false subtleties.
> Thus vainly thinking that she thinks me young,
> Although she knows my days are past the best,
> Simply I credit her false-speaking tongue;
> On both sides thus is simple truth suppressed.
> But wherefore says she not she is unjust,
> And wherefore say not I that I am old?
> O, love's best habit is in seeming trust,
> And age in love loves not to have years told.
>   Therefore I lie with her, and she with me,
>   And in our faults by lies we flattered be.

The speaker tells his story and draws conclusions chiefly by means of wordplay. The short poem teems with double meanings: 'vainly' (l. 5), *futilely* and *with vanity*; 'simply' (l. 7) and 'simple' (l. 8), *plain* and *naive*; 'credit', (l. 7) *believe* and *reward*; 'habit' (l. 10), *custom* and *garment*; 'told' (l. 11), *described*, *counted*, and perhaps *sounded*; and 'faults' (l. 14), *sins* and *cracks*, specifically *orifices*. There are other duplicitous homonyms, such as 'made' (l. 1), meaning *composed*, but with the associations of lunacy ('mād') and purity ('maid'). The quibble from which the poem derives its argument, however, is the verbal phrase *lie with*: falsehoods underwrite the success of the sexual relationship.[1] The exuberance and self-consciousness of Shakespeare's punning in Sonnet 138 suggest an uncommon sensitivity to the ambiguous nature of language and an ability to exploit those ambiguities in a way that delights readers and enriches their experience of the poem. Indeed, the theme of the poem itself is verbal ambiguity, or fictions, or lying— tolerance for loose language being the guarantor of the couple's pleasure. In other words, the sonnet enacts what it argues. But for all his witty pride in this sexual arrangement, the speaker barely conceals a bitterness about its dishonest foundations and a desperate recognition that words can injure: their treachery and their satisfactions are inextricably connected.

Elizabethan and Modern Theory

Language becomes a major topic of Shakespeare's plays early on, as I have indicated in the Introduction, and it is his sense of this inescapable paradox, of the simultaneously creative and destructive power of language, that makes wordplay such a precious artistic tool. What modern criticism has come to know as *polysemy*, the multiple senses of a single verbal sign, was a familiar and pleasing concept to readers of Elizabethan poetry. We might remember, for example, Sir Philip Sidney's elaboration of the adjective 'Rich', the surname of his married sweetheart, in several of the sonnets of *Astrophil and Stella*, or John Donne's playing with his name in the serious 'A Hymn to God the Father': 'When thou hast done, thou hast not done, | For I have none' (ll. 11–12). Sixteenth-century schoolboys would have absorbed a sense of the ambiguities of language from those Latin writers and commentators who formed the core of the humanist curriculum. The greatest of classical rhetoricians, Quintilian, whose *Institutio Oratoria* is constantly cited in the period, recognizes the extent of uncertainty to which language is subject: 'I turn to the discussion of *ambiguity*, which will be found to have countless species: indeed, in the opinion of certain philosophers, there is not a single word which has not a diversity of meanings.'[2] Concerned chiefly with oratory and the speaker's desire for clarity, the Roman devotes most of his commentary to the elimination or at least the restraint of ambiguity. In his English descendants, however, we find a more liberal appreciation for the uses and pleasures of ambiguous verbal constructions.

Early modern poets and pedagogues comment frequently on the susceptibility of language to manipulation and the poetic delights and benefits available to the writer with a gifted ear. George Puttenham, for example, in *The Art of English Poesy* (1589), offers the aspiring poet names, descriptions, and models for various poetic schemes and tropes. Among these are several figures that capture the ability of a word or phrase to convey plural senses, such as the one he calls '*Antanaclasis*, or the Rebound':

Ye have another figure which by his nature we may call the *Rebound*, alluding to the tennis ball which being smitten with the racket rebounds back again, and ... playeth with one word written all alike but carrying divers senses as thus ...

> To pray for you ever I cannot refuse,
> To pray upon you I should you much abuse.

Or as we once sported upon a country fellow who came to run for the best game, and was by his occupation a dyer and had very big swelling legs,

> He is but course to run a course,
> Whose shanks are bigger than his thigh:
> Yet is his luck a little worse,
> That often dyes before he die.

Where ye see this word *course* and *dye*, used in divers senses, one giving the *Rebound* upon th'other.[3]

Puttenham here identifies the intellectual pleasure and exercise associated with polysemy, as his tennis metaphor indicates, and in this appreciation of 'divers senses' he suggests the principle that Shakespeare and his contemporaries enthusiastically exploit. The number of terms employed by the Elizabethan rhetoricians for the several kinds of wordplay attests to their fascination with the variations and subtleties that such figures could be used to achieve: *paronomasia, amphibology, polyptoton, syllepsis, asteismus, agnominatio, skesis*. But writers of the period, even as they make use of the figures, exhibit a healthy irony about the complexity and potential absurdity of the names. As the mock orator in Nashe's *The Unfortunate Traveller* (1594) puts it: 'Why should I go gadding and fizgigging after firking flantado amphibologies?'

Likewise, to the modern reader these names can be downright intimidating, and even if all the variants could be mastered, knowledge of the terms is not sufficient. M. M. Mahood gets it right when she says that 'Naming the parts does not show us what makes the gun go off.'[4] Still, a quick look at the roots of some of these terms can illuminate the way a linguistic sign embraces a multitude of meanings. 'Antanaclasis' comes from the Greek for 'bending back' or 'reflection', as if a unit of sound turns back on itself in yielding another meaning. 'Paronomasia' implies 'naming alongside', or putting two similar nouns next to each other for scrutiny. 'Polyptoton', the trope in which the ending of a word is altered, comes from Greek for 'the changing of cases'. Probably the most useful term is 'amphibology', from the Greek for 'ambiguous meaning': its value in this context is suggested by its prefix, meaning 'on both sides'. 'Bending', 'both sides', 'alongside', 'alteration'—all these words imply the flexibility of the verbal unit and the semantic plurality it bestows. And yet, as useful as it is to reflect on historical attitudes towards linguistic instability and the opportunities it makes available for poetic play, no survey of contemporary theory or example can prepare us for the astonishing range of Shakespeare's wordplay and the profundity of dramatic meaning he is able to derive from it.

The modern equivalents of these earlier terms are fewer in number: 'quibble', 'equivoque', 'double entendre', and the noun most commonly used, 'pun'. Considering the dominance and the familiarity of 'pun', a word not recorded in English until the 1640s, it is interesting to note that its origins are obscure, as the editors of the *Oxford English Dictionary* are forced to admit. They note that the term 'might originally be an abbreviation of the Italian *puntiglio*, small or fine point . . . but nothing has been found in the early history of *pun*, or in the English uses of *punctilio*, to confirm the conjecture'. The operation and value of the pun, however, have been analysed at some length, particularly in relation to modern thinking about communication and the relation between words and meanings. Here is a helpful example of such description:

In any given language, according to the founder of structural linguistics, Ferdinand de Saussure, meaningful words are those units where a signifier and a signified emerge from the otherwise undifferentiated, jumbled planes of sound and ideas, joining together to form a sign. But puns destabilize this neat formulation. . . . It is not that puns expose the arbitrariness of signification (every sign does that) but that puns reveal the discrimination of meaning to be a haphazard, approximate, error-prone affair. A pun subverts the one-to-one relation between signifier (*bat*) and signified (a bald, flying mouse or a stout piece of wood for hitting balls). It fractures the sign and disturbs those neat relations which, in Saussure's diagrams, tie signified and signifier together in tidily serried ranks.[5]

Saussure and most other linguists have little patience with the pun because it is invidious to the goals of clarity and unambiguous specification, and in expressing such distaste they join a long tradition of resistance and doubt to the pleasurable confusion of the figure. Such disapproval, surviving even today in the familiar notion that the pun is the lowest form of humour, reached its apogee in the eighteenth century and received its most notorious expression in Samuel Johnson's *Preface to Shakespeare*:

A quibble is to Shakespeare what luminous vapors are to the traveller: he follows it at all adventures; it is sure to lead him out of his way, and sure to engulf him in the mire . . . . A quibble, poor and barren as it is, gave him such delight that he was content to purchase it by the sacrifice of reason, propriety, and truth. A quibble was to him the fatal Cleopatra for which he lost the world, and was content to lose it.[6]

What these analyses reveal is that the source of uncertainty and the source of pleasure is the same. Wordplay serves to colour the verbal text, offering the rewards of diversion and ornament, but such delights interfere with semantic transparency or certainty of meaning. The pun is a subversive agent, a figure of fun that disrupts the clear passage from signifier to signified. It requires the reader or listener to hesitate, to look in two directions at once, enforcing a momentary shift into another context and thus muddling and/or enriching the meaning of the verbal text. Clowns and smart-mouthed servants are particularly adept at forcibly shifting contexts.

> PANDARUS Friend? You. Pray you, a word. Do not you
> *follow* the young Lord Paris?
> SERVANT Ay, sir, when he *goes before* me.
> PANDARUS You *depend* upon him, I mean.
> SERVANT Sir, I do depend upon the *Lord*.

PANDARUS You depend upon a *notable gentleman*; I must
needs *praise him*.
SERVANT The *Lord be praised*!

(*Troilus and Cressida*, 3.1.1–8)

The mechanics of wordplay make it especially appealing to artists because it demands that the perceiver forget about meaning, at least for a moment, and attend to the surface of the medium. Devoted to the manipulation of words, the writer relishes such attraction to the verbal surface. And given that one of poetry's goals is to concentrate meaning into language and thereby enrich it, the multiple senses available in the structure of the pun make it an especially efficient and productive tool.

The Mechanics of the Pun

Of the many ways of describing the operation of the Shakespearian pun, the most useful is to say that it affords the listener the fundamental poetic pleasure of apprehending likeness in difference. A word, the signifier, has a single sound but refers to two distinct objects or ideas, two different signifieds. The signifiers are and are not alike. Thus puns function as do many poetic properties, notably metaphor, which elucidates an idea or object by figuring it in an image that is like it and not like it; the same relationship obtains in rhyme, where words begin with different sounds but end identically. With all these analogous forms, the act of recognition affords the listener a momentary and minor gratification. According to R. A. Shoaf, puns supply 'the gift of gap', the opportunity to feel ourselves making connections between apparently unrelated and impertinent contexts and meanings, and to delight in those intellectual athletics.[7] Such connections provide us with the temporary experience of comprehension and control, an illusion immediately subverted by the effect of further instability, the appearance of another hole in the text as additional meanings arise.

Shakespeare's attraction to likeness in difference manifests itself everywhere: in his fascination with twins, as in *The Comedy of Errors* and *Twelfth Night*; in his creation of pairs of characters, such as the two noble kinsmen, or Helena and Hermia, who grew like 'twinned cherries'; in his sets of brothers, Claudius and Old Hamlet, or Edgar and Edmund; in his development of parallel circumstances in the experience of Hamlet, Laertes, Fortinbras, and Pyrrhus; in the double plots that enrich many of the comedies and tragedies; in the assignment of female roles to boy actors, and the dressing up of some of these 'young women' (e.g. Rosalind) as young men; and in his consciousness that the dramatist creates a second world which reproduces—or doubles— the actual world. Moreover, to make use of an obvious but important quibble, an artist who set out to write *plays* could hardly fail to respond to the sportful possibilities of wordplay. The key to Shakespeare's use of wordplay is that he finds the instability of language analogous to the ambiguities of human experience generally, and his gift for manipulating the verbal sign permits him to register the intricacies and implications of characters' motives and actions with extraordinary subtlety.

Many of Shakespeare's characters appreciate—although less thoroughly than their creator—the principle of multiple meaning and so use puns deliberately, impressing their listeners with their cleverness. *Romeo and Juliet*, for example, begins (after its Prologue) with a masculine sparring match:

> SAMSON Gregory, on my word, we'll not carry *coals*.
> GREGORY No, for then we should be *colliers*.
> SAMSON I mean an we be in *choler*, we'll draw.
> GREGORY Ay, while you live, draw your neck out of *collar*.
>
> (I.I.I–4)

Waving weapons and looking for trouble, two members of the house of Capulet show off their wit by seeking to best each other mentally and verbally. The initial turns on 'coals' shift as the dialogue continues into a worrying of the word 'moved' (to be angered or to run away in fear) and then into a series of jokes about maids' heads and maidenheads and men's weapons or sexual tools. These bawdy tropes are all fairly conventional—amusing enough, if not as amusing as the jokesters think they are—but they are invaluable in establishing a shifty and contentious atmosphere for the ensuing action. Wordplay here serves as a means of self-assertion, a linguistic version of the physical thrusting and parrying that will follow when Samson and Gregory meet the Montagues. And since the play is fundamentally concerned, as one critic puts it, with 'Coming of Age in Verona',[8] these verbal interchanges prefigure not only the larger feud between the Montagues and the Capulets but the amorous interplay in which Romeo and Juliet themselves will shortly engage.

Early in his career Shakespeare discovered the revelatory possibilities of such amorous tussling, as in the initial meeting between Katherine and Petruccio in *The Taming of the Shrew*:

> PETRUCCIO Come, come, you wasp, i'faith you are too angry.
> KATHERINE If I be waspish, best beware my sting.
> PETRUCCIO My remedy is then to pluck it out.
> KATHERINE Ay, if the fool could find it where it lies.
> PETRUCCIO Who knows not where the wasp does wear his sting?
> In his tail.
> KATHERINE In his tongue.
> PETRUCCIO   Whose tongue?
> KATHERINE Yours, if you talk of tales, and so farewell.
> PETRUCCIO What, with my tongue in your tail?
>
> (2.1.209–16)

For both Petruccio and Katherine, verbal facility implies mental acuity, pride in one's own perception and sensitivity, and the ability to keep others at a distance. And yet their verbal volleys also function as a sign of affinity, a vehicle by which the playwright discloses resemblance and sympathy between the two antagonists. This is a paradox he will develop most brilliantly in the 'merry war' between Beatrice and Benedick in *Much Ado About Nothing*. One of its most original manifestations is the wooing scene (1.2) in *Richard III*, a play written about the same time as *The Taming of the Shrew*: Richard and Anne match each other rhetorically, appropriating each other's words, metaphors, and rhythms, conveying attraction, repulsion, and especially the urge for priority.

A gentler but more sophisticated form of amorous equivocation occurs in *Twelfth Night*, in the first meeting between Olivia and Viola (1.5). Disguised as Cesario, Orsino's messenger, Viola begs to convey her master's intentions—which she describes as 'divinity'—to Olivia in private:

> OLIVIA Give us the place alone, we will hear this divinity.
> Now, sir, what is your text?

> VIOLA Most sweet lady—
> OLIVIA A comfortable doctrine, and much may be said of
>   it. Where lies your text?
> VIOLA In Orsino's bosom.
> OLIVIA In his bosom? In what chapter of his bosom?
> VIOLA To answer by the method, in the first of his heart.
> OLIVIA O, I have read it. It is heresy. Have you no more to
>   say? (1.5.209–19)

Swathed in black and mourning her dead brother, Olivia has professed a desire for privacy and distaste for the Duke's advances. But her willingness to toy with Viola's courtly language unveils an attraction to the speaker that explodes into barely controlled passion by the end of the scene. Her verbal games, which represent advertisements for her wit, imply an erotic engagement that constitutes a return to the world and proclaims her affection for an ironically inappropriate object. In the earlier examples, two speakers wrench each other's particular words for comic purposes, but this genial one-upmanship requires a slightly more liberal definition of wordplay. Olivia and Viola wittily sport with each other's metaphors, taking and giving ironic pleasure by self-consciously adopting and extending a figurative discourse: amorous compliments as holy writ.

Comic wordplay, like comedy in general, is irreverent, even subversive of authority, and thus it often helps to focus issues of class. Servants regularly resort to punning as an outlet for frustration. In *The Comedy of Errors*, Dromio summons the man he thinks is his master, Antipholus of Ephesus, only to be beaten by Antipholus of Syracuse, his master's long-lost twin. Then Adriana, wife of Antipholus of Ephesus, orders the baffled servant to fetch her husband for the second time.

> ADRIANA Back, slave, or I will break thy pate across.
> DROMIO OF EPHESUS An he will bless that cross with
>   other beating,
> Between you I shall have a holy head.
> ADRIANA Hence, prating peasant.
>
>   (2.1.77–80)

Some prating peasants wittily deform their masters' language as a safe kind of backtalk, simultaneously challenging and amusing the authority figure. In *The Taming of the Shrew*, Petruccio orders his servant to knock at a door:

> PETRUCCIO Here, sirrah Grumio, knock, I say.
> GRUMIO Knock, sir? Whom should I knock? Is there any
> man has rebused your worship?
> PETRUCCIO Villain, I say, knock me here soundly.
> GRUMIO Knock you here, sir? Why, sir, what am I, sir,
> that I should knock you here, sir?   (1.2.5–10)

Occasionally the master takes up the punning game, as does Petruccio at the end of this exchange: 'Faith, sirrah, an you'll not knock, I'll ring it ... *He wrings him by the ears.*' Whether or not the authority figure plays along, ambiguity provides the disenfranchised with a cover for defiance; it offers 'deniability', so that servant and master can comfortably spar with each other and still maintain the appointed power relations. Most of the comedies contain exchanges based on a comparable structure: Mote and Armado in *Love's Labour's Lost*, Lance and Proteus in *The Two Gentlemen of Verona*, Feste and almost everyone he meets in *Twelfth Night*.

Feste's entrance line contains bawdy play on being well hanged, and the sexual banter in all of the comedies—indeed, in all of Shakespeare's plays—depends upon the same deniability that protects the impudent servants. Propriety is and is not violated, since one definition is obscene while another remains innocent. Consider Cloten's unwelcome wooing of Innogen in *Cymbeline*, as he instructs the musicians to play an aubade at her window: 'I am advised to give her music o'mornings; they say it will penetrate. *Enter musicians*. Come on, tune. If you can penetrate her with your fingering, so; we'll try with tongue, too' (2.3.11–14). To take offence is to acknowledge that one comprehends the lewd joke: *Honi soit qui mal y pense*.

In little William's Latin lesson in *The Merry Wives of Windsor*, Shakespeare entertains us with Mistress Quickly's salacious misreading of harmless words.

> EVANS What is your genitive case plural, William?
> WILLIAM Genitive case?
> EVANS Ay.
> WILLIAM *Genitivo: 'horum, harum, horum'*.

MISTRESS QUICKLY Vengeance of Jenny's case! Fie on her!
Never name her, child, if she be a whore.
EVANS For shame, 'oman!
MISTRESS QUICKLY You do ill to teach the child such
words. (4.1.52–9)

This instance is especially instructive because it occurs in a scene of
'translation', in which ideas are given new names in a second language.
But the Latinless Quickly (Quick-lay) hears only obscene meanings of
English words she knows: 'genital' for 'genitive'; the sexual sense of
'case' (*vagina*); 'whore' for 'horum'. Linguistic changes over the past
four centuries may prevent us from apprehending many slang terms
and euphemisms common in the early modern period: the word *will*
for sexual organ, mentioned above in the context of Shakespeare's
sonnets; *yard* for penis; *ring* for vagina; *aunt* for prostitute. Shakespeare's clowns manage to corrupt even the most neutral words:
'understand' (erection), 'whole' (hole), 'thing' (penis), and the nearly
infinite number of suggestive nouns ('forehead', 'brow', 'horns') having
to do with cuckoldry.[9] Modern readers should be careful not to over-
look bawdy implications when the speaker or situation calls them to
the surface. Likewise, modern readers should not read sexual innu-
endo into words, even those liable to sexual interpretation, when the
speaker or situation forbids or discourages such meaning. Sometimes a
cigar is just a cigar. Context is everything.

Female characters, like servants, often contest their marginality or
cultural subjection by means of witty words.

DON PEDRO You have put him down, lady, you have put
him down.
BEATRICE So I would not he should do me, my lord, lest
I should prove the mother of fools.

(*Much Ado*, 2.2.264–7)

It is unnecessary to illustrate such jests at any length: all the comic
heroines are celebrated for their verbal talents. What is worth noting is
that, with many of these women, Shakespeare emphasizes their social
transgression with what might be called a visual pun. When Portia
dresses as Balthazar, Rosalind as Ganymede, and Innogen as Fidele,
each disguises her female self (and thus her marginal status in a

patriarchal culture) under the cover of a masculine exterior, giving herself a social liberty and a voice that would be normally unavailable. The masculine disguise thus confers a double meaning on the heroine, creating a likeness in difference corresponding to the dual structure of verbal equivocation: she is and is not female. In the tragedies, where the convention of cross-dressing does not come into play, many of Shakespeare's great women assume and maintain authority by the clever exploitation of words. No one can equal Hamlet for verbal sensitivity, but Cleopatra comes close.

Some of Shakespeare's most charismatic persons fascinate the audience with their verbal dexterity, and skill at manipulating words stands as a symbol of the speaker's ability to influence other characters and to command the attention of the theatre audience. Richard III is an improbable charmer, of course, but it is his mastery of language, particularly his talent for appropriating and reapplying the words of others, that affords him an unparalleled political advantage and renders him theatrically irresistible, despite his physical and moral monstrosity. The play begins with a pun: 'Now is the winter of our discontent | Made glorious summer by this son of York'. The famous opening lines depend upon a conventional quibble (*son/sun*), and as soon as Richard begins to converse with others, he unleashes his unparalleled knack for deforming their speech to suit his own purposes. One of the earliest and clearest instances is his exchange with Brackenbury about King Edward's mistress, Jane Shore:

> RICHARD GLOUCESTER How say you, sir? Can you deny
>   all this?
> BRACKENBURY With this, my lord, myself have naught to
>   do.
> RICHARD GLOUCESTER Naught to do with Mrs Shore? I
>   tell thee, fellow:
>   He that doth naught with her—excepting one—
>   Were best to do it secretly alone.

(1.1.97–101)

Richard seizes Brackenbury's innocent 'naught' (*nothing*) and contaminates it by importing the lewd context of sexual dalliance ('naughtiness'), taking control of the exchange as he will do with each of his antagonists. The action of the play depicts the process of political usurpation, and Richard attains power by usurping words and imbuing them with his own meanings. This process of verbal contention accounts for the extraordinary energy of the first three acts, and its absence may have something to do with the comparative flatness that audiences often sense in the last two: after Richard achieves the crown, taking control of the royal signifier, there is less resistance to his linguistic struggle, and his puns become fewer and more juvenile in their effect:

> STANLEY Richmond is on the seas.
> KING RICHARD There let him sink, and be the seas on him.
>
> (4.4.393-4)

Although Shakespeare makes much of the political dangers of Richard's linguistic usurpation—and will exploit that pattern even more effectively in the second tetralogy—he is also alert to its theatrical implications and opportunities. Skill at wordplay is merely one aspect of a larger gift for verbal domination that Richard shares with many of Shakespeare's other histrionic giants, particularly Hamlet, Iago, Falstaff, Cleopatra. The power of such figures to fill the stage, crowding out other formidable speakers and characters, corresponds to their gift for imposing their own meanings on potentially ambiguous words.

Several early plays could serve to illustrate the brilliant promise of Shakespeare's talent for wordplay—*Love's Labour's Lost* and *Romeo and Juliet* are obvious candidates—but *Richard III* is especially rich for two main reasons. In the first place, it illustrates both the way that Shakespeare uses equivocation to characterize his hero-villain and the way he proceeds beyond character to integrate verbal ambiguity into the structure of the work as a whole. Obviously the play is a brilliant portrait of a verbal wizard. The dialogue becomes an enormous process of substitution as Richard seeks to supplant the rightful monarch; the signifier is thus a battlefield which he must seize from his opponent. But all the Plantagenets attempt the same kind of semantic and political displacement at which Richard is supreme. Old Queen Margaret, Rivers, Queen Elizabeth, even the two young princes— virtually every major figure in the play manages, like Richard, to 'moralize two meanings in one word' (3.1.83). Margaret spends most of her considerable energy lamenting her loss of power and deploring the substitution of Yorks for Lancasters. In the semantic displacements on which wordplay depends Shakespeare finds a structural means of representing the historical struggles of fifteenth-century England. Second, *Richard III* first begins to reveal Shakespeare's increasingly ambiguous attitude towards ambiguity. The violent theft of semantic priority in which the Plantagenets engage attests to his understanding of the vulnerability of language, particularly its susceptibility to political abuse. Richard is a brilliant comedian, delighting the audience, like the clowns of the comedies, with 'the errancy of the word'.[10] As Shakespeare continues to explore the relation between politics and language, his doubts about the perilous consequences of ambiguity begin to intensify.

Puns and Politics

The two parts of *Henry IV* represent one of his most sophisticated examinations of the problem of political language, and in these plays Shakespeare displays the paradoxical effects of wordplay most pointedly in the character of Falstaff. I have already enumerated the forms of his linguistic virtuosity—inventive metaphors, simile competitions, self-mocking rhetorical patterns, biblical allusions, the appropriation of others' voices, and many other tactics. Falstaff uses rhetorical schemes the way he uses his outrageous fictions about his own valour and his copious efforts at self-promotion. All these forms of verbal play serve as sport, a kind of recreation based on linguistic re-creation. And Falstaff is at his most creative with the pun, wielding it mainly as an instrument of self-assertion. His verbal dexterity is a signal of his vivacity as he creates two things from one, multiple meanings from a single sound. At the risk of sounding pretentious, I would suggest that the pun is, for Shakespeare as for Falstaff, a form of imaginative exercise, an artistic stroke, a defence against death.

Falstaff also deploys it pragmatically, as a weapon against his enemies. His first encounter with the Lord Chief Justice in *2 Henry IV* illustrates this function most effectively, as he deflects the censure of his antagonist with a series of verbal evasions. These are taken from Falstaff's first appearance in *2 Henry IV* (1.2):

LORD CHIEF JUSTICE To punish you by the heels would amend the attention of your ears, and I care not if I do become your physician.

SIR JOHN I am as poor as Job, my lord, but not so patient. Your lordship may minister the potion of imprisonment to me in respect of poverty; but how I should be your patient to follow your prescriptions, the wise may make some dram of a scruple, or indeed a scruple itself.
(1.2.125–32)

LORD CHIEF JUSTICE Well, the truth is, Sir John, you live in great infamy.

SIR JOHN He that buckles himself in my belt cannot live in less.

LORD CHIEF JUSTICE Your means are very slender, and your waste is great.

SIR JOHN I would it were otherwise; I would my means were greater and my waist slenderer. (1.2.137–42)

LORD CHIEF JUSTICE There is not a white hair in your face but should have his effect of gravity.

SIR JOHN His effect of gravy, gravy, gravy. (1.2.161–3)

In the first passage, Falstaff converts the Chief Justice's threat to become his physician into a joke about his being unlike Job, that is, being neither patient nor a patient. In the second, he twists the attack on his slender means and wastefulness into a joke about his great waist or girth. In the third, he turns the demand for gravity into a joke about gravy. Each transformation of censure into humour reminds us that puns are tropes, rhetorical figures whereby a unit of sound is *turned* from one sense to another. As the Lord Chief Justice puts it later, 'I am well acquainted with your manner of wrenching the true cause the false way' (2.1.111–13). He recognizes that Falstaff uses the pun brilliantly as a means of deflecting critical attack. But the Chief Justice himself indulges in a good deal of punning—since he is concerned with Falstaff's worthlessness, there is much wordplay about coins—and his various equivocations help to establish the principle that wordplay is by no means only a function of character. To some extent Falstaff's taste for wordplay contaminates his critic—he is not only a punster himself but the cause that puns are in others—but the Lord Chief Justice's predilection for double meanings is shared by others in the plays who have no contact with Falstaff.

In the second tetralogy, Falstaff is the principal agent of linguistic instability, a condition appropriate to a realm in which the overriding problem is political uncertainty. Hotspur's attack on the King as 'this vile politician' reminds us that for centuries the language of politics has been thought of as a species of double talk, a discourse in which words and meanings seldom correspond. Attending to puns teaches us to read between the lines and thus prepares us to interpret the language of the King's party and the rebels. More specifically, awareness of the natural tendency of words to slide from one significational context into another helps to clarify Shakespeare's concern, throughout the tetralogy, with political uncertainty, the problem of whether or not people—monarchs and subjects—will keep their word. From the beginning of *1 Henry IV* Prince Hal is playing a duplicitous game, indulging himself in the life of the tavern while assuring himself and the audience that he will eventually fulfil his courtly responsibilities. The Prince's duality is further articulated in the various twins and foils with which Shakespeare surrounds and compares him: is he Prince Hal, the name by which he is known in the tavern, or Prince Henry, the son who will not imitate his father's sense of duty, or Prince Harry, a rebel to his father's will much like the young Harry Percy, that other Henry to whom he is repeatedly compared?

The most prevalent form of double talk in both parts of *Henry IV* is the broken promise, a difficulty that manifests itself at the very beginning of the tetralogy. Henry Bolingbroke is King of England because in *Richard II* he has violated the assurance that his premature return from banishment, itself a broken promise, is merely an attempt to recover the confiscated property of his dead father. In the third scene of *1 Henry IV* the rebels' distrust of the King is encoded in Hotspur's paronomastic curse on the King's hypocrisy:

> Why, what a candy deal of courtesy
> This fawning greyhound then did proffer me!
> 'Look when his infant fortune came to age',
> And 'gentle Harry Percy', and 'kind *cousin*'.
> O, the devil take such *cozeners*!
>
> (1.3.247–51)

The cousin is a cozener—the kinsman a con-man—and it is acquaintance with Bolingbroke's duplicitous past that leads Worcester to reject the royal offer of clemency in the last act. In withholding the proposal from Hotspur, Worcester justifies his deception by invoking the King's record of promise-breaking: 'It is not possible, it cannot be, | The King should keep his word in loving us' (5.2.4–5). Or, as he puts it to Hotspur, 'I told him gently of our grievances, | Of his oath-breaking, which he mended thus: | By now forswearing that he is forsworn' (5.2.36–8).

The problem of slippery words, as the boasting of Rumour at the beginning of *2 Henry IV* indicates, is one of the chief structural determinants in both parts of *Henry IV*. Glyndŵr defects from the rebellion, claiming that he could not 'draw his power this fourteen days'. Given his tardiness and failure to join the forces of rebellion, one may hear a pun lurking in his first name, especially Falstaff's repetition of it: 'O when? O when?' Hotspur's own father, the Earl of Northumberland, also fails to appear at Shrewsbury, pleading sudden illness. As Rumour puts it, 'old Northumberland, | Lies crafty-sick'. Northumberland's failure to keep his promise creates meaningful symmetry: in the Percy family the father is expected to participate but defaults; in the royal family the son is not expected but comes through splendidly. Recognition of such patterns, all of them further illustrations of likeness in difference, provides the audience the same kind of satisfactions that appreciation of the pun supplies.

The political plot of *2 Henry IV*, which comes to a crisis at Gaultree Forest, turns on Prince John's promise of accommodation: he consents to redress the rebels' grievances, a promise which leads to the peace agreement and dismissal of the armies. The ambiguous language in this scene repays careful scrutiny. Shakespeare's insistence on Prince John's word is inescapable, as we see in his reconciliation with the Archbishop:

> PRINCE JOHN My lord, these griefs shall be with speed
>   redressed;
>   Upon my soul they shall. . . .
> ARCHBISHOP OF YORK I take your princely word for these
>   redresses.
> PRINCE JOHN I give it you, and will maintain my word;
>   And thereupon I drink unto your grace.
>
>   (4.1.285–6, 292–4)

At this point, 'the word of peace is rendered', agreement is reached, and as Prince John puts it, the former enemies 'shall lie tonight together'. But the Prince's word is a lie, or at best an equivocation, and this series of exchanges conceals a minefield of possible meanings, as the rebels immediately discover when the Prince's word explodes in their faces. Westmorland arrests Hastings, York, and Mowbray on charges of treason, and when the rebels ask how the Prince can so easily 'break [his] faith', John replies with a supreme instance of double talk, asserting that he never offered pardon to the rebels themselves, only attention to the substance of their grievances, which he still intends to 'redress'. In the central political event of the play, Prince John employs to his advantage the same verbal ambiguity that the play has been asking its audience to notice, to enjoy, and to be cautious of.

Prince John's alertness to double meanings and the uncertainties of interpretation appears in his objection that his 'father's purposes have been mistook, | And some about him have too lavishly | Wrested his meaning and authority' (4.1.282–4). He uses that verbal sensitivity to perpetrate the deception that mollifies the rebels: 'these griefs shall be with speed redressed'. The verb 'redress' is reiterated in its various forms five times in this scene alone. The word appears one other time in the play, when Falstaff seeks 'redress' against Fang and Snare for endeavouring to arrest him, and that grievance occurs in the midst of Mistress Quickly's complaint that Falstaff has broken his promise to marry her. There is a prior and even more illuminating context for the word, however, one that reveals its sartorial origins and exposes its discursive affiliations with royal duplicity. During Henry's interview with Prince Hal in *1 Henry IV* (3.2), the King proudly recalls his calculated effort to make himself appear regal. He describes how he 'dressed' himself in 'humility', maintaining a mysterious and appealing distance from the people:

> Thus did I keep my person fresh and new,
> My presence like a robe pontifical—
> Ne'er seen but wondered at—and so my state,
> Seldom but sumptuous, showed like a feast,
> And won by rareness such solemnity.
>
> (3.2.55–9)

At the Gaultree meeting Prince John, also mindful of the value of appearance, dresses himself in royal concern for his subjects when he agrees to 'redress' the rebels' grievances.

His offer to accommodate their complaints echoes a conversation between Bardolph and Justice Shallow heard a few moments earlier in the previous scene, a comic analysis of the word 'accommodate':

> SHALLOW He greets me well, sir. I knew him a good
> backsword man. How doth the good knight? May I
> ask how my lady his wife doth?
> BARDOLPH Sir, pardon, a soldier is better accommodated
> than with a wife.
> SHALLOW It is well said, in faith, sir, and it is well said
> indeed, too. 'Better accommodated'—it is good; yea,
> indeed is it. Good phrases are surely, and ever were,
> very commendable. 'Accommodated'—it comes of
> *'accommodo'*. Very good, a good phrase.
> BARDOLPH Pardon, sir, I have heard the word—'phrase'
> call you it?—By this day, I know not the phrase; but I
> will maintain the word with my sword to be a soldier
> like word, and a word of exceeding good command, by
> heaven. 'Accommodated'; that is, when a man is, as they
> say, accommodated; or when a man is being whereby a
> may be thought to be accommodated; which is an
> excellent thing. (3.2.62–79)

'Accommodate' turns out to be a very good word, open to misunderstanding, a soldier-like word, and suitable to the Prince's deceptive purposes. Etymologically it is also associated with costume, like 'dressed' and 'redressed'. The rebels believe that they are being accommodated, furnished with satisfaction of their complaints, but in fact they are victims of double talk, as the Prince keeps the letter of his promise but violates the spirit.

Such verbal duplicity identifies Prince John with Falstaff, who fulfils his duty as recruiting officer in a way that is equivocal and self-serving. Falstaff is a backsword man, a backs-word man, both soldier and liar. He denies his promise to marry Mistress Quickly, reneges on his debt to her, and defaults on the thousand pounds he owes Justice Shallow. The association of word and sword appears not only in Bardolph's rodomontade—'I will maintain the word with my sword to be a soldier-like word'—but also in Prince John's accusation that the religious rebels have turned 'the word to sword and life to death'. Prince John himself, however, is another backs-word man who uses the equivocality of the word to keep from using his sword, employing policy to trick the rebels into surrender. And immediately after the surrender at Gaultree, when Falstaff has captured Coleville of the Dale and yielded him up to Prince John, the old liar declares that if he is not given proper credit for his triumph, then he will devise an elaborate ballad to publicize his own valour and eclipse theirs; and if it does not, then they should 'believe not the word of the noble'. That phrase might serve as the motto for the conclusion of the rebellion in *2 Henry IV.*

All these equivocations and breaches of faith magnify the impact of the one major oath that is actually fulfilled, Prince Hal's promise to banish Falstaff. The famous speech, beginning 'I know thee not, old man', ends with instructions to the Lord Chief Justice that should call to mind the discursive contexts of expectation and oath-keeping: 'Be it your charge, my lord, | To see performed the tenor of our word.' Falstaff, skilled as he is in the chicanery of royal performance, assures his cronies that the Prince's command is like his robe pontifical, that the pretence of severity will be dropped. 'Look you, he must seem thus to the world.' And when Shallow asks for repayment of the debt, Falstaff replies: 'Sir, I will be as good as my word. This that you heard was but a colour.' To which Shallow replies with a complicated and bittersweet pun that emphasizes the desperation of Falstaff's plight: 'A colour that I fear you will die in, Sir John.' The colour is a collar—a hangman's noose—in which Falstaff will d-i-e or d-y-e. Falstaff is mistaken about the new King's tolerance for his moral equivocations. Henry V holds fast to his word ('tenor' derives from the Latin for 'hold'), refusing to permit any slippage of meaning in the terms of Falstaff's banishment.

Equivocation about Equivocation

The *Henry* plays were written, roughly speaking, in the middle of Shakespeare's career, and they disclose, especially in the amusing irresponsibility of Falstaff, the playwright's equivocal attitude towards equivocation. Puns 'divert' an audience by taking them away from the point, by offering a brief holiday from the routine of comprehension.

This is an essentially comic function, and thus the great romantic comedies, written around the same time as the *Henry* plays, depend heavily upon the diversionary effects of wordplay. The brilliant malformations of language audible in the exchanges of Beatrice and Benedick, in the jokes of Touchstone and Feste, and in the witty speeches of Portia and Rosalind contribute a gratifying multiplicity consistent with the affirmations of the comic action. At the same time, however, the susceptibility of words to manipulation and trickery, the province of clowns and a source of infinite mirth in the comedies, becomes a cause of grave concern as the dramatist begins to represent the world through the lens of tragedy. Wordplay becomes an exceptionally sensitive register of Shakespeare's growing anxiety about the potential treachery of language, one of the topics of the next chapter.

There may be a practical explanation for the changing role of equivocation over the course of Shakespeare's career. Will Kemp, who had taken the clown parts since the formation of the Lord Chamberlain's Men in the mid-1590s, left the company at the end of the decade, and his departure coincides with a metamorphosis in the tone of Shakespearian humour. The clown roles were taken over by Robert Armin, an actor who seems to have specialized in a more contemplative and bitter kind of jesting. Even more important, much of the wordplay becomes assimilated into the protagonists' and antagonists' roles. Hamlet, to take the most obvious example, is his own clown, and except for the Fool in *King Lear*, the clowns' roles become much reduced. This is not to say that they are unimportant— the Porter in *Macbeth*, for example, eloquently sets forth the problem of moral equivocation—but gradually Shakespeare begins to make serious wordplay one of the foundational elements in the speech of such figures as Iago, Macbeth, Timon, and Cleopatra.

The effect of this theatrical shift is profound because it signifies his growing concentration on the tragic ambiguities of human experience. After the romantic comedies, the relation between wordplay and character becomes attenuated, an index of this change being Coleridge's claim that he could not find a single pun in *Macbeth*.[11] (Coleridge uses the term in a very limited sense. Double meanings are everywhere in the play.) The point is that equivocation no longer resides mainly in jokes but has become a structural feature of the major tragedies, a verbal instrument for exploring the multiplicity that tragedy frames as inevitably destructive. Recognition of the altered role of equivocal language helps to measure the development of Shakespearian scepticism: what has hitherto been healthy suspicion is metamorphosed into a thoroughgoing tragic conception of human experience, with words at the problematic centre of that understanding. Shakespeare magnifies the troubling separation between surface and meaning, a danger already manifested in the language of the histories, so that in the tragedies he stretches the correspondence between the sign and its referent to the breaking point. The consequences of such linguistic violence are horribly dramatized in *Macbeth*. In addition to the Porter's insistence on the thematic relevance of 'equivocation' (a noun much in the Jacobean air following the Gunpowder Plot of 1605), Macbeth complains about the 'juggling fiends . . . that palter with us in a double sense', and his physical death derives from his misreading of the signifying phrase 'none of woman born'. As much as any of the tragedies, *Macbeth* exposes the distance between words and meanings and conceives of verbal multiplicity as one among many species of fragmentation and failure.

The verbal density characteristic of *Macbeth* emerges most impressively in the great soliloquy before the murder, when Macbeth debates with himself about the ethics and potential consequences of assassination.

> If it were done when 'tis done, then 'twere well
> It were done quickly. If th'assassination
> Could trammel up the consequence, and catch
> With his surcease, success; that but this blow
> Might be the be-all and the end-all, here,
> But here upon this bank and shoal of time,
> We'd jump the life to come.
>
> (1.7.1–7)

These few lines are powerfully resonant. The first sentence, in its teasing of the word 'done', depends upon a verbal turn typical of Shakespeare's serious exploitation of ambiguity. The meaning of the word shifts between its first and second and third soundings: to paraphrase the first sentence, 'If I could be sure that the matter were *finished* when I have *performed* the murder, then I should *take care of it* now.' The sense shifts, although the sound remains the same, because the aural image, like many of the play's visual images, is unreliable. In terms of pure sound, the effect of 'done' is inescapable, echoing as it does through the vital names and speeches of the play: *Duncan* (donekin), *Dunsinane, Donalbain, dunnest smoke of Hell*. An especially disturbing twist occurs in Lady Macbeth's ironic greeting to Duncan as he arrives at the castle: 'All our service, | In every point *twice done* and then *done double*' would be incommensurate with the honour of the King's visit. We hear it later when Lady Macbeth attempts to ameliorate her husband's fears, assuring him that 'What's done is done' (3.2.14), and in the sleepwalking scene, where she madly cautions her absent partner that 'What's done cannot be undone.' The difference between the flatness of the paraphrase and the incantatory quality of Macbeth's line exemplifies what Stephen Booth refers to as the extraordinary 'eventfulness' of Shakespeare's language, the quality that makes it 'exciting to listening minds'.[12] The audience is led repeatedly to traverse the various semantic possibilities of the bare syllable, and such activity is in itself a source of intellectual pleasure.

Semantic patterning is at work as well. The equivocal status of 'done' is crucial to the particular complex of meanings exploited in *Macbeth*, for one of its major themes is the inescapability of 'consequence', the noun that quickly appears in line 3. The etymology of 'consequence', that which 'follows with', makes it especially resonant. *Macbeth* dramatizes the impossibility of controlling the after effects of human action, and the slippage between the three meanings of 'done' exposes what Macbeth intuitively knows although he tries to wish away the knowledge that deeds are never complete. Another way of putting this is to say that *Macbeth* is also about guilt, and the repetition of the monosyllable at the beginning of the soliloquy provides an auditory reminder of what Macbeth will shortly have 'done'. The certainty of Lady Macbeth's 'what's done is done' is undermined by the slippage already noted: the point of the play is precisely the opposite, that what is done is never complete, that it is not possible to 'trammel up the consequence', as the Lady herself discovers. The audience feels the contrary pull of 'What's done cannot be undone', her confident assertion that the past is done with and should be forgotten, and her rueful understanding that misdeeds cannot be re-called.

The importance of this verbal network should encourage us to discard the shopworn notion that *Macbeth* is a study of ambition. It is more properly described as an examination of success, of getting what one wants, of ambition fulfilled. The structure of the play also belies the thematic centrality of ambition. If Shakespeare's main concern were the mechanics of political desire, then most of the action would be given over to the seeking of the crown. But Macbeth gets what he wants in the second act: the play depicts the achievement of desire and sets forth the costs exacted by that achievement. In the 'If it were done' soliloquy, Macbeth wishes that he and Lady Macbeth, by killing Duncan, 'might catch with his surcease, success'. The ramifications of the wordplay here are semantically thrilling. In the first place, there is the aural similarity of the juxtaposed words, 'surcease' and 'success'. Politically, the second (Macbeth's royal future) is dependent on the first (Duncan's demise). But neither noun is stable. Duncan's 'surcease' does not end the matter: as Macbeth will later acknowledge about Banquo's ghost, 'The time has been | That when the brains were out, the man would die, | And there an end' (3.4.78–80). But now the dead return, Banquo as a ghost, and Duncan as a corpse which needs constant tending (additional crimes) to keep it in the earth. 'Success' is even more thoroughly loaded with implications than 'surcease'. Macbeth's letter to his wife opens with his report on meeting the witches, 'They met me in the day of success.' *Victory, achievement, prosperity*—all these senses of the noun apply to Macbeth's military triumph, and they also pertain to his desire for the crown, his attempt to 'catch . . . success'. Finally, further ambiguity arises from the fact that in Shakespeare's day the word 'success' simply meant 'outcome', not necessarily a positive result. The neutrality of the word would have coloured the audience's sense of Macbeth's moral and political trajectory.

Yet another definition of *succeed*—'to follow'—is inevitably called into play and elaborated, not only by the proximity of 'consequence' but also by the principal theme of the speech, the return of misdeeds on our own heads: 'Bloody instructions . . . return | To plague th'inventor' (1.7.8–9). Here 'succession' is both specific (who gets the crown) and abstract (any following series of events). Macbeth has violated the normal process of succession, and therefore what succeeds the murder is an unending succession of further crimes, more misdeeds required to secure the Macbeths' success. In *Richard II*, after the King's confiscation of Henry Bolingbroke's property, York deplores the precedent of such a deed: 'how art thou a king | But by fair sequence and succession?' Whereas the histories underscore the political effects of such violation, *Macbeth* explores the personal, especially the psychological and spiritual consequences. And the outcome is bitter: 'For Banquo's *issue* have I filed my mind.' Perhaps it is this emphasis on consequences and succeeding crimes that accounts for the exceptional degree of verbal repetition in the 'If it were done' speech, beginning with the three instances of 'done' but going on to many other echoes: three uses of 'were' in the first one and a half lines; '*be* the *be-all* and the end-*all*'; 'here, | But here'; even the sequentially repeated consonants in 'but this blow | Might be the be-all'. Alliterative and other homophonic patterns sensitize the audience to the semantic music of the wordplay.

Similar semantic networks enrich, to a greater or lesser extent, virtually all the plays *King Lear*, for example, develops its major themes—the nature of the human species, familial bonds, love, savagery—by exploring the interconnection of words such as *nature, natural, generation, general, kind, kin,* and *king,* thereby refreshing our sense of their meanings. And critics have begun to demonstrate the way in which such wordplay, comic and otherwise, can 'lead us to linkages operating not only within but between Shakespeare's plays, across the often arbitrary boundaries of genre . . . [and] make possible glimpses into the relation between the plays and their contemporary culture'.[13] So sophisticated and meaningful are these verbal networks that they may seem remote from the crude verbal twists of a Grumio or a Pistol—'To England will I steal, and there I'll steal'—but in fact they represent an intensified application of the very principles that motivate such foolery. And the remains of Augustan and Romantic discomfort with wordplay must not be allowed to obscure the centrality of such principles to Shakespearian drama.

If Dr Johnson's judgement about Shakespearian wordplay seems to us too narrow, his instincts were nevertheless sound. Many of Shakespeare's clowns cannot resist a quibble, but the punster who cannot help himself is Shakespeare, and to say that he cannot help himself is to use that phrase in a double sense. His own delight in verbal ingenuity is played out in numerous witty speakers, of course, not to mention the sonnets and narrative poems, but it is also clear that the artist cannot exert control over the multiplicity of meanings that tend to attach themselves to verbal signs. If the flexibility of the word, as

Shakespearian practice suggests, is a function and an emblem of the disorder and duplicity of the world, then it seems clear that intentionality is inadequate to explain the operation of poetic and dramatic wordplay.

Jonathan Culler urges that we separate wordplay from particular speakers and see it instead

as a structural, connecting device that delineates action or explores the world, helping the plays (and also the sonnets) to offer the mind a sense and an experience of order that it does not master or comprehend. We do not know what is the relation between 'guilt' and 'gilding' [in Lady Macbeth's 'I'll gild the faces of the grooms withal, | For it must seem their guilt'], or between the straining of exertion and of filtering [in Portia's 'The quality of mercy is not strained. | It droppeth as the gentle rain from heaven'], but we are urged to conceive an order in which they go together. Insofar as this is the goal or achievement of art, the pun seems an exemplary agent.[14]

The effect of wordplay, as Culler's analysis implies, is inherently paradoxical: double meaning has a double meaning. It is intimately connected with the disorder of language and experience, and yet it also manages to defy that disorder by creating verbal patterns offering the rewards of coherence and comprehension. In other words, the act of representing the multiplicity of the world offers the audience a vehicle for managing that complexity, if only for the duration of the performance.

All of this may seem a little solemn. What needs to be reiterated is that the aural and semantic electricity generated by Shakespeare's wordplay is a source of sensuous delight, intellectual pleasure, and emotional power. We delight in making aural and semantic connections, in observing the fertility of a single signifier as a speaker or a poet forces it to yield up multiple meanings. Above all, we are afforded a feeling of command, an amplified sense of awareness, the thrill of insight and perceived order. Falstaff's extreme self-consciousness about language, especially his pleasure in multiple meanings, is complemented by Mistress Quickly's verbal ignorance, her inability to command even single accurate meanings of discursive signs. Her numerous malapropisms in *2 Henry IV*, *honeysuckle* for *homicidal* (2.1.52), *indited* for *invited* (2.1.28), her confusion of *s-o-m-e* for *s-u-m* (2.1.73–4), and her unconscious obscenities, as in 'Master Fang and

Master Snare, *do me, do me*, do me your offices' (2.1.41–2)—all of these jests are doubly piquant because Mistress Quickly doesn't get it, and what she doesn't get is exactly what we congratulate ourselves for having got. There is danger in such smugness, as we ought to know from watching the fortunes of Falstaff.

But there is another peril as well, the threat of those who do get it but who do not like it. Falstaff's joy in polysemy stands in contrast to the seriousness of Hotspur, whose contempt for 'mincing poetry' is one of his defining traits and is accompanied by a hatred for music and wordplay. He uses puns, to be sure, but he does so as a form of condescension and irony. When his wife wonders what has transported him, 'what carries you away?', Hotspur replies, 'Why, my horse, my love, my horse.' This is wordplay as defensive strategy, a means of getting past unpleasant moments, and he employs the same quibbling tactics against Owain Glyndŵr. When the Welshman brags that he has fought three times against Bolingbroke and 'sent him | Bootless home, and weather-beaten back', Hotspur deflates the boast by shifting from the figurative to the literal with the quibbling 'Home without boots, and in foul weather too!' The point of these final examples is that Hotspur is a sober-sided rationalist, one who values perspicuity, denotation, single meanings, one who does not like to read signs. Hotspur is a killjoy, and Shakespeare, as an entertainer, a joygiver, kills him off. To reject the pleasures of wordplay is to enact the Puritan's response, to attempt to shut down the play, and if there is one thing that Shakespeare insists upon, it is that the show must go on.

Words Effectual,
Speech Unable

Shakespeare's mind, as the preceding chapters have surely demonstrated, seems to have worked antithetically. Or, as Helen Vendler plainly puts it, 'As soon as he thinks of one thing, he thinks of something that is different from it.'[1] Moreover, as Vendler goes on to show, the second thought is often the polar opposite of the first. Such an observation provides a convenient entry into a treatment of Shakespeare's style, for it elucidates not only his poetic choices but also his more general theatrical habits: the innumerable puns, the effect of the iambic rhythms, the alternation between verse and prose, the contrasts in scenic architecture, the ever-present ironies, the complex gender games, the oppositions that furnish dramatic conflict. Antithesis will prove invaluable in taking up the subject of this last chapter, Shakespeare's attitude towards his own medium. The opposing phrases that make up my title, the first from *2 Henry VI*, the second from *King Lear*, represent the two poles of Shakespeare's thinking about the language that gave him his livelihood. From the early days of his career as a playwright, Shakespeare's conception of language was broad and fluid, combining enthusiasm with anxiety, optimism about its benefits with suspicion of its dangers.

His exuberance for the creative potentiality of words emerges most obviously from his early works, especially those, such as *A Midsummer Night's Dream*, written just after his apprenticeship. Conversely, his fears about the limitations of words and their liability to abuse seem much more prominent in the later plays, particularly the tragedies. It would be possible—indeed it is tempting—to develop a teleological argument, a scheme in which Shakespeare's thinking about language enacts a progress from enthusiastic novice to confident young artist to disillusioned adult to reflective but mostly affirmative greybeard. Such a scenario corresponds more or less to the nineteenth-century conception, articulated most explicitly by Edward Dowden, of Shakespeare's 'spiritual biography', with its passage from affirmation to despair to transcendence. But such a tidy scheme, like most tidy schemes, misrepresents the truth, which is always messier and more difficult to quantify and comprehend than we would like it to be.

The truth is that in almost every play Shakespeare's view of language and its possibilities is mixed. His brightest comedies are not without awareness of the limits on human communication, and the tension between confidence and concern animates and complicates those works. Likewise, his bleakest tragedies never succumb to linguistic nihilism, their very existence counterbalancing the intimations of despair. 'Brief sounds determine of my weal or woe', says Juliet, and so it is for Shakespeare in his thinking about the effects of language. My procedure in this chapter will be first to consider Shakespeare's self-consciousness about the word in its early manifestations, and then to examine, in the order given by Juliet, the contradictions in his thinking about language: first the 'weal', Shakespeare's idealism about words, brief sounds, and what they can do *for* us; and then the 'woe', his disillusionment with language and depiction of what words can do *to* us.

Linguistic Idealism

Self-consciousness about words and usage so saturates the works that the difficulty is not how to establish the point but how to limit illustration of it. Thus, a serious occupational hazard for some Shakespeare scholars is the temptation to believe that every play (and each of the sonnets and poems as well) is mainly *about* language. Most playgoers leave the theatre thinking that *Richard III* is about a charismatic killer who usurps the throne, not a demonstration of the satisfactions of anaphora and other rhetorical patterns. Audiences usually infer that *Love's Labour's Lost* stages the follies and confusions of love rather than investigating the permutations of linguistic pretension. They are right to do so. But to study the plays carefully and at length is to recognize that whatever the topic Shakespeare addresses—courtship, power relations, the family, the nature of evil—he is ever mindful of the terms in which these human problems are explored. Some plays, especially those with a strong metadramatic strain, disclose this consciousness more immediately than others. It is not hard to see that *Hamlet* is much concerned with the theatricality of experience and the role of words in the drama of life, and the scrupulous framing of the flattery in the first scene of *King Lear* promises that the topic of language will occupy centre stage. But even when problems of expression do not seem obviously pertinent to the action represented, the playwright's engagement with the linguistic implications of his story is almost always discernible.

Just a few years into his writing career, roughly around 1595 (give or take a year or two), Shakespeare seems to have been suddenly possessed with language as a subject. To be sure, in earlier plays he had speculated on what language can and cannot do: in *The Taming of the Shrew* the battle of the sexes is depicted as a war of words, and in the three *Henry VI* plays he could hardly have missed the political ramifications of his characters' speech. But *Love's Labour's Lost*, *Richard III*, and *Romeo and Juliet* suggest a new degree of self-consciousness about the medium in which he worked. The comedy and the history illustrate Shakespeare's recognition of the extent to which language is implicated in personal and political behaviour. Biron and his fellows must learn to use language responsibly—the women teach them to do so—and their awakening to the need for unaffected language, free of 'taffeta phrases' and 'three-piled hyperboles', becomes a sign of maturity and authentic emotion. In *Richard III*, as I indicated in the chapter on wordplay, the dramatist represents the hazardous nature of political life with slippery rhetorical figures. Characters repeatedly seize meaning from one another by twisting words into an unintended and usually unwelcome sense.

> YORK I pray you, uncle, render me this dagger.
> RICHARD GLOUCESTER My dagger, little cousin? With all
>   my heart.
>
> (3.1.110–11)

Such transmission of meaning occurs between Richard and virtually every character he speaks with, establishing a pattern of displaced power and political instability. Shakespeare's fascination with the range of language takes a variety of shapes, the most ostentatious being Richard's sovereignty over words, but another notable form is Clarence's eloquence. When Richard instructs his hired assassins not to heed the Duke's words, one of the murderers dismisses the warning: 'Tut, tut, my lord, we will not stand to prate. | Talkers are no good doers. Be assured, | We go to use our hands and not our tongues' (1.3.348–50). Ultimately the canon will contradict that claim: Shakespeare comes to believe that talking is a kind of doing. In the theatre, it is the only kind of doing. The linguistic order becomes a simulacrum of the social and political orders, sometimes even of a play's emotional order, and this symbolic relation imposes great thematic weight on the playwright's distribution of words.

For all the verbal exuberance of *Love's Labour's Lost* and *Richard III*, however, it is in *Romeo and Juliet* that Shakespeare explicitly confronts the problem of language: its nature, its virtues, its limitations. 'What's in a name?' asks Juliet, in her great meditation on wherefore Romeo is Romeo (2.2.75–91), and her question immediately impels her and the audience into an impromptu analysis not only of proper names but of all verbal signs, that is, all language. Juliet resolutely adopts the modern, nominalist position in the debate over the proper relation between words and their meanings. Developed most extensively in the twentieth century by the French linguist Ferdinand de Saussure, this view holds that all language is conventional and that verbal signs are entirely arbitrary, representing nothing more than an agreement between members of a discursive group. As Juliet puts it, 'That which we call a rose | By any other word would smell as sweet' (2.2.85–6). The contrary argument, derived ultimately from Plato's dialogue *Cratylus*, contends that some mystical or essential connection obtains between the verbal signifier, i.e. the word, and the signified, i.e. the thing to which it points. Juliet's memorable question and the speech in which it is embedded pose a direct challenge to the meaning of names and labels, focusing the issue that recurs in scene after scene—the question of what we should call things. In fact, throughout Juliet's speech, Romeo's commentary on it, and the dialogue between them that shortly follows, 'name' and 'word' sound repeatedly, sometimes in place of each other, reminding us that what we think of as nomenclature is a specific form of the problems raised by all language. And naming is one of the fundamental concerns of the play: why the Montagues and Capulets call each other names, whether Romeo and Juliet call each other 'enemy' or 'lover', in what sense Romeo will 'lie' with Juliet.

In the very first lines of the play proper (after the Prologue) Gregory and Samson indulge in a series of obvious puns that attune the audience's ears to the instability of language, emphasizing the unfixed relation between name and object, sound and thing. This banter precedes the first street fight, in which Tybalt challenges Benvolio's call for 'peace': 'What, drawn, and talk of peace? I hate the word' (1.1.67). The Prince, after entering to still the riot, condemns the 'Three civil brawls, bred of an airy word' (1.1.86). As the action unfolds, the fixation on words and their referents continues: in the Capulet servant who cannot read the list of party guests, in the Nurse's garrulity and earthy quibbles, in Juliet's asking the name of each departing guest as a way to learn Romeo's identity, in Mercutio's devotion to the witty rhetorical figure and obscene image, in Romeo's fixation on and repetition of the word 'banishèd', in Capulet's extravagant laments at Juliet's apparent death. In addition to these principal examples, there are scores of minor references to names, words, definitions, and linguistic distinctions. Such trouble over appropriate titles serves to draw the audience's attention toward one of the main actions of the play, the discovery of identity seen in Romeo's coming of age in the first two acts, and then brilliantly in Juliet's sudden maturation in the last three.

So vital to this story is the topic of expression that at times Shakespeare seems to be disassembling words so as to inspect them more carefully. Often, that is, he obsessively reiterates sounds and syllables as if wanting to distil the verbal sign to its irreducible components. Each syllable of the name 'Ro-me-o', for example, sounds and resounds through the text. The exclamatory 'O' seems to ring out with unusual frequency, even for tragedy, and a glance at the Concordance confirms that the word occurs 151 times, more than in any other play (*Othello* being a close second, with 150). 'Ay me' is famously spoken by Juliet at her window, but it should be noted that the phrase has been heard only moments before in Mercutio's wild, ironic recitation on the sounds of love: 'Romeo . . . | Speak but one rhyme and I am satisfied. | Cry but "Ay *me*!" Pronounce but "love" and "dove" ' (2.1.7, 8–10). Even the apparently meaningless first syllable gets separated from Romeo's name:

Enter Romeo
BENVOLIO Here comes Romeo, here comes Romeo!
MERCUTIO Without his roe, like a dried herring.

(2.3.34–5)

Then moments later the name is subjected to further deconstruction:

NURSE Doth not rosemary and Romeo begin
Both with a letter?
ROMEO Ay, Nurse, what of that? Both with an 'R'.
NURSE Ah, mocker—that's the dog's name. 'R' is for
the—no, I know it begins with some other letter, and
she hath the prettiest sententiousness of it, of you and
rosemary, that it would do you good to hear it.[2]

(2.3.197–203)

There may even be a pun on 'you' and 'yew' and the letter 'U' in the next to the last line, and one editor has suggested that the phrase ' "R" is for the—' moves towards and then retreats from 'arse'. The Nurse's playing with letters and syllables represents a form of flirtation, as she teases Romeo by affectionately toying with his name.

Such syllabic dissection creates a rich context for Juliet's verbal explosion in Act 3, when she must endure the Nurse's baffling announcement of the deadly swordfight and its aftermath. Immediately after the 'Gallop apace' soliloquy (3.2.1–30), each of the next four speeches—Juliet's exchange with the distraught Nurse who has just entered—begins with a single syllable: 'O . . . Ay, ay . . . Ay me . . . Ah, welladay!' (3.2.31–7). Thinking Romeo dead, Juliet suffers a kind of phonic convulsion:

Hath Romeo slain himself? Say thou but '*Ay*',
And that bare vowel '*I*' shall poison more
Than the death-darting *eye* of cockatrice.
I am not *I* if there be such an '*Ay*',
Or those *eyes* shut that makes thee answer '*Ay*'.
If he be slain, say '*Ay*'; or if not, 'No'.
Brief sounds determine of my weal or woe.

(3.2.45–51)

The effect of such reiteration is to distance us from the most familiar sounds we know, recreating the experience of looking too long at a familiar word until it begins to seem bizarre.³ And the conclusion to Juliet's burst of verbal fireworks, its last line, has a pertinence that extends far beyond this passage. The lovers' bondage to 'brief sounds', the verbal system that represents the social realm, is a primary expression of their inability to escape the limits and snares of the mortal world.

Here it might be appropriate to follow Shakespeare's development of this self-scrutinizing impulse through the romantic comedies, the later histories, the dark comedies, the tragedies, and the late romances or tragicomedies. Such a survey would consider the shuffling of names in the forest of Arden; the nature of slander in *Much Ado* or *Cymbeline*; Master Ford's mad diatribe on 'terms! names!' in *The Merry Wives*; the contest between loquacity and silence in *Coriolanus*; the sophisticated poetics of *The Tempest*; Falstaff; and just about every other line in *Hamlet*. But a systematic review of Shakespearian reflexivity is unnecessary, especially for readers who have got this far in this book. Some of these episodes and plays will receive attention in the ensuing pages, but rather than compile a heap of examples of Shakespearian linguistic self-consciousness, I shall instead glance at one play in which both strains of Shakespeare's linguistic thinking obviously compete for dominance.

Henry V represents a kind of showcase for the tension between linguistic optimism and suspicion, and it is not surprising that this should be so. As the last in the second tetralogy of history plays, it extends the intermingling of the linguistic and the political order developed in the preceding three. Chronologically, it appears near the mid-point of Shakespeare's writing career (1599), when his thinking about language and its uses begins a radical shift. Having banished Falstaff from *Henry V*, Shakespeare disperses the character's extraordinary linguistic energy through a range of characters and episodes. Speech can be colourful and various, as we hear in the dialects of the English, Irish, Scots, and Welsh soldiers in Henry's army. It is often ridiculous, as it is in Nim's monomaniacal repetitions ('that's the humour of it'), or Mistress Quickly's malapropisms. It may be effete and trivial, as in the conversation of the arrogant French Dauphin and his camp. Or it may be foreign: since Princess Catherine speaks no English, one entire scene (3.4) and part of another are spoken in French. Even Falstaff makes a cameo appearance in Mistress Quickly's recital of his last words. Shakespeare asks the audience to entertain contrary responses to these multiple accents. As with the questions of monarchy, succession, patriotism, war, heroism, and politics, he complicates the linguistic theme so thoroughly that any satisfactory conclusion or even compromise becomes very difficult.

The competing strains of affirmation and doubt are held in almost perfect balance in *Henry V*. In practically every scene the virtues of language are balanced against its vices. Shakespeare's unusual decision to begin with a Chorus (and to bring him back again and again) suggests a positive spin. The Chorus identifies the linguistic origins of what we see, implying that the audience's 'fancy' must respond to the playwright's verbal stimuli: 'Think, when we talk of horses, that you see them' (Prologue, l. 26). Numerous verbal episodes in the ensuing story confirm that apparent optimism. The young King is known for his forensic attainments, his 'sweet and honeyed sentences' (1.1.51). When the three traitorous lords urge that the King forgo mercy in the case of a drunkard who railed against him, Henry traps them with their own words, preserving his person and political stability with verbal legerdemain. Then the action moves to France, where the King's forensic gifts will sound thrillingly in the St Crispin's Day speech before Agincourt (4.3.18–67). A more troubling oration, however, is the one he delivers earlier at the gates of Harfleur, detailing the horrors that await the citizens unless their governor surrenders the city:

> look to see
> The blind and bloody soldier with foul hand
> Defile the locks of your shrill-shrieking daughters
> .   .   .   .   .
> Your naked infants spitted upon pikes.
>
> (3.3.116–18, 121)

In threatening rape, infanticide, and what amounts to an early modern version of a scorched-earth policy, the passionate speech paradoxically reveals the capacity of the word to help prevent such terrors. King Henry's brutal threat saves lives. It is a verbal performance that, in bringing about a bloodless English triumph, displaces actual injury into a virtual realm. The linguistic imagination serves positive social and political ends.

Yet verbal misuse is equally prominent. The Archbishop of Canterbury and the Bishop of Ely, fearing the crown's assault on their treasury, encourage Henry to pursue a very tenuous claim to the throne of France. Obfuscating where he ought to simplify, extending where he ought to abbreviate, the Archbishop concludes a fifty-line genealogical proof with the disingenuous 'as clear as is the summer's sun' (1.2.86), a phrase that almost always gets a laugh in the theatre and seems to invite disgust at religious circumlocution and hypocrisy. The placement of this lineal mumbo-jumbo—Act 1, scenes 1 and 2—and the degree of attention given to it mark it as crucial, even though the comic stage business that usually accompanies it can efface its thematic importance. Later, before Agincourt, when the soldier named Williams begins to imagine 'all those legs and arms and heads chopped off in a battle' (4.1.134–5), we take a more negative view of the clergy's linguistic distortions and self-interest. Similarly disturbing, entertaining though it may be, is Pistol's sublime bluster, especially when heard in the context of a national crisis. Big words cannot disguise his cowardice, although Captain Fluellen is briefly taken in, and Pistol's encomium to Bardolph ('a soldier firm and sound of heart, | Of buxom valour' (3.6.24–5)) cannot change the fact that Bardolph and Pistol are no better than common thieves.

Shakespeare's doubts about language overshadow the final scene, the wooing by King Henry of Princess Catherine. Looked at out of context, the exchange may seem a delicate and charming interview in which the warrior-king hesitantly moves towards a proposal that he hopes will be accepted. But as a conclusion to *Henry V*, the scene is a sham: the marriage has been agreed to and will take place, regardless of the bride's feelings, as a consequence of Henry's victory and as a symbolic union of England and France. Is the language of courtship delightful, or is it intolerably false? Is Henry really comparable to Alexander the Great, or, to borrow a phrase from Captain Fluellen, to Alexander the Pig? Shakespeare's divided attitude towards language in *Henry V* is encoded in his ambivalent depiction of the King and his victories. The comic concord suggested by the marriage is undercut by the kinds of actions represented. Although the second tetralogy may have begun as an enormous comic project, a celebration of the career of Henry V, in the course of its creation Shakespeare seems to have lost some of his positive conviction, and his changing view of words is one of the clearest proofs of this gradual disillusionment.

The Virtues of Illusion

Shakespeare's enthusiasm for the immense creative possibilities of the word, opportunities both theatrical and poetic, was shared by most early modern writers and by Elizabethan literate culture in general. As indicated in Chapters 1 and 2, the newly dignified status of the vernacular at the end of the sixteenth century had led to an outpouring of theoretical defences and poetic celebrations of English, and, by implication, of language in general. In 1591 Sir John Harrington identified the virtues of imaginatively ordered language:

> in verse is both goodness and sweetness, rhubarb and sugar candy, the pleasant and the profitable.... he that can mingle the sweet and the wholesome, the pleasant and the profitable, he is indeed an absolute good writer: and such be Poets, if any be such; they present unto us a pretty tale, able to keep a child from play, and an old man from the chimney corner.[4]

Harrington's argument is congruent with most of the other such defences of the time, and in fact he has filched several choice phrases from that greatest of all Elizabethan treatises, Sir Philip Sidney's *Apology for Poetry*. Sidney's defence was prompted by Stephen Gosson's attacks on the supposed iniquities of the stage, and thus the line of argument is moral. The poet—and by 'poet' Sidney means the writer of fiction generally—arranges words in an artful form that will delight the mind and create an effective vehicle for conveying truth. This contention may be traced back to the Roman poet Horace, whose terms for the purposes of poetry were *utile* and *dulcere*, to be useful and sweet, or to teach and delight. The shapes and forms of poetry (and, to a lesser but still significant extent, prose) beguile the reader or audience, captivating them with aural and semantic patterns to which the mind seems naturally to respond.

Although most Elizabethan commentators tenaciously proclaim the morality of art, their discussions often seem to veer, as does Harrington's, into the realm of delight. They do not say so explicitly, but it is clear that for most of these apologists the great power of poetic language rests in its ability to keep a child from play, its power to enchant. Thomas Campion refers to this irresistible response in 1602 when he asserts that 'The world is made by symmetry and proportion, and is in that respect compared to music, and music to poetry.'[5] In dedicating his treatise to Lord Buckhurst, Campion succinctly declares that reason and speech separate humans from animals and that poetry is the highest form of human expression, 'the chief beginner and maintainer of eloquence, not only helping the ear with the acquaintance of sweet numbers, but also raising the mind to a more high and lofty conceit'.[6] The moral component in Campion's argument appears somewhat softer than in most such defences, where the musical and sensuous qualities of language are considered instrumental virtues, that is, effective delivery systems for moral precepts.

Most of the Elizabethan defences were composed by poets or schoolmasters. As a professional playwright earning his living in the commercial theatre, Shakespeare seems to have cared less about theory than about praxis. The occasional prologue excepted, drama affords few opportunities for theoretical commentary, and so commercial dramatists rarely joined these controversies, at least until Ben Jonson came to prominence around the turn of the century. Even Shakespeare's sonnets, which might seem more hospitable to such commentary, and which do occasionally refract contemporary views of poetry, are presented by a speaker whose persona makes the poems fundamentally dramatic and oblique. Although he left no poetic *apologia* on the uses and value of poetic language, the plays make it plain that Shakespeare favoured, to use Harrington's terms, the sugar-candy over the rhubarb. All his works reveal an unfailing relish for verbal artifice. 'Symmetry', 'proportion', 'sweet numbers'—Campion's chosen properties, as well as other unnamed forms of patterning, are discernible in every play. But to what end? It is on this point that Shakespeare evidently parts company with the theorists. His aim was to entertain, to attract paying audiences to the public theatre in which he held a financial share. The patterns of language that excited him and that still excite playgoers are devoted not to instruction but to the primary goal of moving, delighting, commanding the imagination of an audience. This is not to say that the plays lack moral interest, but the inculcation of lessons is not their main motive. Shakespeare would probably have agreed with Sam Goldwyn, the Hollywood producer of the 1930s, who defended his movies against charges of frivolousness by saying that if he wanted to send a message he'd call Western Union.

Poetic patterns depend upon the configuration of verbal or aural elements, and Shakespeare's idealism about his medium is grounded in a reverence for human relatedness. From the earliest plays to the end of the career, he never surrenders his faith in the benefits of *communication*, liberally defined. He maintains a belief in the ability of language to strengthen human ties, which is to say that he understands the vital relation between communication and community. Thus, dialogue becomes a register of human interaction generally, and the comic harmony and social unity achieved at the end of comedy are often represented in linguistic terms. The happy ending frequently depends upon the education of the main characters, with the schooling of the heart frequently taking the form of a language lesson.

Antipholus of Syracuse in *The Comedy of Errors*:

> I'll *say* as they *say*. . .
> (2.2.218)

Katherine in *The Taming of the Shrew*:

> What you will have it *named*, even that it is,
> And so it shall be still for Katherine.
> (4.6.22–3)

Rosalind in *As You Like It* ·

> What would you *say* to me now an I were your very, very Rosalind? (4.1.65–7)

From *All's Well that Ends Well*:

> HELEN 'Tis but the shadow of a wife you see,
> The *name* and not the thing.
> BERTRAM   Both, both O, pardon!
> (5.3.309–10)

It might be said that in all the plays, regardless of mode, learning a language betokens other forms of understanding or awakening. But such lessons are never simple, and languages can be misunderstood, as we remember from the Latin lesson in *The Merry Wives of Windsor*, where Quickly's corruption of little Will's innocent speech provides a foretaste of more serious contamination of the word.

Reciprocal speech creates understanding and agreement that remove comic obstacles to the characters' fulfilment. As the witty exchanges between Katherine and Petruccio or Beatrice and Benedick suggest, the give and take of dialogue often acts as a substitute for the sexual coupling promised at the end of most comedies. That sexual union, as Northrop Frye has taught us, is integral to the comic artist's affirmative vision of experience,[7] and such a comic conviction presupposes a faith in the capacity of language to reveal, to unify, to create harmony. The tongue, in other words, becomes a sexual organ, an instrument of reproduction:

> PORTIA   It is almost morning,
> And yet I am sure you are not satisfied
> Of these events at full. Let us go in,
> And charge us there upon inter'gatories,
> And we will answer all things faithfully.
>
> (*The Merchant of Venice*, 5.1.295–9)

Since the marriages are not yet consummated, the promised satisfactions would seem to be both verbal and sexual, and often the connection between speech and fertility is secured by diction common to the two discourses, such as 'deliver', 'pregnant', and 'gossip' (which originally referred to a godparent at the baptism of an infant). The explanatory stories promised at the end of many of the comedies attest to the characters' and the playwright's faith in the future, and such a conception of social unity depends upon shared speech and unanimity of definition. All of Shakespeare's comedies imply that the necessary terms can be mastered, that comic characters can learn to read the world, but as the comic endings become more shadowy and complex, the language lessons built into the action, unlike Quickly's bawdy annotations, become more painful. For example, Malvolio's humiliation in *Twelfth Night* derives from misreading, and Paroles ('words') in *All's Well* is brutally mocked with gibberish:

> INTERPRETER   *Boskos thromuldo boskos.*
> PAROLES   I know you are the Moscows regiment,
> And I shall lose my life for want of language.
>
> (4.1.69–71)

Such rogues and misfits threaten the harmony of the societies they inhabit, and thus Shakespeare ironically underscores the interdependence of verbal and social bonds.

Falstaff's verbal gifts permit him to create his own community in the tavern, a kind of shadow court. A brilliant if irregular tutor of the Prince, he never permits the audience to forget the extent of his verbal talent. His various speech is an exposition of the multiple ways that words can invigorate and delight the mind. The unmixed delight he takes in his own linguistic skill is matched by his linguistic self-awareness, his recognition of his own fallibility and skill at masking it with words. In this combination of talent and self-consciousness he seems a stand-in for, or a displaced version of, the playwright sensitive to the opportunities and liabilities of his occupation. But Falstaff is not the only impressive speaker in the *Henriad*. Shakespeare has carefully assigned distinctive styles of speech to many of the principal figures: Richard II, Hotspur, Shallow, Pistol, Mistress Quickly, the Lord Chief Justice, and the various soldiers in *Henry V*. All these idioms help to join the political and linguistic themes, and with each of these speakers as a symbolic model, the royal education of Prince Hal is figured as the acquisition of a language. Like many of the comedies, the tetralogy proposes that a healthy community requires proper verbal relations. And in fact the tragedies make the same point, but with negative examples and bitter irony.

Falstaff's tall story about his valour in the robbery suggests another positive function of language for Shakespeare—its role in the creation of illusion. To take up such a topic is to consider a subject as large as theatre itself: through the verbal medium the artist generates a virtual reality in which the audience temporarily, but pleasurably and profitably, loses itself. The experience of losing oneself in illusion is, of course, one of the cornerstones of Shakespearian comedy: the two Syracusans in *The Comedy of Errors* 'wander in illusions' (4.3.43); Katherine in *The Taming of the Shrew* suffers a phantasmagoric stay at Petruccio's house in the process of learning 'gentle' behaviour; Sebastian in *Twelfth Night*, distrusting his own sanity when swept up by Olivia, submits to the 'wonder that enwraps' him. Not only are such surrenders theatrically satisfying, they are also revelatory, both for the characters who accept the fantasy and the spectators who observe them. Such is the function of the supernatural high jinks in *A Midsummer Night's Dream*, where Helena is guided through the forest 'By some illusion' (3.2.98). That play dramatizes as well as any the paradoxical power of illusion to clarify, to expose, and to stimulate revision of opinion and behaviour. But supernatural illusions are exceptional in Shakespeare.

Play-worlds fabricated from words, however, appear everywhere, as plays-within-plays: the mechanicals' performance of 'Pyramus and Thisbe' at the end of *Dream*; the pageant near the end of *Love's Labour's Lost*; the tavern skit in *1 Henry IV*; the masquerading that enlivens many of the romantic comedies; 'The Murder of Gonzago' in *Hamlet*. All of these instances depend, as does theatre generally, upon the cooperation of the visual and the verbal. They also reveal the dramatist in the act of contemplating his own professional enterprise. An episode that captures the complex valences of linguistic creativity is the Pageant of the Nine Worthies in *Love's Labour's Lost*. When the clowns and fools enter as ancient heroes, the discrepancy between themselves and their roles is enormous.

> *Enter Holofernes the pedant as Judas, and the boy Mote as*
> *Hercules*
> HOLOFERNES   Great Hercules is presented by this imp,
>   Whose club killed Cerberus, that three-headed
>   *canus*,
> And when he was a babe, a child, a shrimp,
>   Thus did he strangle serpents in his *manus*.
> *Quoniam* [Since] he seemeth in minority,
>   *Ergo* [Therefore] I come with this apology.

(5.2.582–7)

Forced to cast a child as Hercules, the schoolmaster resorts to words to cover the incongruity, but his speech is absurd, and throughout the performance the amateur actors must suffer the gibes of the court.

It might seem peculiar, then, to have chosen the Pageant of the Nine Worthies to demonstrate the power of verbal illusion since the playlet is a disaster, the speeches preposterous. But the theatrical catastrophe, the failed verbal construct, is a foil to the larger, affective value of linguistic illusion. The irony is that by means of his words—both those of the buffoons and those of their tormentors—Shakespeare has induced the theatre audience to credit a chimera. Elizabethan audiences took boys for women, and modern audiences at least agree to accept an actor for a king. The illusion of *Love's Labour's Lost* has moved us not only to laughter but also—improbably—to sympathy.

At the height of the mockery, Holofernes issues a frustrated protest that carries a huge emotional charge: 'This is not generous, not gentle, not humble' (5.2.622). The complexity of that moment vividly substantiates the affective and moral power of language.

A still more sophisticated case, one relying upon the same ironic means, is found in the last act of *Antony and Cleopatra*, where the Egyptian Queen warns her handmaiden of the public humiliation they will face as captives in Rome. She fears the exaggerated misrepresentation of the players, 'the quick comedians' who will 'stage' her love affair with an intoxicated Antony. Worst of all, 'I shall see | Some squeaking Cleopatra boy my greatness | I'th' posture of a whore' (5.2.215–17). The key word in the speech is 'boy', a relatively rare instance of this noun's use as a verb. Since the lines were spoken from the stage of the Globe by a boy actor, Shakespeare insists on the potential discrepancy between the theatrical image of Cleopatra and the 'real' Cleopatra, indicating that what we see is a mockery. But the speaker, the 'real' Cleopatra, is an image created mainly with the poet's words. His exotic and sensuous language has persuaded the audience of Cleopatra's reality and of her 'greatness'.

Implicit in the extravagant beauties of the Egyptian tragedy is faith in the positive effect of words. The existence of the play itself constitutes a justification of the power of language; this is a version of the sonneteer's claims for the power of poetry to sustain life. The triumph of verbal illusion documents an effect of language generated by every play, even the bleakest of the tragedies. *Coriolanus*, for example, a portrait of a hero who despises words, is almost relentless in its exposure of the defects and inadequacy of language. Nevertheless, the stark power of the play's attack on words is, of course, a paradoxical assertion of what words can achieve. Shakespeare's scepticism cannot destroy his fundamental belief in the power of language to convey his scepticism about, among other things, language.

Cleopatra's vision of herself mimicked in Rome captures what may be the most valuable of all the positive functions of language—its capacity to make an audience experience the impossible. The verbal illusion affords us imaginative participation in another realm, a liberation from the restrictions of the material world. In Campion's suggestion that poetry not only delights the ear but 'rais[es] the mind to a more high and lofty conceit' his verbal phrase identifies the infallible source of Shakespeare's faith in language, its kinetic effect on the human intellect. The forms and patterns of dramatic speech expand the mind of the listener, and the strenuously pleasurable exercise associated with the expansion is the effect that kept Shakespeare writing, the product that has kept him in business over the past four centuries. Stephen Booth argues that 'clarification' or 'epiphany' or whatever spiritually charged term we choose has little to do with the real value of Shakespeare's use of language.[8] This argument resembles the position taken in his later years by the philosopher Ludwig Wittgenstein: in the principle he called 'the language game', he proposed that the virtue of language resides chiefly in its power to amuse and insisted that we should not attempt to overstate its explanatory capacities.[9] For Booth, it is the *experience* of the clarification that matters, the pleasure of making the discovery, not the content of the revelation. Process is all. Speaking of the first scene of *Twelfth Night*, he contends 'that to experience that scene is to be given a small but metaphysically glorious holiday from the limitations of the ordinary logic by which sentences determine what they will be understood to say, and that that holiday is a brief and trivial but effectively real holiday from the inherent limitation of the human mind'.[10] The artifice of the dramatic language ensures that we never entirely lose ourselves, that we recognize even as we watch that we are on holiday, and this double vision gives the spectator an immense sense of pleasure.

The Perils of Illusion

The unreliability and inadequacy of language have become familiar themes in Shakespeare studies, with much more critical attention paid to Shakespeare's suspicion of the word than to his celebration of it. This emphasis arises partly from the axiom that, artistically speaking, evil is usually more interesting than good. It may also follow from our own age's scepticism about the possibility of any genuine communication, doubts registered in literature by Samuel Beckett and Harold Pinter, in criticism by Jacques Derrida and other theorists. Many critics have yielded to the temptation to see in Shakespeare the radical kind of linguistic scepticism that would appear in the work of Thomas Hobbes in the middle of the seventeenth century; others go so far as to turn the Renaissance playwright into a proto-modernist who happened to anticipate our own (sensible) opinions by some four centuries.[11] We should not allow such ahistorical errors to go unchallenged. Neither should we accept the claim that, bound by the discursive restraints of his culture, Shakespeare uncritically shared the enthusiasm for language and its virtues exhibited by some of the humanist boosters of the English tongue. Nor, finally, should we mislead ourselves into believing that self-consciousness about the theatre made language his exclusive topic.

The plays indicate that Shakespeare thought seriously and subtly about a wide range of vast subjects—love, hate, death, theatre, beauty, heroism, evil, to name a few—and that he arrived at multiple and often contradictory views about all of them. It is reasonable to conclude that he thought intensely about the artistic materials he employed, the words which gave him his livelihood and which he lived with day after day. An appropriate analogy might be with the painter who never abandons his interest in representation, but whose fascination with the colours and textures of paints and brushes can seem to dominate his canvases so thoroughly as to occlude other subjects. And I believe that, without equating his views with our own, we may conclude that Shakespeare's fierce concentration on the instruments of his art led to grave anxiety about the infidelity and perversity of words (see Fig. 3). So pressing are these concerns that they seem to have induced in him a serious struggle, indeed a kind of professional crisis, over the uses and value of language, especially the language of the stage. The major tragedies pose the greatest challenge to any kind of linguistic security, and in them the playwright returns consistently to three specific faults of language: the futility and inadequacy of speech, particularly compared to deeds; the unreliability of the verbal sign and its consequent vulnerability to manipulation; and finally—the negative side of one of its principal virtues—its guilty role in the stimulation of dangerous illusion.

'Words, words, words': the phrase represents one of the central problems in *Hamlet*, the wordiest (i.e. the longest) of all Shakespeare's plays, a tragedy in which the hero's eloquence may also be one of his principal vices. The longstanding cultural axiom that assumes the inferiority of words to deeds is responsible for the familiar, oversimplified charge that Hamlet does not act, that he only talks. Shakespeare grasps the perils of this argument, of course, subverting it in the

No Heart can thinke, to what strange ends,
The Tongues *unruely* Motion *tends.*

3. Shakespeare's interest in the unreliability of the word was a concern he shared with his culture at large. This illustration from George Wither's *A Collection of Emblems* (1635, but based on a Dutch emblem book of ? 1611) depicts the perils of the wayward tongue. The Latin motto surrounding the image reads 'Where is your tongue taking you?'

reckless bravado of Laertes or the even more dangerous aggression of Fortinbras. But clearly he is disturbed by the potential futility and ineffectuality of words. So is Hamlet. Disgusted at his own hesitation, or caution, or passion for rightness, or whatever label it is assigned, he impugns his verbal brilliance with similes connoting waste and power-lessness. 'This is most brave', he says, contrasting his own behaviour with that of the player, 'That I ... | Must, like a whore, unpack my heart with words | And fall a-cursing like a very drab, | A scullion!' (2.2.585–6, 588–90). The bitter contrast opposes actor to prince, actor to non-actor, man to woman, hero to whore, action to language. For both Shakespeare and Hamlet, gender comes into play as well, in the cliché of the womanish wagging tongue; as an anonymous sixteenth-century poem puts it, 'Women are words, Men deeds.'[12] While Shakespeare does not subscribe unthinkingly to that position, Hamlet's metaphor of the foul-mouthed whore implies a sense of rage at the frailty of the word ('frailty, thy name is woman'), at having nothing more potent than words to combat the horrors of the world. King Lear's experience on the heath bespeaks a similar debility. His first speech commanding the elements to destroy the world (3.2.1–9), ferocious as it is, has no effect on the apparently heedless gods; the second instalment (3.2.14–24) seems feebler still, poetically conveying the theme of futility and frustration. Lear's self-inflicted loss of power is encoded in his speech, so that the vocabulary and syntax of madness which begin to dominate his speech introduce yet another variation on the inadequacies of the word.

If Hamlet and Lear lament the futility of language, Coriolanus feels contempt for its practical inadequacy, particularly its inferiority to feats of war: 'oft | When blows have made me stay I fled from words' (2.2.71–2). For the military hero, the courageous warrior who uses his arm rather than his tongue, words fail to capture the magnitude of his achievements. He objects to hearing a recital of his victory, claiming that he cannot bear to hear his 'nothings monstered'. When Coriolanus is urged to fulfil the expected ritual and ask the people directly for the consulship, he balks at the verbalizing of his desire. He mocks the citizens' 'voices', repeating the noun seven times in a single six-line speech (2.3.125–30). Later he identifies language with a 'harlot's spirit', imagines his 'throat of war' converted 'into a pipe | Small as an eunuch or the virgin voice | That babies lull asleep!' (3.2.112–15), thinks of words as no better than the tools of flatterers and mountebanks. Coriolanus conceives of all representation as misrepresentation, and while Shakespeare certainly challenges the validity of such an absolute view, he also considers it seriously in creating Coriolanus' most annoying adversaries, Sicinius and Brutus. These tribunes are the people's representatives, but their style of political representation involves mostly self-interest and envy, and language for them has no integrity at all. Evidence of the force of Shakespeare's linguistic doubts is that Hamlet and Coriolanus, probably Shakespeare's most and least appealing tragic figures, should share a discomfort with words and express their suspicions so eloquently.

Words are not merely poor substitutes for deeds but even at their best are unreliable and vulnerable to distortion. In the last of the romantic or festive comedies, the Clown announces the treachery of language when he says that 'words are very rascals', that they are 'grown...false' (*Twelfth Night*, 3.1.20, 23), and one aspect of this treachery is their capacity to mimic the benefits of language, to devastating effect. A great pleasure of language, one with which Shakespeare entertains his audience from his earliest plays, is the ironic discrepancy between a verbal sign and the context in which it appears: we might think of Petruccio's 'gentle Kate', or Orsino's addressing Viola as 'boy'. In tragedy, however, this incongruity turns sinister. A famous example of this characteristic of words is Shakespeare's repetition, in *Othello*, of the brutally ironic adjective, 'honest' Iago: in that form the phrase appears five times; several variations of it, each referring to Iago, recur some fifteen more times. The playwright could hardly do more to widen the gap between the name and the thing.

The wicked daughters in the first scene of *King Lear*, exploiting this gap, depend on their father's linguistic *naïveté*, his childish belief that meanings correspond to words. In fact the connection is much more complex, and the hazards of that relation are implicit in the structure and function of the pun. Having established that the semantic multiplicity associated with a single sound affords the audience intellectual exhilaration and momentary freedom, we are obliged to pursue the further implications of that effect. The trope allows not only duality but also duplicity. Coriolanus, arrogant and self-dedicated though he is, has a valid claim in condemning the people and their 'voices' for their 'uncertainty', their lack of integrity or unity.

> my soul aches
> To know, when two authorities are up,
> Neither supreme, how soon confusion
> May enter 'twixt the gap of both and take
> The one by th'other.
>
> (3.1.111–15)

In linguistic terms, this is an appropriate critique of the uncertainty of the signifier and also a useful definition of 'equivocation', speaking with two equal voices.

In *Macbeth*—the play in which 'equivocation' plays a demonic role—we see just how false words have become as Shakespeare imagines their corruption in the service of evil. Here Shakespeare searches into the dangers of verbal duplicity, particularly the consequences of trusting 'the equivocation of the fiend | That lies like truth' (5.5.41–2). Almost to the end of the play Macbeth is confident of his safety, since the witches have told him that he will be in no danger 'till Birnam Wood | Do come to Dunsinane' (5.5.42–3), and that 'none of woman born | Shall harm Macbeth' (4.1.196–7). But both of these prophecies are fulfilled equivocally; the puns prove to be lethal. Macbeth discovers the utility of unstable words to the forces of evil, those 'juggling fiends... | That palter with us in a double sense' (5.10.19–20). As I demonstrated in Chapter 7, the prominence of puns in *Macbeth* forces us to think dubiously about the intellectual risks of wordplay. Since the relation between sound and meaning is arbitrary, a verbal sign or word can have two meanings. But if a unit of sound signifies two distinct senses then it can surely signify more than two. Potentially, at least in theory, the same sound can generate an infinite number of meanings, and so the feature that produces the invigorating flexibility of language could also bring about semantic chaos. What might have been the transcendence of limits begins to look more like insecurity and even meaninglessness, a vast collection of sounds 'signifying nothing'.

The third liability of the word is also based on an inversion: if the stimulation of illusion is one of the greatest strengths of language, it is also one of its greatest threats. Illusion is the basis of all fiction, and an unflattering term for a fiction is a lie. The Puritans' recognition of this relation accounts in large part for their opposition to the stage, to images in worship, and to other forms of artistic representation. That illusion can beguile us into pleasurable imaginary realms also means that it can deceive and ensnare us. Many of the great Shakespearian villains, from Richard III to Iago to Goneril and Regan and Giacomo, are gifted liars. They appreciate the malleability of language, the affective power of images, the importance of context in the interpretation of a word, the usefulness of multiple senses, and their superior understanding confers upon them a kind of evil authority. Their innocent opponents, King Lear, Othello, and other naïfs, credit the illusion that words and performances should be kin. In a throwaway scene in *Othello*, Shakespeare foregrounds not only the uncertainty of the signifier but also the enormity of verbal illusion in that play. It is the exchange between Desdemona and the utterly unimportant Clown over 'where Lieutenant Cassio *lies*': 'I know not where he lodges, and for me to devise a lodging and say he lies here, or he lies there, were to lie in mine own throat' (3.4.11–13). Words are both untrustworthy and subject to perversion.

They are the tools of both the villain and the artist. Shakespeare's liars share much with their creator—the maker of fictions, manipulator of words, and master of his audience.

> APEMANTUS Art not a poet?
> POET Yes.
> APEMANTUS Then thou liest.
>
> (*Timon of Athens*, 1.1.223–5)

It seems clear that Shakespeare is reassessing the meaning and value of his medium, and indeed of his professional life in general. Several years earlier in *As You Like It* Touchstone had made a similar claim, that 'the truest poetry is the most feigning' (3.3.17–18), but the analogy between poet and pretender now seems oppressive, perhaps even debilitating. *Timon* ends with another notice of the relation between language and pain. Broken by the discovery of his friends' ingratitude, disillusioned with their flattery, a victim finally of empty promises, Timon retreats into a desert cave, leaving the stage with a curse: 'Lips, let four words go by, and language end' (5.2.105). Some scholars have argued that *Timon* seems unpolished, incomplete, a skeleton of a great play that might have been, and that Shakespeare's desperate view of communication accounts for his inability to finish it. Perhaps the playwright is contemplating the futility of his own words. But the end of language would be the end of the theatre, and despite his growing sense of impotence and fear of inevitable misrepresentation, Shakespeare continues to write.

A glance at the greatest of his liar-artists, Iago, confirms the vulnerability of language in the hands of a gifted illusionist. Shakespeare represents his extraordinary imaginative talent as a kind of negative creativity: Iago's 'I am not what I am', spoken to Roderigo in the opening scene (l. 66), is an evil parody of the Creator's 'I am that I am', from Exodus 3: 14. Sensitivity to the affective power of words and the importance of timing are crucial to the success of his hateful scheme to destroy Othello, and as his plot begins to take shape, he himself notes that its brilliance lies in the irony of its verbal patterning. While Cassio 'plies' or entreats her for help, Iago will 'pour... pestilence' about Desdemona and Cassio into Othello's ear: 'And by how much she strive to do him good | She shall undo her credit with the Moor' (2.3.349–50). Paradoxically, that is, the more Desdemona begs, the guiltier her pleas make her appear. Iago also recognizes the power of visual images and knows when to deploy them. Of all his tactics, these verbal pictures have an immediate and visceral effect:

> IAGO Would you, the supervisor, grossly gape on,
>   Behold her topped?
> OTHELLO   Death and damnation! O!
>
>   (3.3.400–1)

Later it is Iago's byplay on 'lie with her, on her, what you will' that triggers Othello's seizure. Such a sense of the well-timed word is characteristic of the wicked. Desdemona does not share it: her insistent pleading that Othello recall and pardon Cassio denotes an insensitivity to audience. Her innocence prevents her from recognizing Othello's unreceptive mood, and the more insistent she becomes, the more her words manage to 'undo her credit'.

Finally, Iago knows the value of a good story. In the tale we refer to as 'Cassio's dream', he confides to Othello that Cassio, while sleeping in the barracks, has murmured love talk to Desdemona in his sleep, and that then he would 'lay his leg o'er my thigh, | And sigh, and kiss, and then cry "Cursèd fate | That gave thee to the Moor"' (3.3.428–30). That narrative, among Iago's most effective weapons, is a virtuoso demonstration of the destructive effects of illusion. It may be worthwhile, however, to ask whether or not Iago's tale is indisputably fictional. We know that Iago uses whatever he finds, and we know that Cassio admires Desdemona ('She's a most exquisite lady'). Above all, the ontology of theatre makes it impossible to ascertain whether or not something like what Iago relates actually happened in the barracks. The play urges us to be wary of the uncertainties of language, insists on the difficulty of discriminating between truth and fiction. 'Cassio's dream' is almost certainly Iago's invention, but there is virtue in 'almost', and categorically to call it a lie is to simplify Shakespeare's complex presentation of the relation between language and truth.

Desdemona's father is wrong when he rejects the Duke's consolation by denying the power of language: 'But words are words. I never yet did hear | That the bruised heart was piercèd through the ear' (1.3.217–18). Words are considerably more than words. And the murderer in *Richard III* is mistaken in thinking that 'talkers are no good doers'. A look at one more twist in Shakespeare's thinking will suggest that if 'action is eloquence', to borrow Volumnia's phrase from *Coriolanus*, eloquence is also action.

The End

Although I have attempted to avoid constructing a neat chronological system, it is obvious that the comedies tend to promote the benefits of the word, while the tragedies expose its liabilities. The reader will also have noticed the infrequency of references to the late plays, *Pericles*, *Cymbeline*, *The Winter's Tale*, *The Tempest*, and then the two surviving collaborations, *Henry VIII, or All is True*, and *The Two Noble Kinsmen*. I have reserved discussion of these texts for two reasons. The first is that they disclose a vital development in Shakespeare's thinking about the compensatory powers of language, specifically theatrical language, and its place in the world. The second is that this expanded conception of speech brings into a new state of balance the competing strains of linguistic idealism and pessimism. I begin with the second of these points and then take up the first.

Shakespeare's late views of language can be approached with the help of two quotations. The first is by M. M. Mahood:

The world of words had once seemed to Shakespeare tragically incompatible with the world of things. Now he finds in the world built from Prospero's words of magic the truth of what we are. Belief in words is foremost among the lost things which are found again in Shakespeare's final comedies.[13]

The second is by Anne Barton:

Unlike M. M. Mahood, whose book *Shakespeare's Word-Play* I have otherwise found extremely illuminating, I cannot see the final romances as embodying a renewed faith in words after the scepticism of the tragedies.... Not even Prospero, the magician dramatist who orders this play-world, can bring about a true coherence of minds. He stands among characters sealed off in private worlds of experience, worlds which language is powerless to unite. It seems at least possible that *The Tempest* was Shakespeare's last non-collaborative play because in it he had reached a point in his investigation of the capabilities of words beyond which he found it difficult to proceed.[14]

Shakespeare scholars, like most academic critics, often disagree, but the stark opposition of these two views is unusual. Both the authors are distinguished critics with a particular commitment to the study of Shakespeare's language, their opinions were published within fifteen years of each other, and yet their responses to the same plays could hardly be more different. How can the contradiction be reconciled?

It is not the case, for once, that the proper interpretation lies somewhere between their two positions. I would contend, rather, that both Mahood's and Barton's arguments are right. Both critics are responding genuinely to stimuli and evidence inherent in the last plays. I have chosen these two passages because they convey very clearly the vigour with which each of Shakespeare's conflicting opinions emerges from this group of plays. Shakespeare's faith in language seems to have been fortified or renewed after the experience of writing the tragedies, the change that Mahood perceives; but this resurgence of confidence does not diminish the powerful scepticism that still characterizes much of his thinking, the emphasis to which Barton responds. One guide to understanding the disagreement is the name of the dramatic mode represented by most of these plays: tragicomedy. Each critic may be said to emphasize one half of the term.

Awareness of previously delineated vices still obtains in the late plays: humans use language for lying, slandering, deceiving others, and deluding themselves. Caliban learns to curse; *Pericles* begins with a grotesque and mystifying riddle about incest between father and daughter; in *Cymbeline* Giacomo slanders the chaste Innogen, which prompts her fiancé to a misogynistic outburst; Leontes in *The Winter's Tale* destroys his family by viciously accusing his innocent wife of infidelity, and in the same play the con-artist Autolycus bamboozles the country folk with 'true' ballads about fictitious events; the cagey Wolsey employs deceptive speech and indulges in a good bit of smug irony while 'serving' Henry VIII. Throughout these plays language is abused as often as it is used constructively. Moreover, the reunions and consequent joyful endings are more often a function of providential intervention or an outpouring of grace than a result of some verbally induced persuasion or clarification. In other words, the restoration of lost children and other such repeated actions do not come about because of language; they seem independent of it or even beyond expression.

But speech justifies itself despite its infirmities. Language may not be the primary means of reconciliation, but it serves as a way of marking the union or reunion, as a vehicle for identifying, understanding, and maintaining the links between people. Moreover, Shakespeare's artful arrangement of moving words is the engine that generates immense emotional and theatrical power. The events depicted are often extremely moving, and usually it is the form of expression that augments the emotional effect. Interestingly, many such moments depend for their effect on simplicity of statement. A good example would be Hermione's defence against her husband's charges of adultery.

> Since what I am to say must be but that
> Which contradicts my accusation, and
> The testimony on my part no other
> But what comes from myself, it shall scarce boot me
> To say 'Not guilty'.
>
> (*The Winter's Tale*, 3.2.21–5)

This passage is unusually pertinent because Hermione flatly declares the futility of speech, admits her inability to *say* anything that will have any practical effect. Ironically, of course, the lines do have a practical effect—on the audience—and the plainness of expression, especially in contrast to the tortuous syntax of her husband, largely accounts for its affective power.

The emotional charge is frequently released at the moment of reunion, and while there may be a striking image or some other rhetorical flourish, most of these climaxes also depend upon economy of means.

Posthumus to Innogen:

> *She throws her arms about his neck*
> Hang there like fruit, my soul,
> Till the tree die.
>
> (*Cymbeline*, 5.6.263–4)

Leontes, about Hermione:

> O, she's warm!
>
> (*The Winter's Tale*, 5.3.109)

Palamon to Arcite:

> I am Palamon,
> One that yet loves thee dying.
>
> (*The Two Noble Kinsmen*, 5.6.89–90)

It is as if Shakespeare is replaying some of the methods of the tragedies, notably the distillation of meaning apparent in Cordelia's speech. And keeping in mind the notion of naming as a subspecies of all language, a point discussed in connection with *Romeo and Juliet*, we may also recall that many instances of verbal power in the last plays derive from the speaking of a name. The most memorable, and one of the most moving, is the single line that crowns the recognition between father and daughter in the last act of *Pericles*. 'My name is Marina.'[15] The restoration of the lost may be the most urgent emotional force in the romances, and their existence depends upon Shakespeare's having recovered his balance in the way he thinks about language.

Or maybe the change occurred the other way around. Instead of suggesting that a re-evaluation of the word is responsible for Shakespeare's turn to tragicomedy, perhaps we should say that, whatever considerations led him to adopt the new mode—commerce? fashion? novelty? collegiality? maturation?—it was the experience of telling tragicomic stories that prompted him to revise his sense of language. In either case, the artistic ramifications of this rehabilitated (or at least broadened) viewpoint are so great because his evaluation of language is intimately tied to his sense of his own professional status. The commitment to the tragicomic mode signifies a belief in the capacity of words to create an alternative realm of experience. Language, whatever else it may be, has become an instrument for constructing a harmonious, protected realm within a bare and hostile world.

This theatrical world of words is now seen not only as a form for reflecting experience but as a vehicle for creating reality. In the tragedies, the most valuable property of language was implicit in the dramatic experience: the existence of the play amounts to a triumphant exposure of the limitations of language. In the late plays, Shakespeare makes this implicit value explicit so that *awareness* of the expository and affective functions of the words is made a central feature of the dramatic experience. Hence the flagrant self-consciousness apparent in the last scene of *Cymbeline*, or in Prospero's wedding masque in *The Tempest*. The playwright seems eager to declare his conviction that artistically controlled language adds pleasure to the actual world and is therefore as legitimate an element of that world as any of its natural phenomena. He encourages us to see the Globe not merely as a representation of the globe but as a smaller, working version of it.

The last plays reward the audience by temporarily granting wishes that the conditions of mortality normally forbid. Lost children are found, a dead wife is returned to her penitent husband, disastrous political errors are forgiven and amended, all in defiance of the rules of human experience. Language permits these impossible joys a momentary reality, and Shakespeare 'not only does not try to conceal, he positively emphasizes the fact that his material is the archetypal stuff of legend and fairy-tale'.[16] As beautiful as the end of *The Winter's Tale* may be, its distance from what *is* can be discouraging as well as uplifting. A double vision is required of the audience: we are invited to lose ourselves in the virtual world, but at the same time are reminded of its fragility and temporal brevity. This double vision also corresponds to the positive and negative assessments of language that seem to stand in perfect poise throughout this last phase. Ultimately the virtual world is merely verbal; but then the actual world is merely physical.

INTRODUCTION

1. Sigurd Burckhardt, *Shakespearean Meanings* (Princeton: Princeton University Press, 1968), 24.
2. Patricia Parker, *Shakespeare from the Margins: Language, Culture, Context* (Chicago: University of Chicago Press, 1995), 3. Also see her *Literary Fat Ladies: Rhetoric, Gender, Property* (London: Methuen, 1987).
3. *Shakespeare from the Margins*, 1.
4. *Shakespearean Negotiations* (Oxford: Oxford University Press, 1988), 4.
5. *Shakespearean Meanings*, 28.
6. George T. Wright, *Shakespeare's Metrical Art* (Berkeley and Los Angeles: University of California Press, 1988), 258–9. For much of the material in this paragraph (and elsewhere in this book) I am deeply indebted to Wright's extraordinary stylistic study.
7. 'Certain Notes of Instruction on the Making of Verse', in Brian Vickers (ed.) *English Renaissance Literary Criticism* (Oxford: Clarendon Press, 1999), 162 (there retitled 'A Primer of English Poetry').

CHAPTER I. THE LANGUAGE SHAKESPEARE LEARNED

1. Quoted in Richard Foster Jones, *The Triumph of the English Language* (Stanford, Calif.: Stanford University Press, 1953), 17. I have retained the original spelling in this and a few other quotations in this chapter to give a flavour of the original. The lack of standardized spelling is one of the prominent features of sixteenth-century English and an important element of its perceived crudeness, especially compared to the fixed spelling of the classical languages.
2. For many of these examples and ideas I have relied on chapters I and II of Jones's *Triumph of the English Language*.
3. *The Worckes of Thomas Becon* (London, 1564), fo. 475^v.
4. *The First Part of the Elementarie which Entreateth Chefelie of the Right Writing of our English Tung, Set Furth by Richard Mulcaster* (London, 1582), 254.
5. Ibid..
6. George Gascoigne, 'Certain Notes of Instruction on the Making of Verse', in Brian Vickers (ed.), *English Renaissance Literary Criticism* (Oxford: Clarendon Press, 1999), 166 (there retitled 'A Primer of English Poetry').

7. *The Arte of Reason, Rightly Termed, Witcraft, Teaching a Perfect Way to Argue and Dispute* (London, 1573), especially books II and IV. Charles Barber, *Early Modern English*, 2nd edn. (Edinburgh: Edinburgh University Press, 1997), 63–4, provides helpful commentary on the controversy.

8. Bryan A. Garner, 'Shakespeare's Latinate Neologisms', in Vivian Salmon and Edwina Burness (eds.), *A Reader in the Language of Shakespearean Drama* (Amsterdam: John Benjamins, 1987), 209.

9. Thomas Digges, *A Geometrical Practical Treatize Named Pantometria* (1571/91), quoted in Jones, *Triumph of the English Language*, 76.

10. Thomas Wilson, *The Arte of Rhetoric (1560)*, ed. with notes and commentary by Peter E. Medine (University Park: Pennsylvania State University Press, 1994), 189.

11. For more complete and specific discussion and illustration of verb endings, see Barber's *Early Modern English*, 164–8, to which I am much indebted.

12. 'Certain Notes of Instruction', 168.

13. *The Motives of Eloquence: Literary Rhetoric in the Renaissance* (New Haven: Yale University Press, 1976), 2.

14. George Puttenham, *The Arte of English Poesie*, ed. Gladys Doidge Willcocks and Alice Walker (Cambridge: Cambridge University Press, 1936), 298–302.

15. *Pierce's Supererogation* (1593) in Smith (ed.), *Elizabethan Critical Essays*, ii. 277.

16. *The Art of Rhetoric*, 43.

17. *Poems and 'A Defence of Ryme'*, ed. Arthur Colby Sprague (Cambridge, Mass.: Harvard University Press, 1930), ll. 939–50.

18. *The Art of Rhetoric*, 147–8.

19. The most useful modern guide to such terms is Richard Lanham's *A Handlist of Rhetorical Terms* (Berkeley and Los Angeles: University of California Press, 1968).

20. *On Copia of Words and Ideas*, trans. Donald B. King and H. David Rix (Milwaukee: Marquette University Press, 1963), 16–17.

21. Richard Sherry, *Treatise of the Figures of Grammar and Rhetoric* (London, 1555), fos. 57^v and 58^r.

22. Lanham, *The Motives of Eloquence*, 7.

23. *The Emperor of Men's Minds: Literature and the Discourse of Rhetoric* (Ithaca, NY: Cornell University Press, 1995), 15.

CHAPTER 2.   SHAPING THE LANGUAGE

1. 'Shakespeare's Language and the Language of Shakespeare's Time', *Shakespeare Survey 50* (1997), 1.

2. *The Complete Works of Christopher Marlowe: Tamburlaine the Great, Parts 1 and 2*, ed. David Fuller (Oxford: Clarendon Press, 1998). I have modernized the spelling.

3. 'Shakespeare and the Arts of Language', in *The Cambridge Companion to Shakespeare Studies* (Cambridge: Cambridge University Press, 1986), 63.

4. *Palladis Tamia: Wit's Treasury* (1598).

5. The anonymous overstater is mentioned by Bryan Garner, 'Shakespeare's Latinate Neologisms', in Vivian Salmon and Edwina Burness (eds.), *A Reader in the Language of Shakespearean Drama* (Amsterdam: John Benjamins, 1987), 209–11. For much of the material on this topic I have relied on Garner's helpful article.

6. Ibid. 216–25.

7. Jane Donawerth, *Shakespeare and the Sixteenth-Century Study of Language* (Urbana: University of Illinois Press, 1984), 4–5; see also Judith Anderson, *Words that Matter: Linguistic Perception in Renaissance English* (Stanford, Calif.: Stanford University Press, 1996), 2–3, 230 1.

8. 'Shakespeare's Use of Rhetoric', in *A New Companion to Shakespeare Studies* (Cambridge: Cambridge University Press, 1971), 86.

9. Sister Miriam Joseph, *Shakespeare's Use of the Arts of Language* (New York: Columbia University Press, 1947); Brian Vickers, *In Defence of Rhetoric* (Oxford: Oxford University Press, 1989); Peter G. Platt, 'Shakespeare and Rhetorical Culture', in David Scott Kastan (ed.), *A Companion to Shakespeare* (Oxford: Blackwell, 1999), 277–96.

10. S. T. Coleridge, *Shakespearean Criticism*, ed. T. M. Raysor (London: J. W. Dent, 1960), i. 86.

11. *Shakespeare's Universe of Discourse: Language Games in the Comedies* (Cambridge: Cambridge University Press, 1984), 242.

12. Wayne A. Rebhorn, *The Emperor of Men's Minds: Literature and the Discourse of Rhetoric* (Ithaca, NY: Cornell University Press, 1995), 57.

13. 'On the Value of *Hamlet*', in Norman Rabkin (ed.), *Reinterpretations of Elizabethan Drama* (New York: Columbia University Press, 1969), 149.

14. See Platt, 'Shakespeare and Rhetorical Culture', 278.

15. Rebhorn, *The Emperor of Men's Minds*, 14.

CHAPTER 3.   WHAT IS THE FIGURE?

1. The facsimile is reproduced in Caroline Spurgeon, *Keats's Shakespeare* (Oxford: Oxford University Press, 1928; repr. 1966), 28–9.

2. To John Hamilton Reynolds, 3 Feb. 1818, in *The Letters of John Keats*, ed. Hyder Rollins (Cambridge, Mass.: Harvard University Press, 1958), i. 223.

3. *Preface to 'Troilus and Cressida'*, in *The Works of John Dryden*, ed. Alan Roper and Vinton Dearing (Berkeley and Los Angeles: University of California Press, 1984), xiii. 225.
4. 'Prefaces, Biographical and Critical, to the Works of the English Poets', in *Samuel Johnson*, ed. Donald Grene, Oxford Standard Authors (Oxford: Oxford University Press, 1984), 690.
5. Terence Hawkes, *Metaphor* (London: Methuen, 1972), 60.
6. *Shakespearean Meanings* (Princeton: Princeton University Press, 1968), 24.
7. For an informed and sophisticated analysis of these Renaissance views, see Anne Ferry, *The Art of Naming* (Chicago: University of Chicago Press, 1988), especially chapter 3.
8. John Hoskins, *Directions for Speech and Style*, ed. Hoyt H. Hudson (Princeton: Princeton University Press, 1935), 8.
9. *The Art of Naming*, 95.
10. *The Philosophy of Rhetoric* (Oxford: Oxford University Press, 1936), 95 ff.
11. *More than Cool Reason* (Chicago: University of Chicago Press, 1989), chapter 1.
12. *The Garden of Eloquence* (London, 1593), 23–4.
13. Preface to *Lyrical Ballads* (1800), in *The Prose Works of William Wordsworth*, ed. W. J. B. Owen and Jane Worthington Smyser (Oxford: Clarendon Press, 1974), 148.
14. R. A. Foakes, 'Poetic Language and Dramatic Significance', in Philip Edwards, Inga-Stina Ewbank, and G. K. Hunter (eds.), *Shakespeare's Styles* (Cambridge: Cambridge University Press, 1980), 82.
15. Thomas McLaughlin, 'Figuration', in Frank Lentricchia and Thomas McLaughlin (eds.), *Critical Terms for Literary Study* (Chicago: University of Chicago Press, 1990), 88.

CHAPTER 4. A WORLD OF FIGURES

1. (Cambridge: Cambridge University Press, 1935), 204. Spurgeon also sought to use the identification of strains of imagery in deciding questions of authorship in disputed texts.
2. *The Development of Shakespeare's Imagery* (Cambridge, Mass.: Harvard University Press, 1951). The book was originally published in German, as *Shakespeares Bilder*, in 1936.
3. Brooks's essay was published first as 'Shakespeare as a Symbolist Poet' in the *Yale Review*, 34 (1944–5), 642–65. I quote from the version reprinted as 'The Naked Babe and the Cloak of Manliness' in Brooks's *The Well-Wrought Urn* (New York: Harcourt, Brace & World, 1947). The quotations appear, respectively, on p. 35 and p. 23 of that book.

4. (Princeton: Princeton University Press, 1969). The quotations are on p. 6 and p. 5.

5. 'The Naked New Born Babe and the Cloak of Manliness'. See n. 3.

6. The classic treatment is that of Anne Righter (Barton), *Shakespeare and the Idea of the Play* (London: Chatto & Windus, 1962).

7. See George Lakoff and Mark Turner, *More Than Cool Reason* (Chicago: University of Chicago Press, 1990), chapter 1, for a treatment of hidden metaphors.

8. *Structure and Society in Literary History* (Charlottesville: University of Virginia Press, 1975), 195.

9. See Thomas McLaughlin, 'Figuration', in Frank Lentricchia and Thomas McLaughlin (eds.), *Critical Terms for Literary Study* (Chicago: University of Chicago Press, 1990), 84 for a discussion of words with 'histories' and the contribution of such associations to poetic power.

10. James R. Siemon, *Shakespearean Iconoclasm* (Berkeley and Los Angeles: University of California Press, 1985), 14. Siemon conducts a detailed and persuasive analysis of Brutus' speech, pp. 153–7.

11. Barbara Lewalski, *Protestant Poetics and the Seventeenth-Century Religious Lyric* (Princeton: Princeton University Press, 1979), 78.

12. See Louis Montrose, *The Purposes of Playing* (Chicago: University of Chicago Press, 1996).

13. Quoted in Keir Elam, *Shakespeare's Universe of Discourse* (Cambridge: Cambridge University Press, 1984), 299.

14. See particularly Annabel Patterson, *Shakespeare and the Popular Voice* (Oxford: Basil Blackwell, 1989), 120–53.

CHAPTER 5.   LOOSENING THE LINE

1. George T. Wright, *Shakespeare's Metrical Art* (Berkeley and Los Angeles: University of California Press, 1988), 48–9.

2. *A History of English Prosody from the Twelfth Century to the Present Day*, 3 vols. (London: Macmillan, 1906), ii. 6.

3. *The Making of Shakespeare's Dramatic Poetry* (Toronto: University of Toronto Press, 1981), 62.

4. In line 286 I depart from the Oxford text to accept the proposed emendation of 'low' for 'love' on the grounds that the pun in the next line ('loathes') indicates a compositor's misreading of 'love' for the authorial 'low'.

5. Granting the uncertain status of punctuation in early printed texts, I here depart from the modernized text to present the passage as it seems to have been aurally perceived by contemporary audiences, as represented by the work of either a scribe or compositor.

6. *Shakespeare's Apprenticeship* (Chicago: University of Chicago Press, 1974), 230.

7. 'Rabbits, Ducks, and *Henry V* ', *Shakespeare Quarterly*, 28 (1977), 279–96, repr. in *Shakespeare and the Problem of Meaning* (Chicago: University of Chicago Press, 1981).

8. See especially Lytton Strachey's declaration that Shakespeare was 'bored with people, bored with real life, bored with drama, bored, in fact, with everything except poetry and poetical dreams', in 'Shakespeare's Final Period', in *Books and Characters* (New York: Harcourt Brace, 1922), 64; and James Sutherland's belief that the irregularities come from '[s]peed, . . . an increasing impatience to get the thing down on the paper, with a consequent danger of confusion, and an interesting tendency to be satisfied with a sort of impressionism', in 'The Language of the Last Plays', in John Garrett (ed.), *More Talking of Shakespeare* (New York: Theatre Arts Books, 1959), 147.

9. See Wright, *Shakespeare's Metrical Art*, 220.

10. See Anne Barton, 'Leontes and the Spider', in *Essays, Mainly Shakespearian* (Cambridge: Cambridge University Press, 1994), 161–81. Barton mainly discusses asymmetries of syntax rather than rhythm, but her remarks are helpful in explaining the imbalance and originality of the style after 1608 or so.

CHAPTER 6.   HERE FOLLOWS PROSE

1. See R. W. David, 'Shakespeare and the Players,' *Proceedings of the British Academy*, 47 (1961), 139–59.

2. *Euphues: The Anatomy of Wit*, in Paul Salzman, *An Anthology of Elizabethan Prose Fiction* (New York: Oxford University Press, 1987), 98.

3. 'Of Truth', in *The Essayes or Counsels, Civill and Morall*, ed. Michael Kiernan (Cambridge, Mass.: Harvard University Press, 1985), 8–9. I have modernized the spelling.

4. *Ben Jonson and the Language of Prose Comedy* (New York: Norton, 1970), 23.

5. *Richard II* is an exception, and its relatively early date (*c*.1595) separates it from the rest of the tetralogy: most of its characters are associated with the court, and even the extended scene with the gardeners is spoken in verse.

6. Barish, *Ben Jonson and the Language of Prose Comedy*, 31.

7. *The Arte of English Poesie*, ed. Gladys Doidge Willcocks and Alice Walker (Cambridge: Cambridge University Press, 1936), 201–2.

8. For a fascinating analysis of the rhetorical implications of Shallow's language, see Patricia Parker, *Literary Fat Ladies* (London: Methuen, 1987), 70–2.

9. For more specific commentary on the particulars of Shakespeare's parodic style, see the notes to the Arden edition of *Love's Labour's Lost* by Richard David (London: Methuen, 1951), and the more recent Arden edition by H. R. Woudhuysen (London: Thomas Nelson, 1998).
10. See Brian Vickers, *The Artistry of Shakespeare's Prose* (London: Methuen, 1968), 241–5, for a thorough analysis of the complexities of this speech.
11. Ibid. 61.

CHAPTER 7. DOUBLE TALK

1. Sonnet 138 is positioned among a group of poems in which wordplay insistently advertises itself, notably the famous 'will' sonnets, nos. 135 and 136, in which the poet exploits with dazzling ingenuity the various meanings of the apparently innocent signifier. In addition to the obvious 'wish', 'desire', and the auxiliary for 'intention', there are also the more arcane (to us) sexual uses of the word: to the early modern ear, the word 'will' could also designate the penis, the vagina, or specifically sexual desire. And this is not to mention the most brilliant and extended verbal joke, the play on the poet's first name.
2. Book 7.9. *The Institutio Oratoria of Quintilian, with an English Translation by H. E. Butler*, 4 vols. (London: William Heinemann, 1921), iii. 153.
3. *The Arte of English Poesie*, ed. Gladys Doidge Willcocks and Alice Walker (Cambridge: Cambridge University Press, 1936), 207.
4. *Shakespeare's Wordplay* (1957; repr. London: Routledge, 1980), 19.
5. Catherine Bates, 'The Point of Puns', *Modern Philology*, 96 (1999), 424.
6. *The Norton Anthology of English Literature* (New York: W. W. Norton, 1986), i. 2413.
7. 'The Play of Puns in Late Middle English Poetry: Concerning Juxtology', in Jonathan Culler (ed.), *On Puns: The Foundation of Letters* (Oxford: Blackwell, 1988), 53.
8. Coppélia Kahn, 'Coming of Age in Verona', in Carolyn Ruth Swift Lenz, Gayle Greene, and Carol Thomas Neely (eds.), *The Woman's Part: Feminist Criticism of Shakespeare* (Urbana: University of Illinois Press, 1980), 173–91.
9. Readers interested in this topic should consult Gordon Williams, *A Glossary of Shakespeare's Sexual Language* (London: Athlone Press, 1997).
10. Thomas Greene, *The Light in Troy* (New Haven: Yale University Press, 1988), 11.
11. See Mahood, *Shakespeare's Wordplay*, 130.
12. 'Shakespeare's Language and the Language of Shakespeare's Time', *Shakespeare Survey 50* (1998), 5.

13. Patricia Parker, *Shakespeare from the Margins* (Chicago: University of Chicago Press, 1996), 1.
14. 'The Call of the Phoneme', in Culler (ed.), *On Puns*, 8.

CHAPTER 8. WORDS EFFECTUAL, SPEECH UNABLE

1. *The Art of Shakespeare's Sonnets* (Cambridge, Mass.: Harvard University Press, 1997), 33.
2. The probable sense of 'she hath the prettiest sententiousness of it' is: 'she makes the prettiest sentences out of those two words.'
3. Anne Barton makes this point about repetition in *King Lear* in her very pertinent essay 'Shakespeare and the Limits of Language', published first in *Shakespeare Survey 24* (1971) and reprinted in her *Essays, Mainly Shakespearian* (Cambridge: Cambridge University Press, 1994), 51–69.
4. This excerpt is from the preface to his translation of the Italian poet Ariosto, printed as *A Brief Apology for Poetry* in G. Gregory Smith (ed.), *Elizabethan Critical Essays* (Oxford: Clarendon Press, 1904), ii. 208.
5. *Observations in the Art of English Poesie* (1602), in Smith (ed.), *Elizabethan Critical Essays*, ii. 329.
6. Ibid. 327.
7. 'The Argument of Comedy', *English Institute Essays 1948* (1949), 58–73.
8. *Precious Nonsense: The Gettysburg Address, Ben Jonson's Epitaphs on his Children, and 'Twelfth Night'* (Berkeley and Los Angeles: University of California Press, 1998), *passim*.
9. For an illuminating discussion of Wittgenstein and his attempts to come to terms with Shakespeare, see Jonathan Bate, *The Genius of Shakespeare* (Oxford: Oxford University Press, 1998), 319–23.
10. *Precious Nonsense*, 122–3.
11. For a critique of such proleptic arguments, see Margreta De Grazia, 'Shakespeare's View of Language: An Historical Perspective', *Shakespeare Quarterly*, 29 (1978), 374–88.
12. The poem is from *Howell's Devises 1581, with an Introduction by Walter Raleigh* (Oxford: Clarendon Press, 1906), 31.
13. M. M. Mahood, *Shakespeare's Wordplay* (London: Methuen, 1957; repr. London: Routledge, 1988), 188.
14. 'Shakespeare and the Limits of Language', 66 and 69.
15. For an excellent analysis of this economical strategy, see Inga-Stina Ewbank, ' "My Name is Marina": The Language of Recognition', in Philip Edwards, Inga-Stina Ewbank, and G. K. Hunter (eds.), *Shakespeare's Styles: Essays in Honour of Kenneth Muir* (Cambridge: Cambridge

University Press, 1980). In citing the sentence I have departed from the Oxford text in favour of the reading of the 1609 quarto.

16. Anne Barton, 'Leontes and the Spider: Language and Speaker in Shakespeare's Last Plays', in *Essays, Mainly Shakespearian*, 180.

REFERENCE WORKS

The Oxford English Dictionary is probably the single most useful tool for studying Shakespeare's language; it is now available in an electronic version. Also invaluable are such general works as Alex Preminger (ed.), Frank J. Warnke and O.B. Hardison, Jr. (assoc. eds.), *The Princeton Encyclopedia of Poetry and Poetics* (Princeton: Princeton University Press, 1996), and Frank Lentricchia and Thomas McLaughlin (eds.), *Critical Terms for Literary Study* (Chicago: University of Chicago Press, 1990). Stephen Booth's edition of the *Sonnets* (New Haven: Yale University Press, 1977) has hundreds of pages of helpful notes, with a multitude of contemporary examples. Essential reference books concerned specifically with Shakespeare are C. T. Onions, *A Shakespeare Glossary*, enlarged and revised by Robert D. Eagleson (Oxford: Clarendon Press, 1986) and, although it is well over a century old, E. A. Abbott's *A Shakespearian Grammar; an Attempt to Illustrate Some of the Differences between Elizabethan and Modern English. For the Use of Schools* (London: Macmillan, 1870; repr. New York: Haskell House, 1966). Gordon Williams's *A Glossary of Shakespeare's Sexual Language* (London: Athlone Press, 1997), a redaction of a three-volume set covering all of Renaissance drama, is now the standard work, replacing Eric Partridge's *Shakespeare's Bawdy* (London: Routledge & Kegan Paul, 1955), still an entertaining book.

N. F. Blake's *Shakespeare's Language: An Introduction* is an uncommonly readable survey of such linguistic features as grammar, syntax, pronouns, and verb forms. The anthology of articles (all previously published) called *A Reader in the Language of Shakespearean Drama*, ed. Vivian Salmon and Edwina Burness (Amsterdam: John Benjamins, 1987), contains a number of pieces on technical linguistic matters, but also collects useful pieces on more general topics (e.g. Anne Barton's 'Shakespeare and the Limits of Language'). Volumes 7, 24, and 50 of *Shakespeare Survey* concentrate chiefly on language and interpretation and contain several admirable pieces by distinguished scholars.

A succinct summary of many interpretative issues raised by language study is Inga-Stina Ewbank, 'Shakespeare and the Arts of Language', in Stanley Wells's *The Cambridge Companion to Shakespeare Studies* (Cambridge: Cambridge University Press, 1986), 49–66. General works treating language as a route to thematic analysis include B. Ifor Evans's *The Language of Shakespeare's*

Plays (London: Methuen, 1952) and F. E. Halliday's *The Poetry of Shakespeare's Plays* (London: Duckworth, 1964). Madeleine Doran's *Shakespeare's Dramatic Language* (Madison: University of Wisconsin Press, 1976) is organized so as to give a chapter each to several major plays. G. R. Hibbard's *The Making of Shakespeare's Dramatic Poetry* (Toronto: University of Toronto Press, 1981) examines the uses of language in the first ten plays or so, particularly the early histories. Keir Elam's *Shakespeare's Universe of Discourse: Language Games in the Comedies* (Cambridge: Cambridge University Press, 1984), uses *Love's Labour's Lost* and other comedies as a way of understanding Elizabethan ideas of discourse and helpfully relates that thinking to modern theory. As for tragedy, Lawrence Danson's *Tragic Alphabet* (New Haven: Yale University Press, 1974) considers the particular speech patterns of the tragic heroes. Many fine critics practise their reading skills on particular passages—and, in the best pieces, move impressively beyond the passage—in Philip Edwards, Inga-Stina Ewbank, and G. K. Hunter (eds.), *Shakespeare's Styles* (Cambridge: Cambridge University Press, 1980), Anne Barton's *Essays, Mostly Shakespearian* (Cambridge: Cambridge University Press, 1994) collects a number of essential essays (particularly 'Leontes and the Spider: Speaker and Language in the Last Plays' and 'Shakespeare and the Limits of Language').

EARLY MODERN LANGUAGE AND RHETORIC

For decades the standard work on the emergence of English from the Middle Ages to the eighteenth century was R. F. Jones's *The Triumph of the English Language* (Palo Alto, Calif.: Stanford University Press, 1953). Charles Barber's *Early Modern English*, 2nd edn. (Edinburgh: Edinburgh University Press, 1997) offers a more recent approach to many of the same problems, and does so thoroughly and with admirable clarity. Also helpful with many linguistic particulars is *A Reader in the Language of Shakespearean Drama*, mentioned above. Helge Kökeritz, *Shakespeare's Pronunciation* (New Haven: Yale University Press, 1959), is not considered invariably reliable, but provides a comprehensive treatment of the subject. Wayne Rebhorn's *The Emperor of Men's Minds: Literature and the Renaissance Discourse of Rhetoric* (Ithaca, NY: Cornell University Press, 1995) is a clear and ambitious survey of early modern theoretical issues, with a healthy emphasis on continental sources. His *Renaissance Debates on Rhetoric* (Ithaca, NY: Cornell University Press, 2000), an anthology of primary sources—polemics, essays, and dialogues—is a welcome collection of material. One of the most stimulating studies of early modern thought about language is Richard Lanham's *The Motives of Eloquence: Literary Rhetoric in the Renaissance* (New Haven: Yale University Press, 1976). Also, his *A Handlist of Rhetorical Terms* (Berkeley and Los Angeles: University of

California Press, 1968) is an indispensable tool for dealing with the nomen-
clature of tropes and schemes, and it is nicely cross-indexed. Also worth noting
are Sister Miriam Joseph, *Shakespeare's Use of the Arts of Language* (New York:
Columbia University Press, 1947); Brian Vickers, *In Defence of Rhetoric*
(Oxford: Oxford University Press, 1989); and Peter G. Platt, 'Shakespeare
and Rhetorical Culture', in David Scott Kastan (ed.), *A Companion to Shakespeare* (Oxford: Blackwell, 1999).

For examples of early modern commentary about language and poetry, the
basic text is now Brian Vickers's *English Renaissance Literary Criticism*
(Oxford: Clarendon Press, 1999), which supplants the two-volume G. Gregory Smith (ed.), *Elizabethan Critical Essays* (Oxford: Clarendon Press, 1904).
Renaissance attitudes to language are surveyed in Jane Donawerth, *Shakespeare
and the Sixteenth-Century Study of Language* (Urbana: University of Illinois
Press, 1984), the first chapter of which is especially helpful. Some analytical
works that seek to bridge the distance between Tudor-Stuart thinking about
language and modern theories of discourse include Anne Ferry's *The Art of
Naming* (Chicago: University of Chicago Press, 1988), much of which is
devoted to Spenser, and Judith Anderson, *Words that Matter: Linguistic Perception in Renaissance English* (Stanford, Calif.: Stanford University Press, 1996).

VERSE AND PROSE

The authoritative study of Shakespeare's verse is George T. Wright's *Shakespeare's Metrical Art* (Berkeley and Los Angeles: University of California Press,
1988): Wright is both sensible about technical matters—there is none of the
rigidity that damages other studies—and able to move easily to the semantic
implications of metre. The notes and index are also uncommonly informative.
A good general introduction to the sounds of verse and their functions is Paul
Fussell's *Poetic Meter and Poetic Form* (New York: Random House, rev. edn.
1979). In George Saintsbury's *A History of English Prosody from the Twelfth
Century to the Present Day*, 3 vols. (London: Macmillan, 1906–10), the 'present
day' is the end of the nineteenth century, but the analyses are still fascinating,
and Shakespeare's metrical habits are treated in historical context. Other
critics have written helpfully about prosody here and there: see James Sutherland, 'The Language of the Last Plays', in John Garrett (ed.), *More Talking of
Shakespeare* (New York: Theatre Arts Books, 1959); O. B. Hardison, Jr., 'Blank
Verse before Milton', *Studies in Philology*, 81 (1984), 253–74; and Derek
Attridge, *The Rhythms of English Poetry* (London: Longman, 1982). The major
modern study of Shakespeare's prose is Brian Vickers's *The Artistry of Shakespeare's Prose* (London: Methuen, 1968). For a brilliant analysis of Shakespearian syntax, especially as it contrasts with that of his main theatrical rival, see

Jonas Barish's *Ben Jonson and the Language of Prose Comedy* (New York: Norton, repr. 1970), especially chapter 2, 'Prose as Prose'.

IMAGERY, METAPHOR, SYMBOL

Since much of the New Criticism was concerned with imagery, there is no shortage of material on the subject. Caroline Spurgeon, *Shakespeare's Imagery and What it Tells Us* (Cambridge: Cambridge University Press, 1935) set the terms of the modern discussion; her arguments were modified and improved by Wolfgang Clemen in *The Development of Shakespeare's Imagery* (Cambridge, Mass.: Harvard University Press, 1951; originally published in German, as *Shakespeares Bilder*, in 1936). Other important studies include I. A. Richards's *The Philosophy of Rhetoric* (Oxford: Oxford University Press, 1936) and Cleanth Brooks's *The Well-Wrought Urn* (New York: Harcourt, Brace & World, 1947). Almost any of Kenneth Burke's books, e.g. *The Philosophy of Literary Form* (Baton Rouge, La.: LSU Press, 1941) contains pertinent and rewarding commentary. More recent work on figurative language has tilted towards philosophy and psychology, in accord with other recent research into the origins and significational powers of language. Terence Hawkes's *Metaphor* (London: Methuen, 1972) is a trenchant introduction to some of these issues. A more popular approach that links figuration to forms of everyday speech is found in George Lakoff and Mark Turner's *More than Cool Reason* (Chicago: University of Chicago Press, 1989). A persuasive (though challenging) analysis of metaphoric language from a materialist perspective is Robert Weimann's 'Shakespeare and the Study of Metaphor', *New Literary History*, 6 (1974), 149–67; it is reprinted in Weimann's *Structure and Society in Literary History* (Charlottesville: University of Virginia Press, 1975).

WORDPLAY

The study of puns in the twentieth century begins with William Empson, first in *Seven Types of Ambiguity* (London: Chatto & Windus, 1949) and later in *The Structure of Complex Words* (London: Chatto & Windus, 1951): Shakespeare plays a large role in the second. Kenneth Muir's 'The Uncomic Pun', *Cambridge Journal*, 3 (1950), 472–85 succinctly articulates Renaissance views of wordplay that may seem foreign to us; these views are acutely considered at greater length in M. M. Mahood's *Shakespeare's Wordplay* (London: Methuen, 1957). More recent contributions, both excellent, are by Catherine Bates, 'The Point of Puns', *Modern Philology*, 96 (1999), 1–22, and Stephen Booth, 'Shakespeare's Language and the Language of Shakespeare's Time', *Shakespeare Survey* 50 (1997), 1–17.

In the past three decades, post-structuralist thinking about the instability of language has prompted a healthy reconsideration of the pun. Some of the most stimulating work has been done by Patricia Parker in *Literary Fat Ladies* (London: Methuen, 1987) and *Shakespeare from the Margins* (Chicago: University of Chicago Press, 1996). Philippa Berry's *Shakespeare's Feminine Ending* (London: Routledge, 1999) extends Parker's concern with gender and equivocation. A very lively collection of essays in which Shakespeare figures prominently is Jonathan Culler (ed.), *On Puns: The Foundation of Letters* (Oxford: Blackwell, 1988). The most taxing (although brilliant) work in this line has been done by Joel Fineman in a series of essays collected as *The Subjectivity Effect in Western Literary Tradition* (Cambridge, Mass.: MIT Press, 1991). His earlier *Shakespeare's Perjured Eye* (Berkeley and Los Angeles: University of California Press, 1986) is also relevant. Fineman's work is much influenced by the ideas of Jacques Lacan and other French thinkers.

Index